IMAGES
of America

MARION

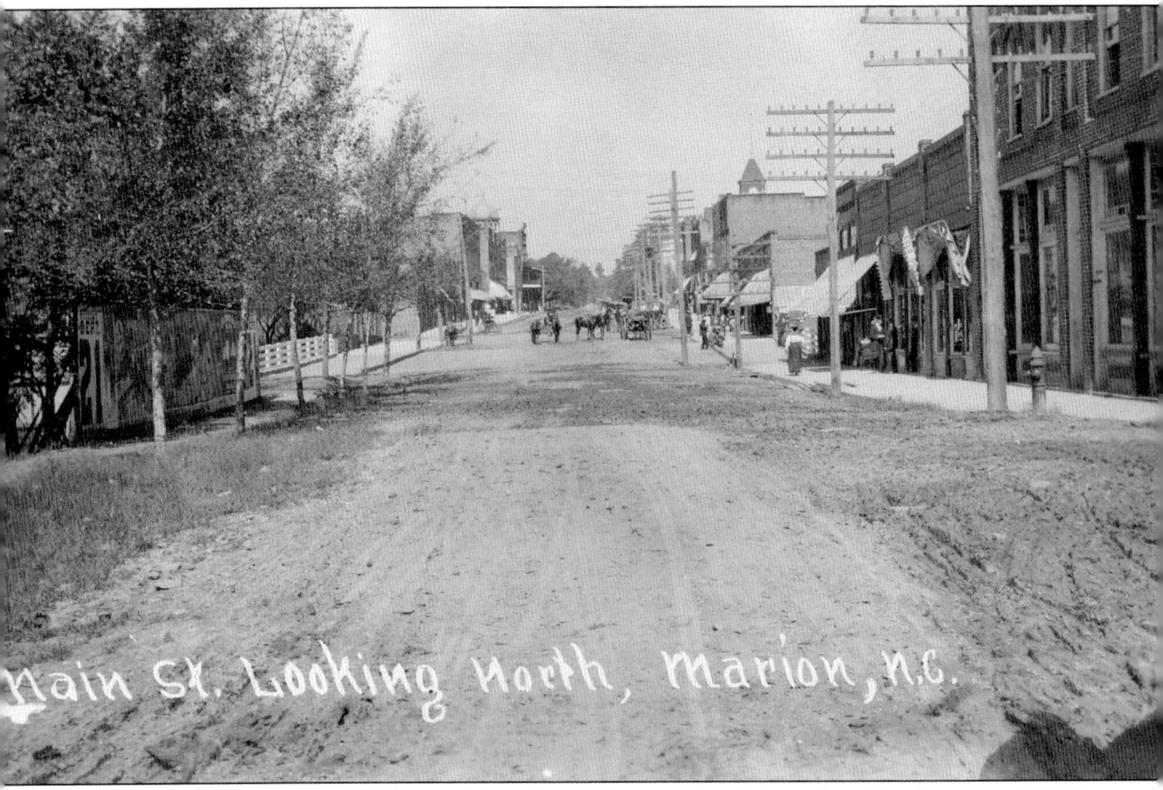

This view of Marion is looking up Main Street from south of the railroad bridge around 1908. The cupola of the remodeled courthouse is visible at the upper right. Even though automobiles had not yet arrived in Marion, electricity had begun to illuminate homes and businesses. The Marion Power and Light Company was established by J. Lafayette Morgan and R.H. Bennett, who built a dam at Tom's Creek Falls to produce electricity. (Courtesy of McDowell County Public Library, Joyce Decker Corbett Collection.)

ON THE COVER: This view from atop the McDowell Hotel looks south on Main Street in 1931. Although modern viewers of the scene may assume that a special event was taking place, this number of automobiles and pedestrians was typical for a Saturday morning of the era. (Courtesy of City of Marion.)

IMAGES
of America

MARION

Kim Clark and the McDowell House
Project Advisory Committee

ARCADIA
PUBLISHING

ISBN 978-0-7385-9793-5

Published by Arcadia Publishing
Charleston, South Carolina

Printed in the United States of America

Library of Congress Control Number: 2012942688

For all general information, please contact Arcadia Publishing:
Telephone 843-853-2070
Fax 843-853-0044
E-mail sales@arcadiapublishing.com
For customer service and orders:
Toll-Free 1-888-313-2665

Visit us on the Internet at www.arcadiapublishing.com

Contents

Acknowledgments

This volume would not have been possible without the assistance of many knowledgeable and generous people. Numerous images in this book come from private collections, and I thank the wonderful people who took the time to bring them to me at the McDowell County Public Library and who welcomed me into their homes. It was a pleasure to meet and visit with each one of them, and their identities are noted in the captions of the photographs. I am also indebted to Bob Boyette, Freddie Killough, Anne Swann, and Margaret Adams for steering me toward historical nuggets in the public archives. Todd and Melanie Buckner were also very kind to share some of the incredible images that have been captured by Eckenrod Studio over the years.

As any fledgling historian soon discovers, much history is not written in books. The most important and enlightening stories are often held only in the memories of those who lived them or in the records of those who have taken the time to listen to the telling. I thank the following for sharing their knowledge and for helping me play "history detective": James Haney, Jim Long, Terrell Finley, Annette Bryant, Alvin Hawkins, Edna Wall, Jetta Webb Walker, Steve Little, and Jack Wood. A special thanks goes to Louis Wall, whose incredible memory provided more information about Marion than a roomful of books and unlimited high-speed Internet ever could.

Crucial to the success of this project was the unconditional support of director Elizabeth House and the staff of the McDowell County Public Library. Patti Holda of the library's Abe Simmons North Carolina History and Genealogy Department was an indispensable ally. Without her pulling out boxes of old photographs, helping me with research, and giving me the run of her department, this book simply would not exist.

Deep appreciation is also extended to the McDowell House Project Advisory Committee, whose members set me off on this rewarding adventure.

INTRODUCTION

There is an old saying that "time is like a river." In many ways, it is, flowing endlessly from yesterday to today to tomorrow. Some moments in history have an exceptional effect on the flow of our destiny, just as the river speeds up when it comes to rapids or finds a way around an obstacle in its path. Although some events and circumstances affect the flow of history more than others, every moment is a part of it.

The first important moment for Marion and McDowell County was when the McDowells and the Carsons found their way into this rich and rugged wilderness in the 1700s. "Hunting" John McDowell and fellow explorer Henry Weidner first came through on a hunting expedition sometime in the 1740s. A friendly wrestling match settled the matter as to who would be the first white man to lay claim to the prime tract of land along the Catawba River that both fancied. McDowell flipped Weidner with a leg wrap and established a home near present-day Highway 70 West. His son Joseph, born in 1758, became a courageous Overmountain man in the Revolutionary War and was later a physician and statesman. His neighbors honored his memory by naming the county after him when it was formed.

John H. Carson arrived in what is now McDowell County about 30 years after Hunting John. He built a home on Buck Creek in the 1780s, and it quickly became a center of community and civic activity. When McDowell County was formed in 1843, the Carson House was designated as the seat of county government until the town of Marion could be laid out and a courthouse built.

Marion remained relatively rural until the railroad arrived in 1870. Until that time, businesses in town were mostly limited to general stores and the offices of doctors and lawyers. With the trains came substantial economic growth. By 1892, commercial business in Marion included a telegraph office, insurance agencies, livery stables, bars, pool halls, barbershops, hotels, and restaurants. Construction of a resort hotel to rival the Battery Park Hotel in Asheville was begun, but financing for that and similar projects collapsed after the onset of a nationwide financial panic in 1893.

Perhaps the most dramatic moment in time for Marion has been the moment on the morning of November 25, 1894, when a prisoner in the old McDowell County jail yelled "Fire!" A blaze had broken out in a dilapidated building behind the courthouse, and high winds rapidly pushed it south down Main Street. It traveled the length of the business district, crossed the street, and headed north again in a seemingly deliberate effort to make the destruction of downtown complete. When it was over, every building except one between the courthouse and the Episcopal church had been destroyed.

After the initial shock wore off, Marion's citizens began rebuilding their town, essentially from scratch. Remarkable and rapid progress was made. When one views photographs of Marion taken in the very early 1900s, it is difficult to believe that the city had been lying in ruins less than a decade before.

Marion continued to grow exponentially into the 1920s. Main Street was home to a new courthouse, several hotels and banks, two movie theaters, hardware stores, speciality merchants, automobile repair shops, and much more. Cotton mills, furniture factories, and hosiery mills were attracting newcomers looking for a steady paycheck and a pleasant environment in which to raise their families. It is perhaps not a coincidence that the main newspaper of the period was the *Marion Progress*.

World War II forever changed Marion, just as it greatly altered the rest of the nation and the world. Everyone pitched in during the war years. Businesses curtailed hours and services, schoolchildren collected scrap metal, their mothers conserved sugar and coffee, and the men who were not away fighting engaged in civil defense training. Most public events included an exhortation to "buy victory bonds." A sense of community, purpose, and patriotism was instilled in the citizens of that time that they still carry with them today.

The economic boom of the postwar years ushered in a period of unprecedented affluence, comfort, and ease for the majority of Marion's people. There was a job for everyone who wanted to work and plenty of money for hamburgers and soda pop. In a fitting metaphor for the time, the stately Main Street homes built by Marion's founding families were razed in the 1950s and 1960s to make room for service stations, banks, and other commercial enterprises. The world had changed into one that would have been scarcely recognizable to those early residents.

Countless everyday moments have also greatly influenced Marion's direction. This book is largely a collection of those moments: moments in the lives of moonshiners and mayors, of laborers and merchants, of businessmen and children, and of teachers and soldiers. Although perhaps less dramatic than the milestones discussed above, the people, places, and events pictured in this collection have also served to guide the flow of history of Marion, North Carolina.

This book is a project of the McDowell House Project Advisory Committee and was produced as a means to raise funds for the restoration of the McDowell House property. The committee was appointed by McDowell County and is made up of members from various realms of interest: county and city government, the National Park Service, museums and historic sites, tourism, the McDowell Trails Association, McDowell family descendants, and the local school system.

The committee was tasked with determining the best and most feasible use for the McDowell House and with securing financing for the endeavor. In partnership with the National Park Service, which has designated the house as a certified site on the Overmountain Victory Trail, the committee has charted a course to restore the house, to install historical exhibits, and to maintain the property for public visitation.

Committee members are Chuck Abernathy, McDowell County manager; Bob Boyette, Marion City manager; Terrell Finley, Mountain Gateway Museum director; Dr. James L. Haney Jr., Historic Carson House Board chairman; Arthur Campbell, owner of Springhouse Farms; Kristina Bartlett, student representative; Marc Cook, Marion businessman; Michael Lavender, McDowell County commissioner; Rod Birdsong, McDowell County Chamber of Commerce director; Carol Price, McDowell County Tourism Development Authority director; Margaret Adams, McDowell family descendants; Frank Dean, McDowell Trails Association; Paul Carson, superintendent of the Overmountain Victory National Historic Trail; and Anne Swann, McDowell Historic Preservation Commission chairman.

One

Beginnings

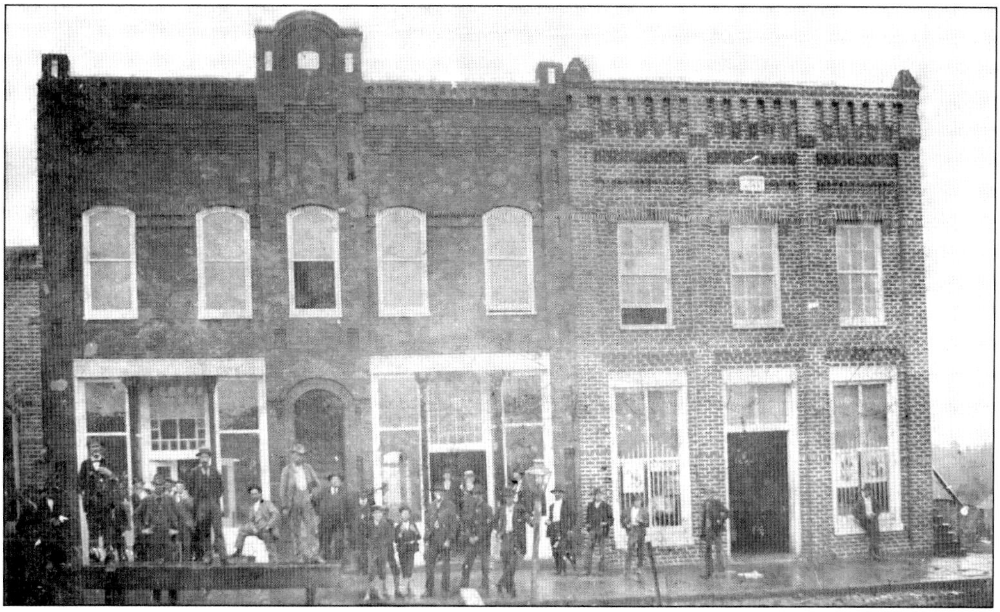

Businesses located on the east side of Main Street south of Henderson Street are seen here in early 1894. These buildings would be gutted by fire just months after this photograph was taken. Note the horse-watering trough to the left and the gas streetlamp near the center of the image. Marion's lamplighter lit the lanterns every evening at dusk and snuffed them out at dawn. (Courtesy of McDowell County Public Library, Greenlee Collection.)

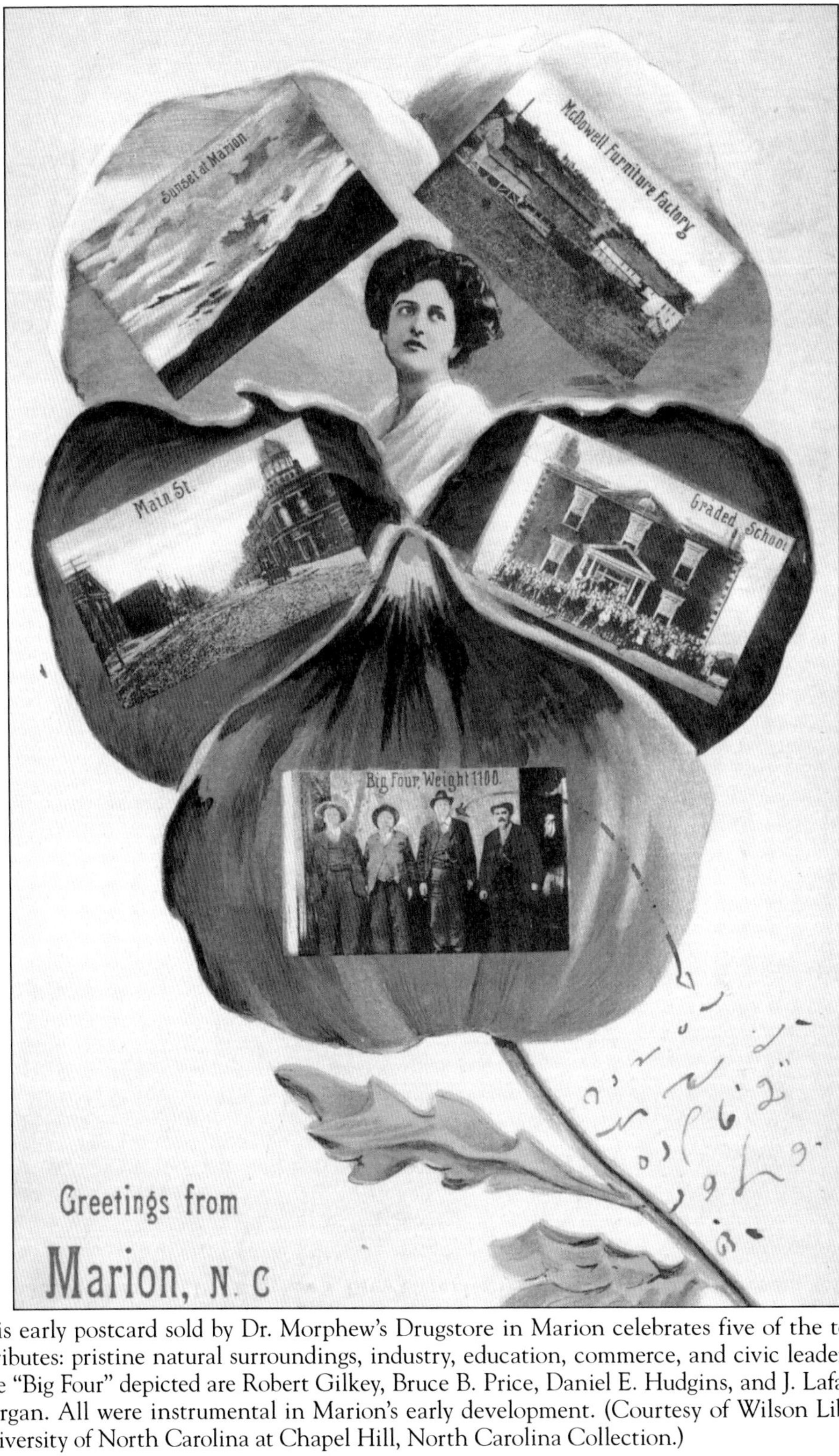

This early postcard sold by Dr. Morphew's Drugstore in Marion celebrates five of the town's attributes: pristine natural surroundings, industry, education, commerce, and civic leadership. The "Big Four" depicted are Robert Gilkey, Bruce B. Price, Daniel E. Hudgins, and J. Lafayette Morgan. All were instrumental in Marion's early development. (Courtesy of Wilson Library, University of North Carolina at Chapel Hill, North Carolina Collection.)

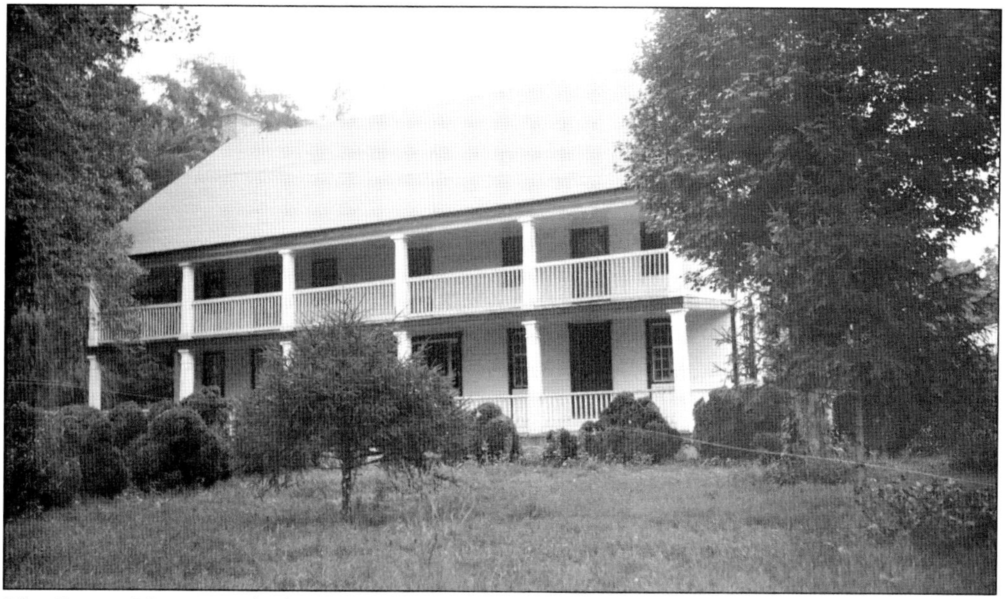

The Carson House was built on Buck Creek around 1793 by John Hazzard Carson, who had come to America from Ulster, Ireland. The 1808 Price-Strother map of Western North Carolina marks only one site between Morganton and Asheville, which is "Carson." The legislation creating McDowell County in 1842 stipulated that court sessions be held at the home until a town could be established and a permanent courthouse built. (Courtesy of Library of Congress, Prints & Photographs Division, HABS.)

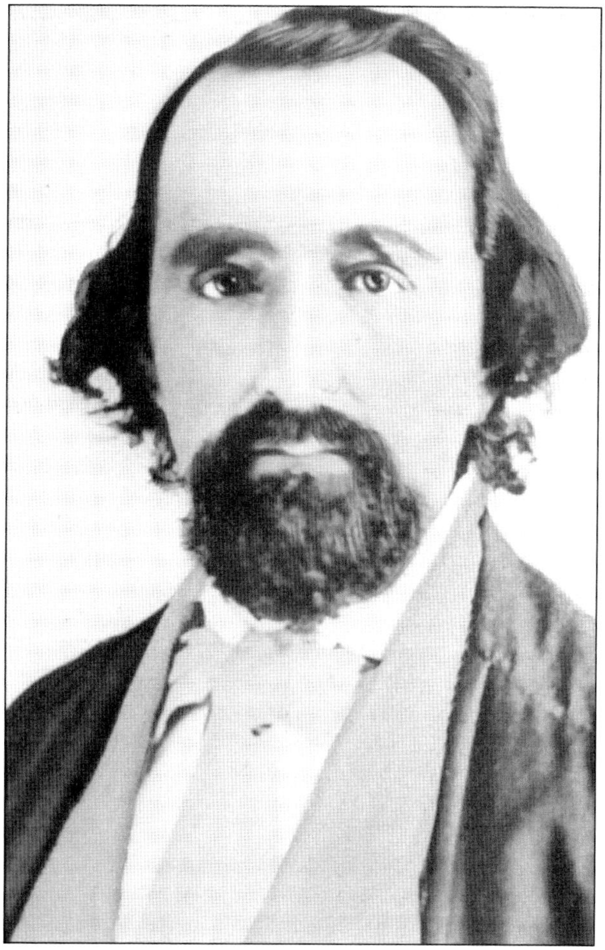

Jonathan Logan Carson was the youngest son of John and Mary Carson and inherited the Carson House and substantial land holdings upon the death of his father in 1841. Early citizens favored locating the permanent county seat near the Carson home, but J.L. Carson feared that having a town nearby would disrupt plantation life. He instead donated 50 acres near the geographical center of the county for the town of Marion. (Courtesy of Historic Carson House.)

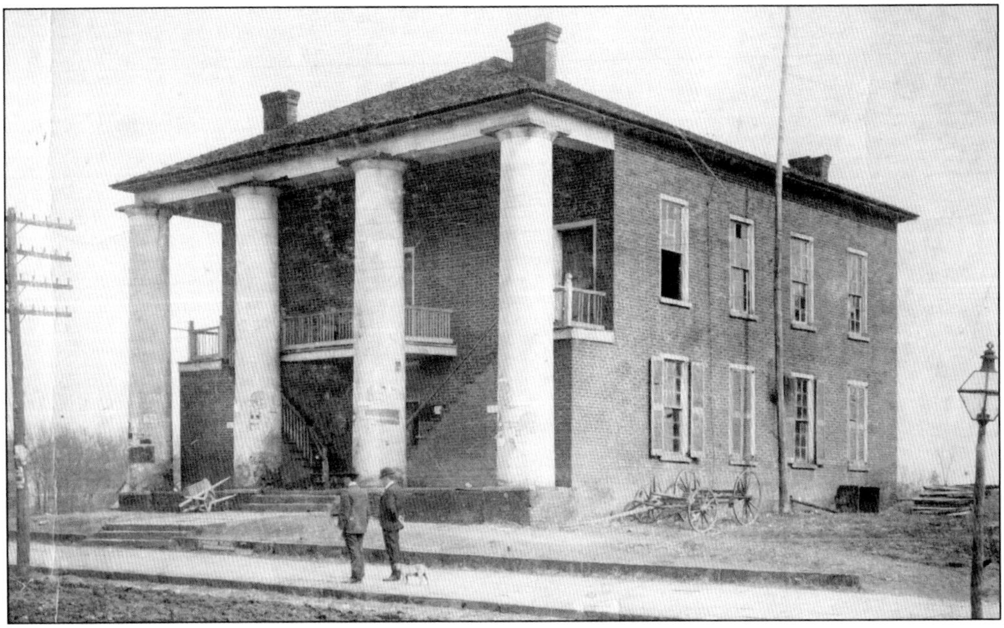

The original McDowell County Courthouse was built shortly after the town of Marion was established. Court sessions moved here from the Carson House in May 1845. This photograph was taken just before the courthouse was remodeled in 1902. This was a time of transition to electric power, as evidenced by the single power pole with no wires yet strung and the gas streetlight. (Courtesy of McDowell County Public Library.)

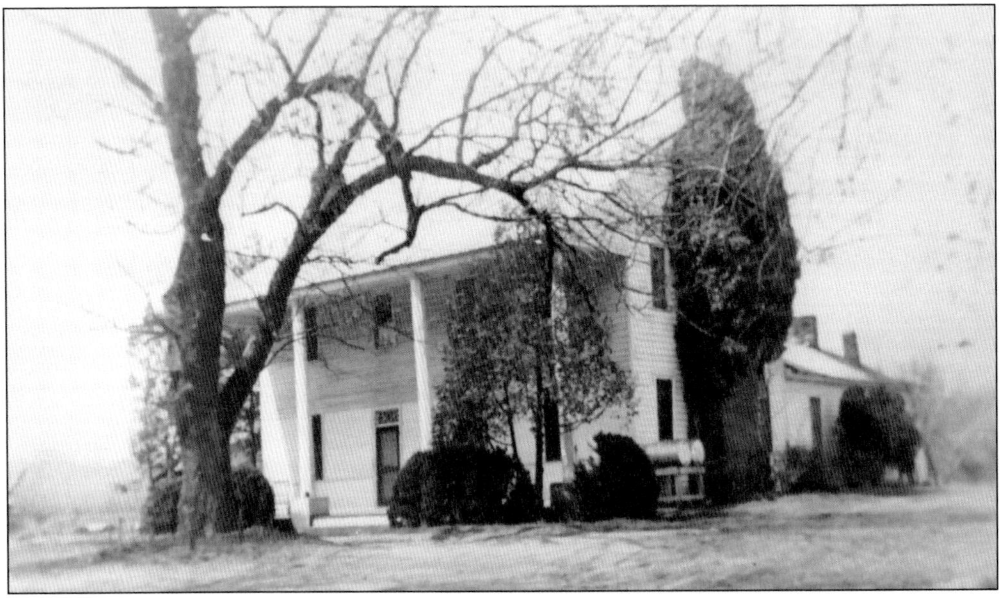

McDowell County takes its name from Joseph McDowell, whose father "Hunting" John McDowell settled the rich bottomlands along the Catawba River in the mid-1700s. Joseph McDowell was an Overmountain man and an officer at the Battle of Kings Mountain, which turned the tide of the Revolutionary War. He later served in the US Congress. The McDowell family called their home Pleasant Gardens, and this historic residence on the property is known as the McDowell House. (Courtesy of Mountain Gateway Museum.)

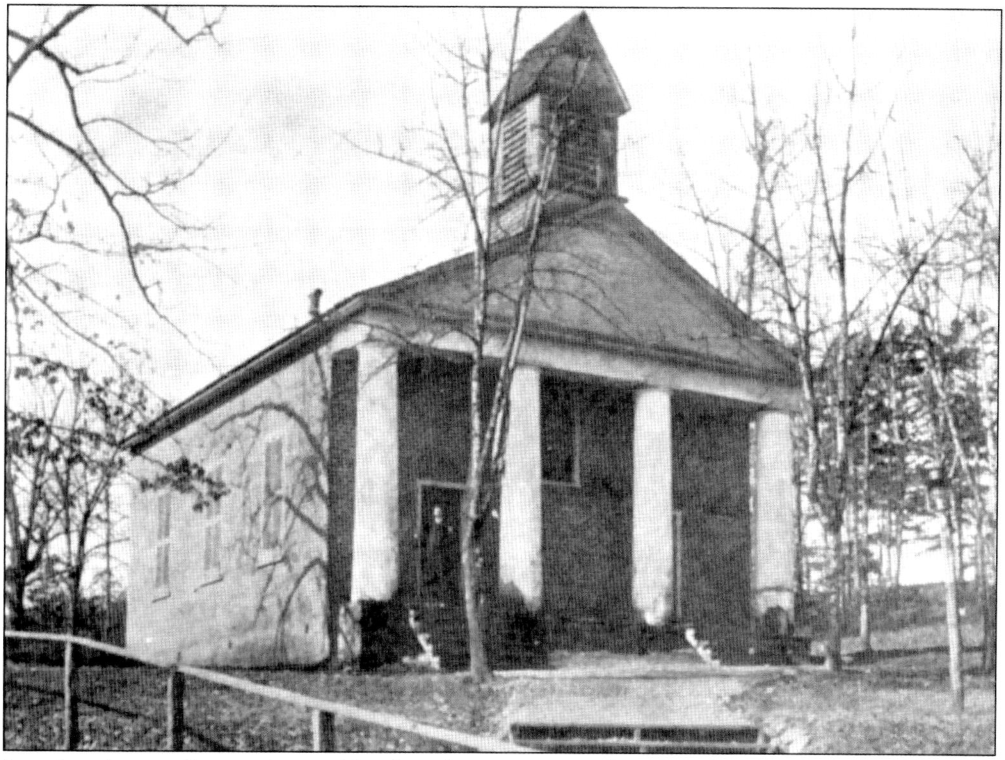

Jonathan Logan Carson donated land in the new town of Marion for a Presbyterian church in 1847. The original structure seen in this rare photograph was the first church building in town. It was demolished in 1923 to make way for a larger facility at the same Academy Street location. The Carson family also donated a site for a Methodist church. (Courtesy of McDowell County Public Library, Robin Hood Collection.)

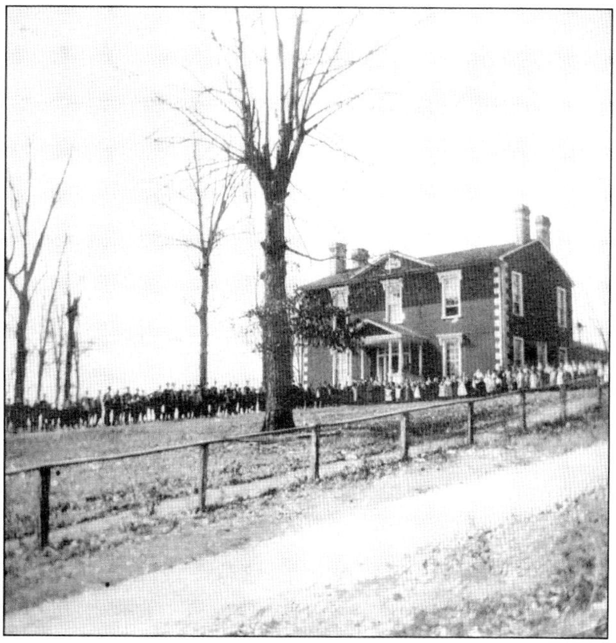

The Marion Academy was constructed beside First Presbyterian Church in 1857. Emmett and Martha Wright Guy taught there beginning in 1895 and were the last private school instructors in McDowell County prior to the advent of a public school system. The institution became the Marion Graded School in 1901. It was torn down in 1913 to make room for a modern facility, which served as a high school until 1923. (Courtesy of McDowell County Public Library.)

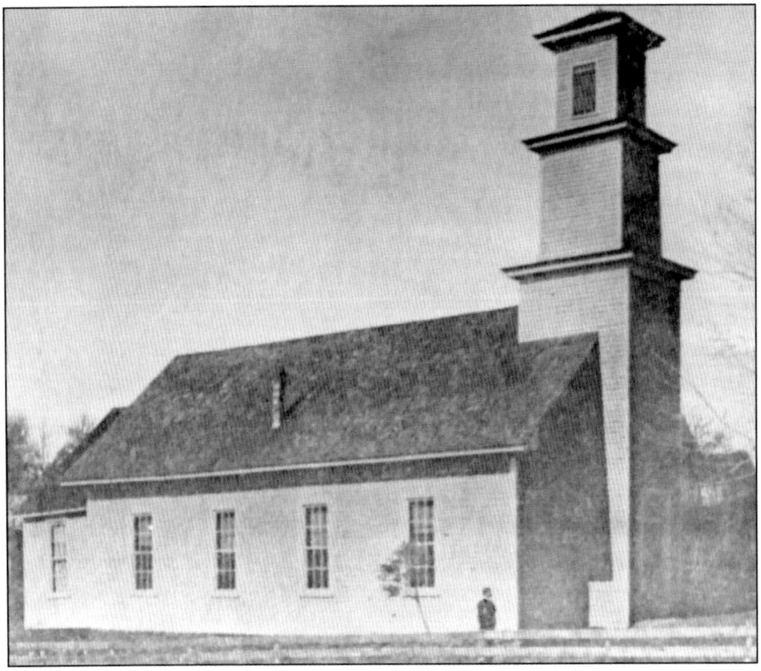

The First Baptist Church of Marion was organized on July 21, 1862, in the courthouse. Its first building was this 1878 wooden structure located on North Main Street. The church later purchased the adjoining corner lot and in 1913 built the brick Gothic Revival structure that is seen today. (Courtesy of McDowell County Public Library, Robin Hood Collection.)

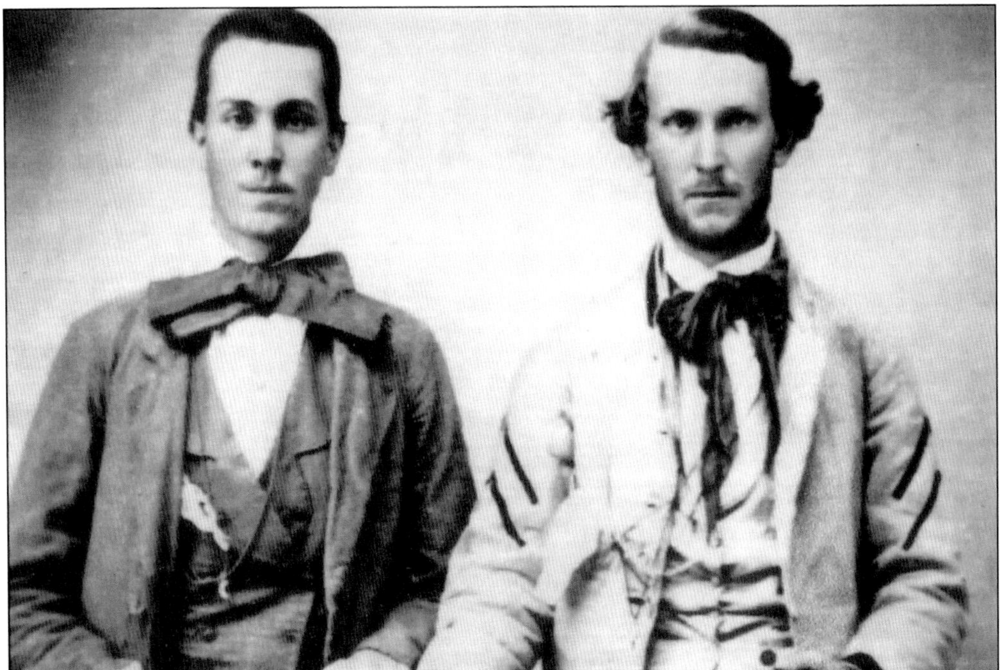

The town of Marion was less than 20 years old when the Civil War began. Pictured here are brothers David H. Davis (left) and Marion Francis Davis, who both enlisted in the Confederate army. Marion Francis served in the 22nd North Carolina Infantry, Company K, known as "the McDowell boys." Injured in the Battle of Chancellorsville in 1863, he died in Windsor Hospital, Virginia. Over a thousand McDowell men fought in the War Between the States. Approximately 300 gave their lives. (Courtesy of David Vess.)

Martin California Carson (1862–1956) was born into Carson plantation slavery, the son of Jefferson and Mahala Ervin Carson. He was educated in McDowell County schools and the State Normal School in Salisbury. He taught in Burke County public schools beginning in 1883 and later became an ordained Methodist minister. He served churches in five Western North Carolina counties. (Courtesy of Historic Carson House Library.)

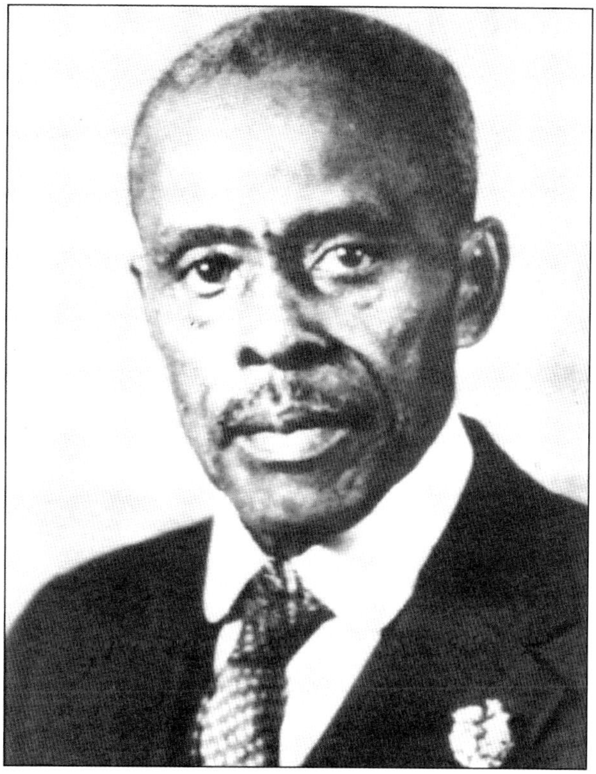

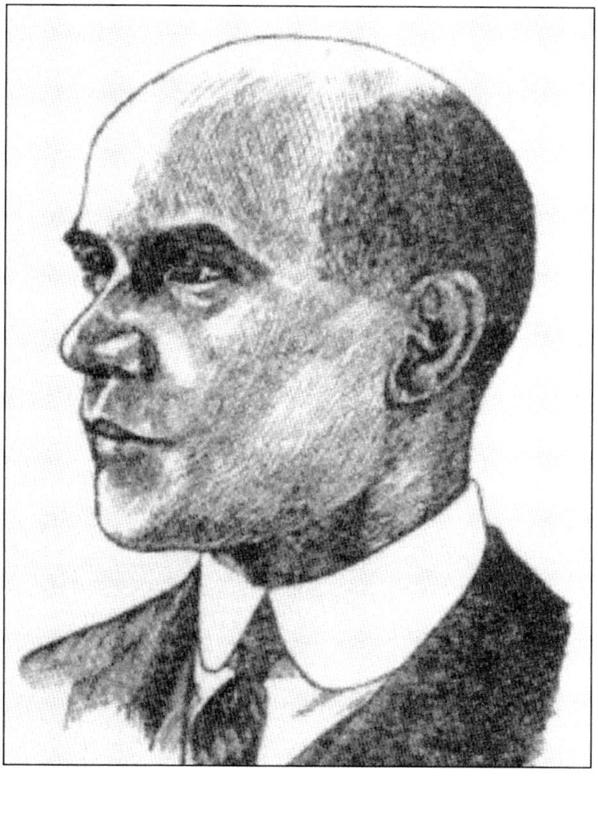

Simeon Lewis Carson (1882–1954) was the son of Carson House slaves Martin and Harriet. He graduated from the University of Michigan Medical School in 1903. In 1910, he became the first surgeon in Washington, DC, to use spinal anesthesia. He founded the Carson Private Hospital in Washington and presided over it until 1938. He also served as clinical professor of surgery at Howard University Hospital. (Courtesy of Historic Carson House Library.)

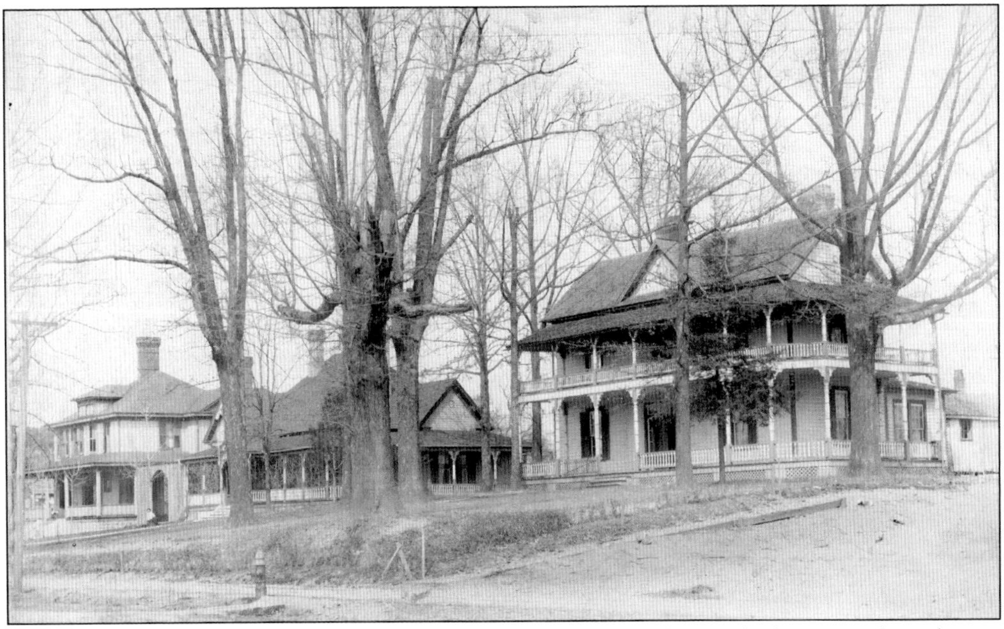

These stately homes on North Main Street were owned by the Gilkeys. The house on the right was built by Dr. John Harvey Gilkey and his wife, Adele Thomas Gilkey, around 1870. The middle home belonged to J.H. Gilkey's sister Mary and her husband, E.H. Dysart. The home at far left was owned by John Quince Gilkey, an ardent conservationist who played a key role in establishing Lake Tahoma and Linville Caverns. (Courtesy of McDowell County Public Library, Greenlee Collection.)

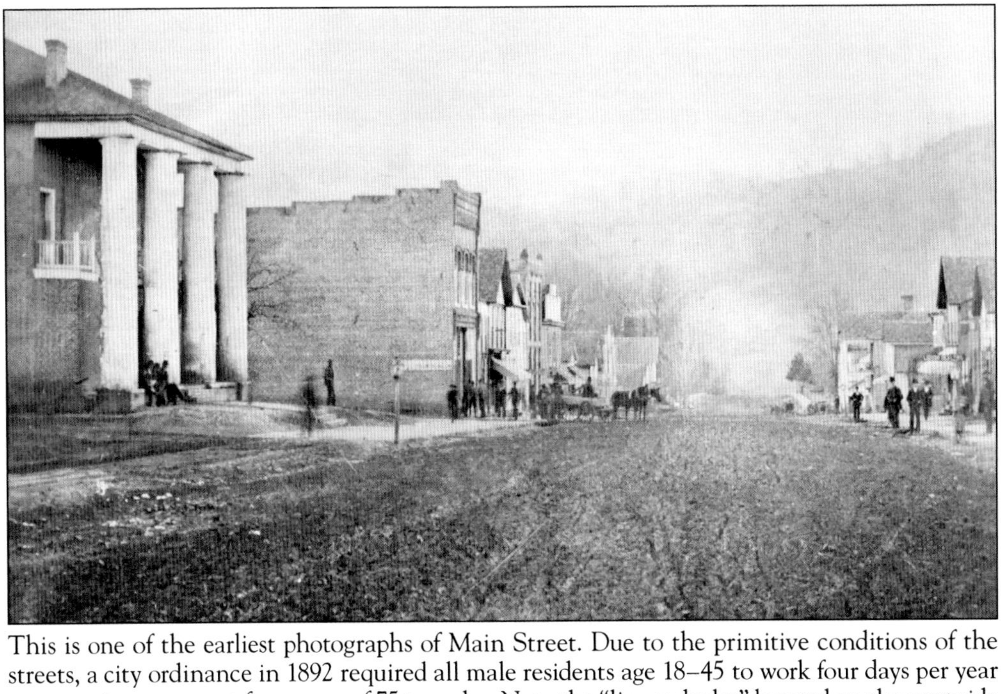

This is one of the earliest photographs of Main Street. Due to the primitive conditions of the streets, a city ordinance in 1892 required all male residents age 18–45 to work four days per year on street improvement for a wage of 75¢ per day. Note the "liquor dealer" located on the west side of the street. Alcohol flowed freely in Marion in the early days. (Courtesy of McDowell County Public Library.)

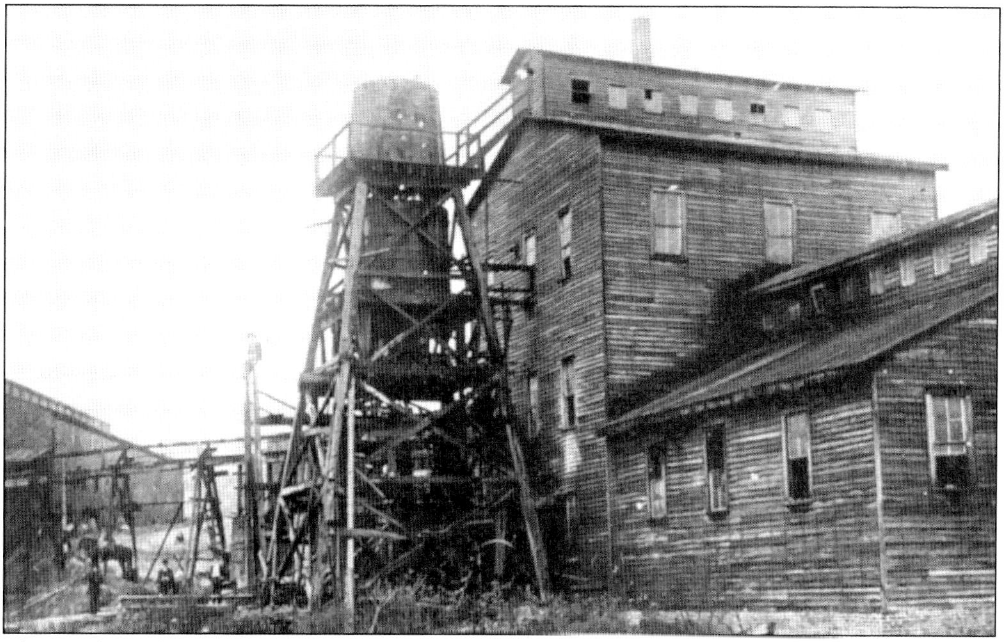

This is the only known photograph of the Blue Ridge Distillery, established by J. Lafayette Morgan and R.H. Bennett in what would later be the Cross Mill community. Distilleries were an important part of the economy in McDowell County in the late 1800s. In 1908, North Carolina became the first Southern state to outlaw the manufacture and sale of "intoxicating liquor," thus closing McDowell's legal distilleries and Marion's three bars. (Courtesy of McDowell County Public Library.)

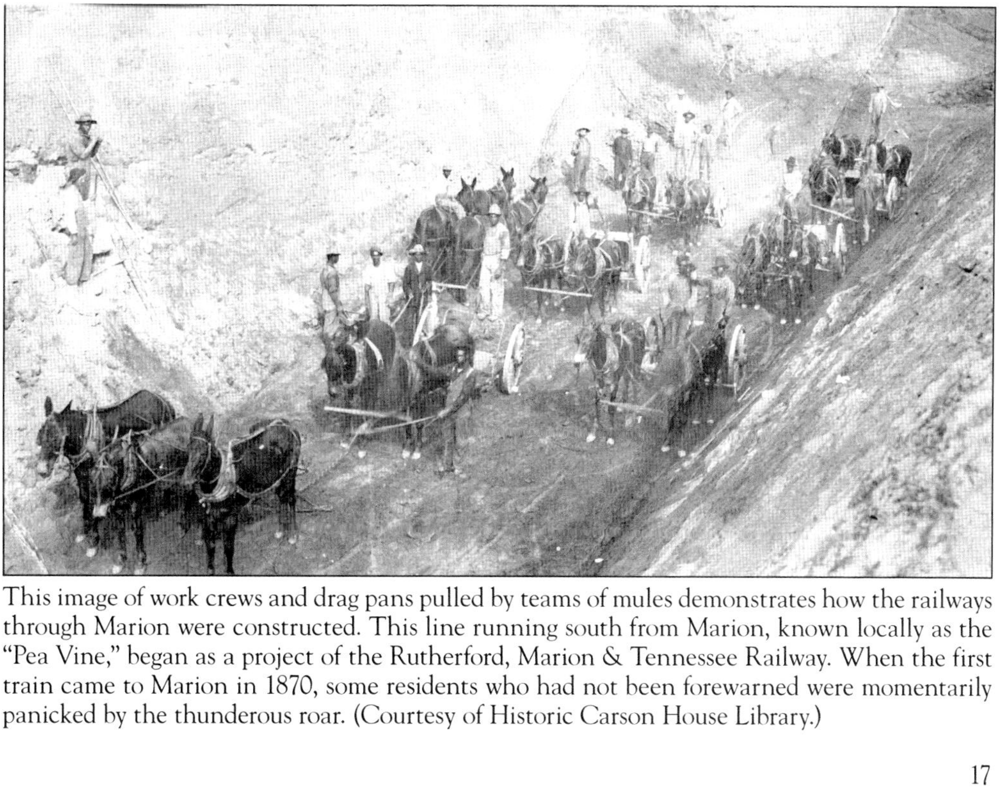

This image of work crews and drag pans pulled by teams of mules demonstrates how the railways through Marion were constructed. This line running south from Marion, known locally as the "Pea Vine," began as a project of the Rutherford, Marion & Tennessee Railway. When the first train came to Marion in 1870, some residents who had not been forewarned were momentarily panicked by the thunderous roar. (Courtesy of Historic Carson House Library.)

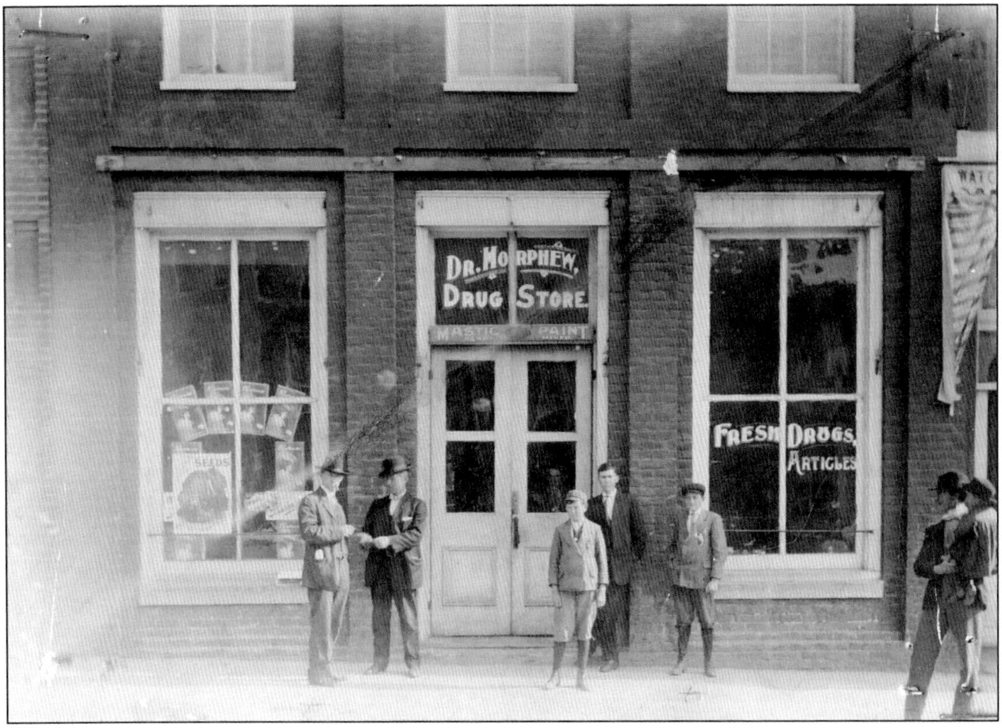

Dr. Morphew's Drugstore on South Main Street served the people of Marion and McDowell County during the last quarter of the 19th century and the early 20th century. This photograph predates the 1894 fire that destroyed most of the town. Just before the fire, Morphew's business partner was J.W. Streetman, who would go on to have a drugstore of his own. (Courtesy of Mountain Gateway Museum, Warren Hobbs Collection.)

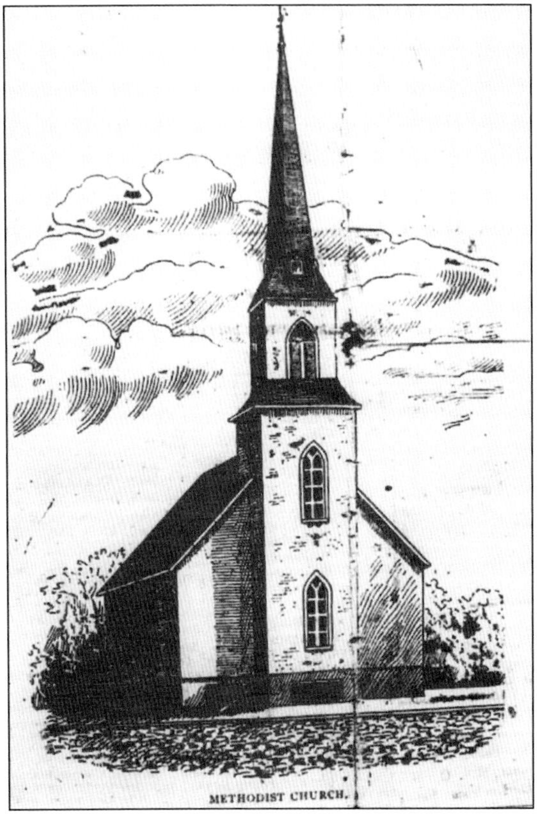

The First Methodist Church built this structure at the corner of Court and Logan Streets after its building on East Court Street was condemned in 1896 due to a cracked foundation. This line drawing is from the *Western Free Lance*, an early Marion newspaper. The congregation's third home would be erected in 1909 at the corner of Fort and Logan Streets. (Courtesy of James L. Haney.)

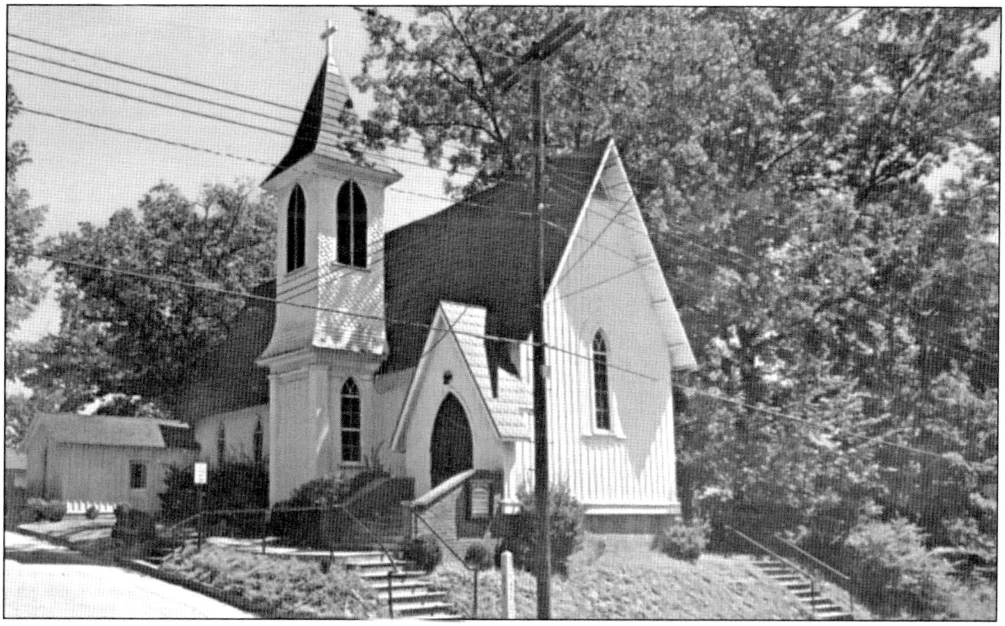

St. John's Episcopal Church was built in 1883 on South Main Street and is the oldest existing church building in Marion. Rector Charles T. Bland built the church with the help of one carpenter, William Dellinger. During the fire of 1894, flames crossed the railroad bridge and burned buildings on both sides of the street. They turned just before reaching the Episcopal church. (Courtesy of McDowell County Public Library.)

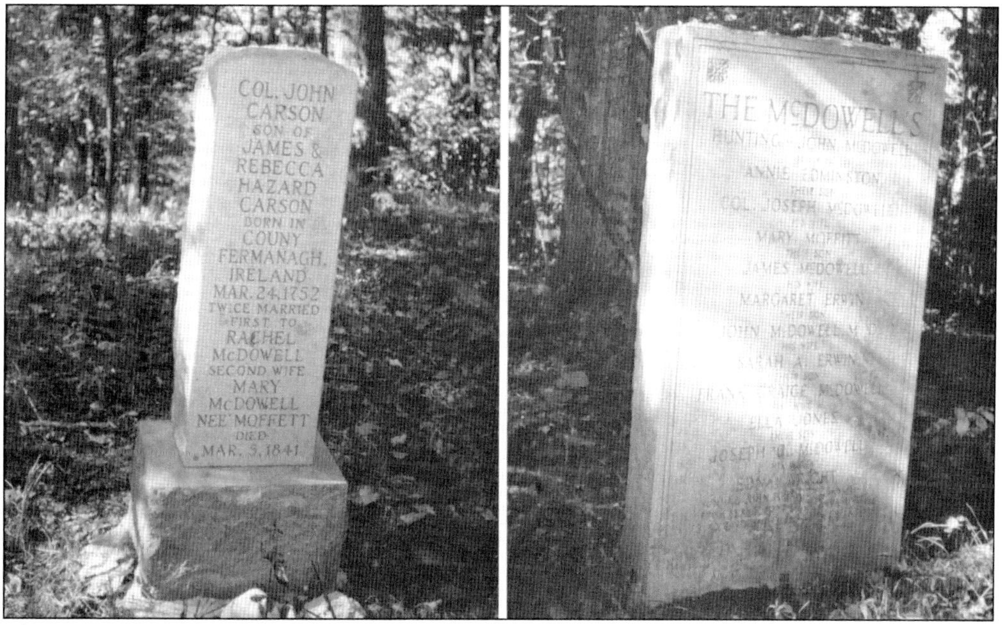

These markers at Round Hill, located a few hundred yards from the McDowell House, suggest that the mound is the final resting place for some of the members of McDowell County's founding families. Evidence indicates that the mound is an ancient Cherokee burial ground as well. In 1978 and 1986, archeologists excavated part of a nearby field and found proof of a Native American village. (Courtesy of Margaret Adams.)

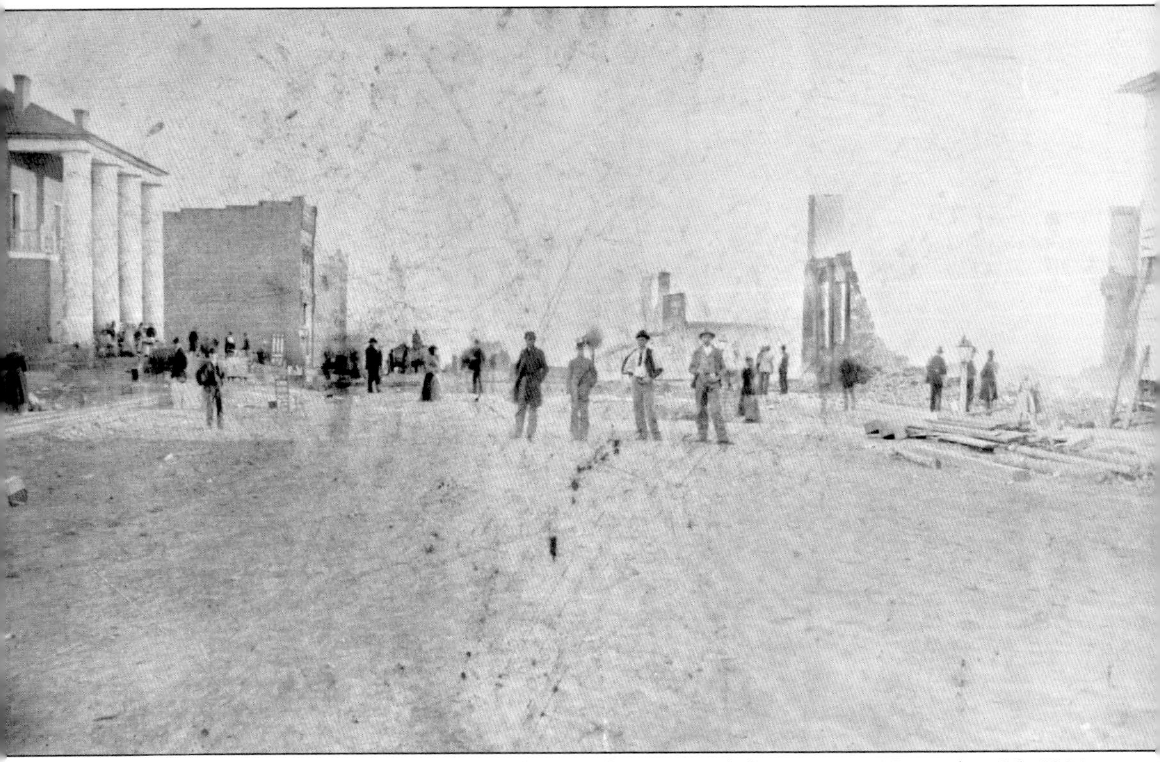

Marion residents take stock following the fire that ravaged the town on November 25, 1894. The blaze started in a dilapidated tenement house beside the jail and rapidly spread south down Main Street, devouring businesses and homes. High winds blew embers all the way to Mount Ida, igniting woods fires. An Asheville-bound train was held for three hours as burning debris fell from the railroad bridge. Those aboard disembarked and helped combat the flames. One passenger, J.B.S. McIntosh, later described the scene to the *Asheville Daily Citizen*: "The wells supplying the bucket brigades were soon drawn dry . . . the people, in their excitement, seemed to lose their heads. Merchandise was taken from buildings and deposited in the street between walls of flames, to be consumed." After the fire, residents whose homes had been spared took in their less fortunate neighbors until they could rebuild. (Courtesy of City of Marion.)

Two

Out of the Ashes

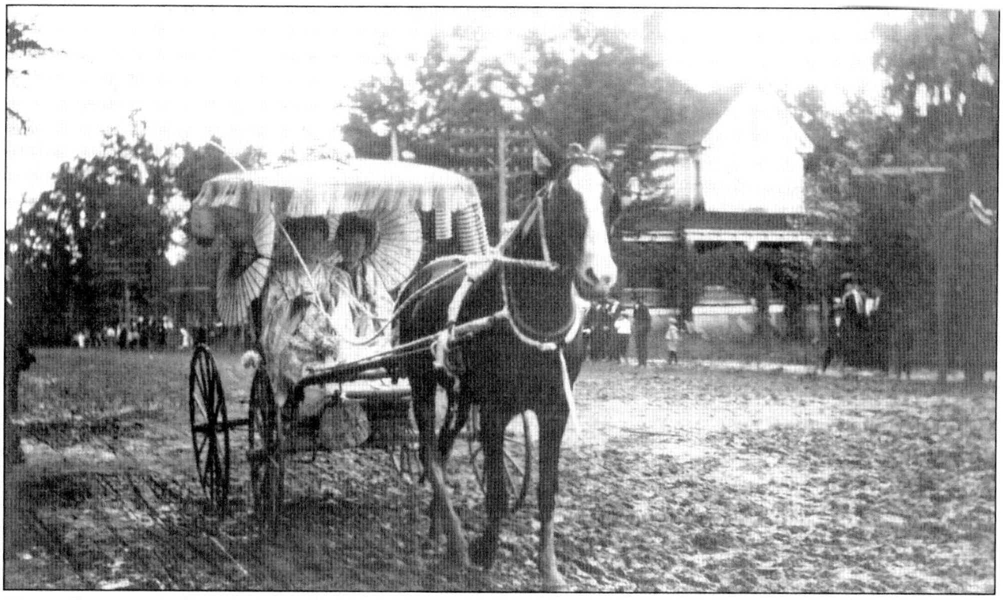

Once the town of Marion got back on its feet following the great fire, residents were in the mood to celebrate. Fairs and parades abounded in the early 20th century. These two young ladies adopted an oriental theme for their turn in front of the onlookers lining the parade route. (Courtesy of McDowell County Public Library.)

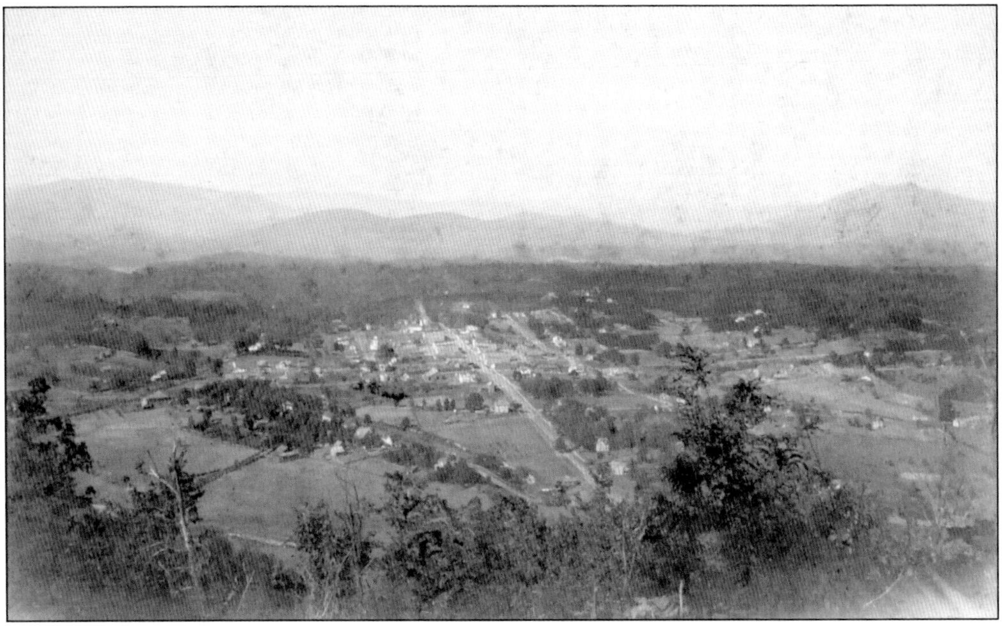

This is a view of Marion from Mount Ida four years after the fire. Around 1890, when the national economy was booming, a group of developers from the railroad planned to run a trolley line to the top of the peak. The financial crash of 1893 doomed the enterprise. In 1913, rumors circulated that a resort hotel was planned for the summit, but it never materialized. (Courtesy of McDowell County Public Library.)

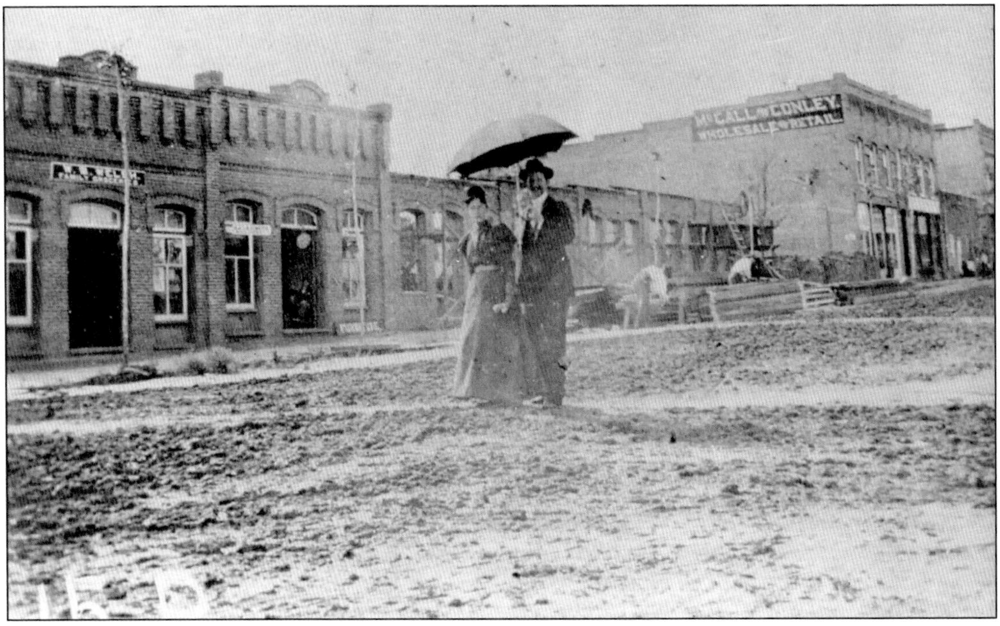

Businessman John Yancey and his wife stroll down a muddy Main Street in 1898. Before the streets were improved, stepping stones were placed at key crossing areas but were of little help. They usually became deeply immersed in the mud and could not be seen, or they were so slippery that they sent pedestrians sliding into the muck despite their best efforts. (Courtesy of McDowell County Public Library, Robin Hood Collection.)

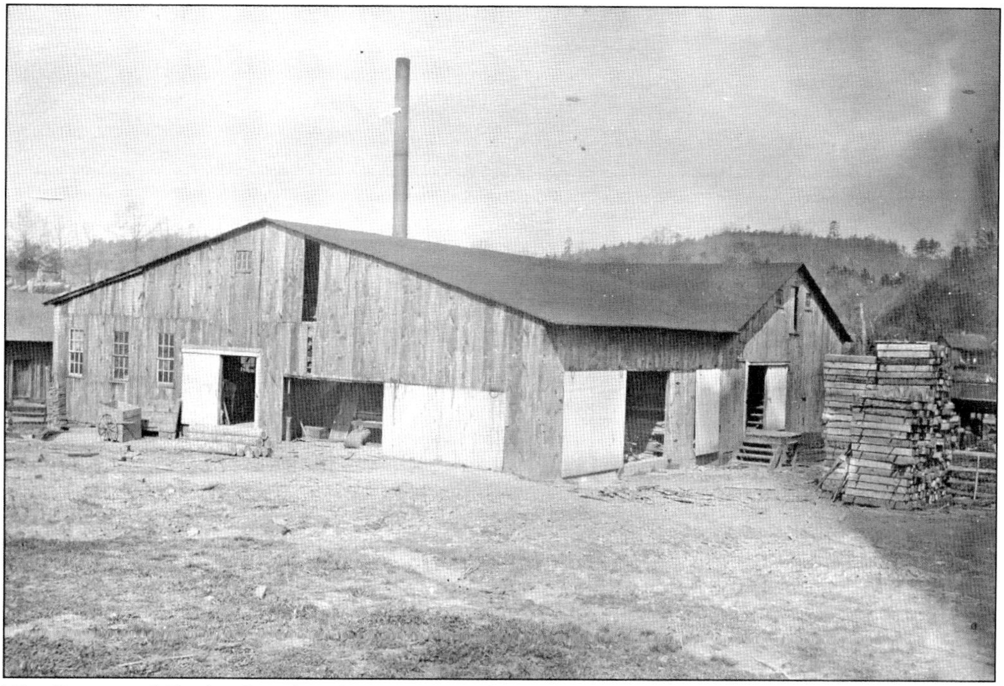

The Payne and Decker Lumber Company was located just off of Morgan Street near the Marion depot. Established in 1897, the firm manufactured interior building materials. With forests being rapidly depleted in the North, demand for Southern materials to be shipped northward was steadily increasing. (Courtesy of McDowell County Public Library, Joyce Decker Corbett Collection.)

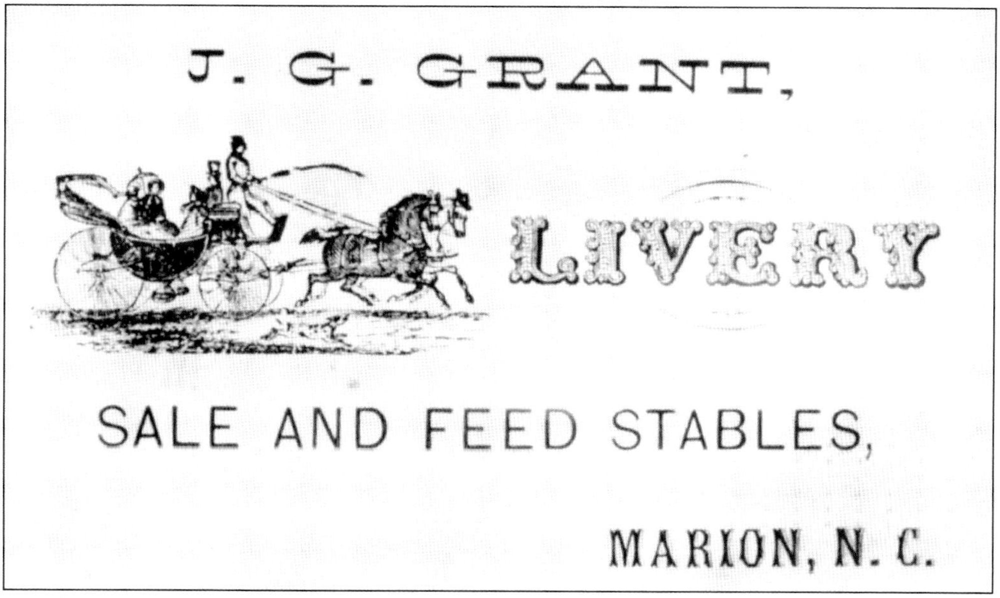

As advertised on this business card, Joseph G. Grant (1852–1910) was the proprietor of a livery stable. Before the advent of the automobile, livery stables supplied transportation between the train station and hotels and also offered horses, buggies, and carriages for rent to visitors. In addition, travelers could have their own horses boarded and fed when they stopped for the night. (Courtesy of McDowell County Public Library, Warren Hobbs Collection.)

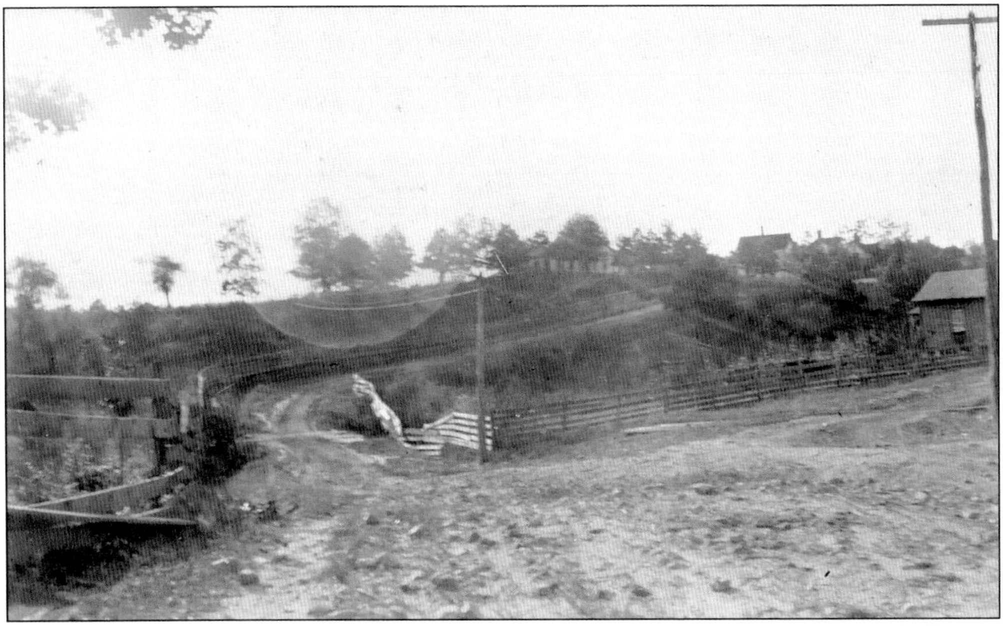

This 1898 view of the intersection where South Main Street (right) and Morgan Street (left) meet Rutherford Road attests to the challenging condition of public throughways in Marion's early days. Led by Dr. B.L. Ashworth and J.Q. Gilkey, an aggressive program to improve Marion's streets and sidewalks was begun a few years after this photograph was taken. (Courtesy of McDowell County Public Library, Joyce Decker Corbett Collection.)

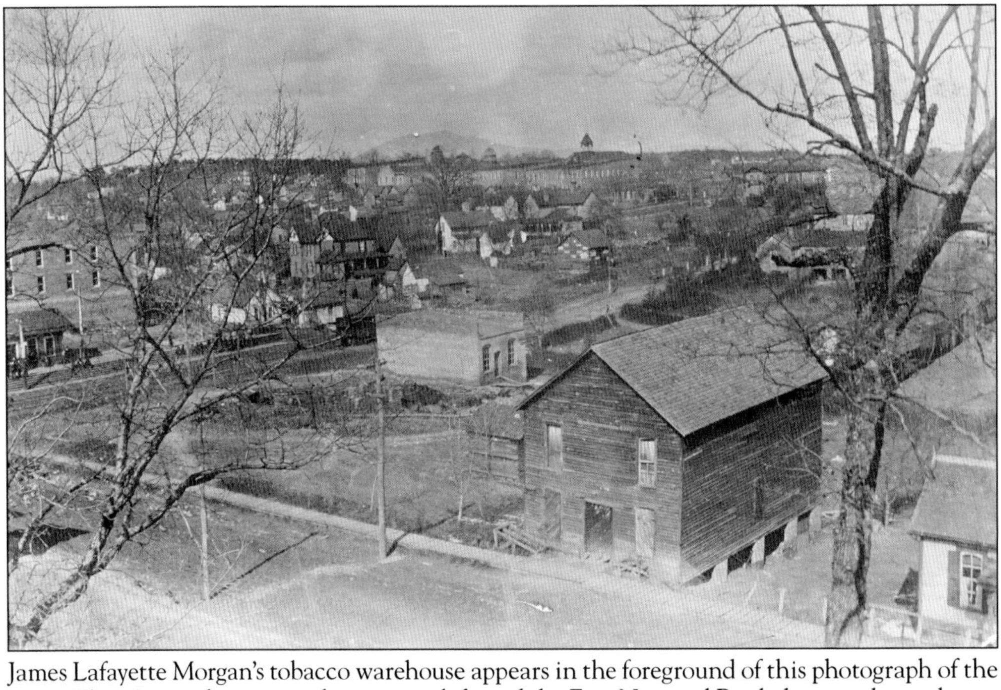

James Lafayette Morgan's tobacco warehouse appears in the foreground of this photograph of the town. The Marion depot is on the extreme left, and the First National Bank dome and courthouse cupola are visible in the distance. Note the wooden sidewalk alongside Morgan Street. (Courtesy of McDowell County Public Library.)

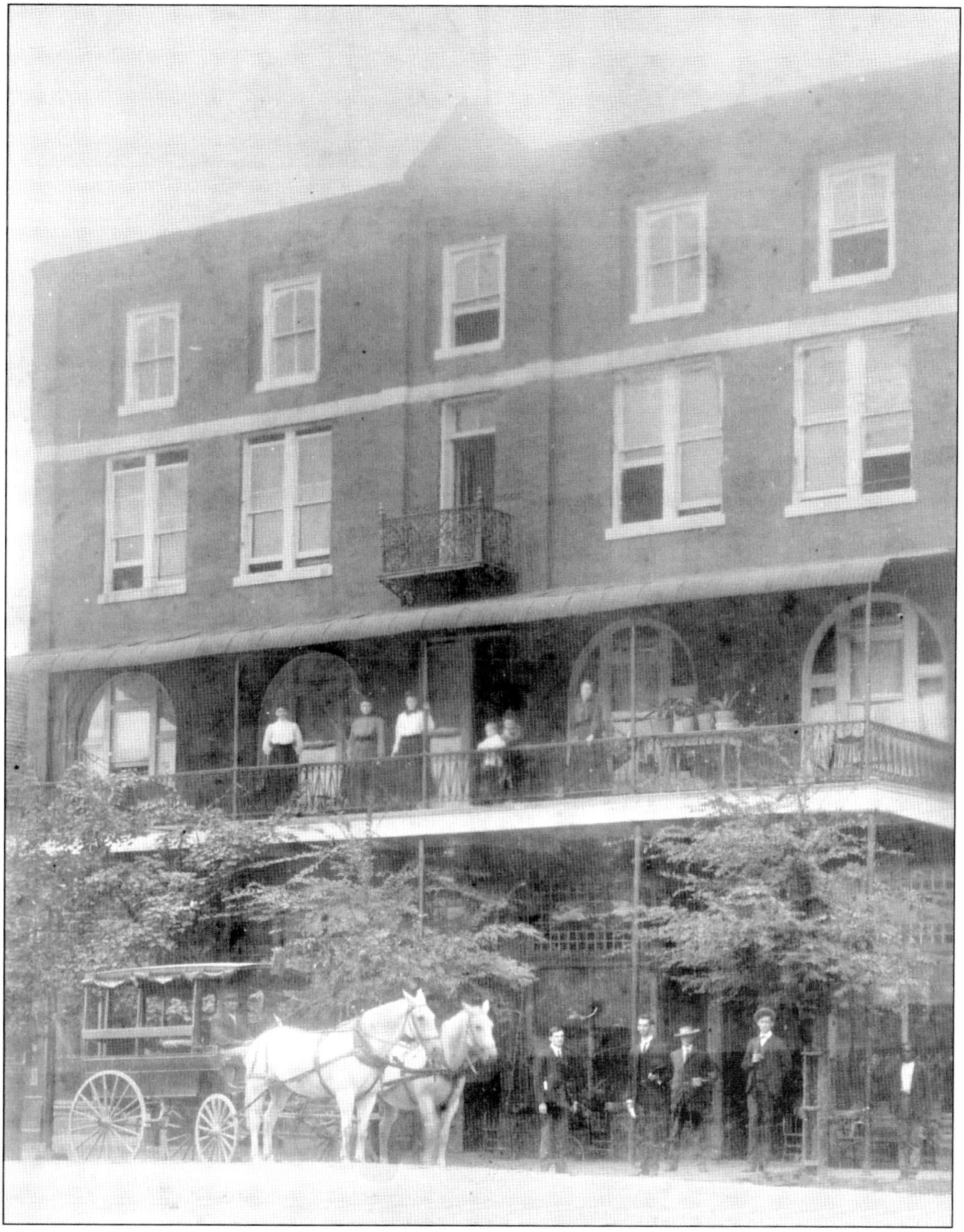

Construction of the Eagle Hotel on North Main Street was completed in October 1892. Commenting on the high-quality accommodations, the *Marion Record* states that "the Eagle Hotel is now preparing to accommodate the traveling public in a manner heretofore unknown." The Eagle also served as a temporary jail after the 1894 fire. In this c. 1905 image, a hack driven by "Uncle" Chisolm waits out front. The man nearest to the horses is W.A. Colvert, the hotel manager. Mrs. Colvert is on the balcony with their son in her lap, and Mrs. R.H. Bennett is to her left. The African American gentleman at the far right on the street was known as Uncle Charlie. The Eagle became the McDowell Hotel in 1917. (Courtesy of Historic Carson House Library, Warren Hobbs Collection.)

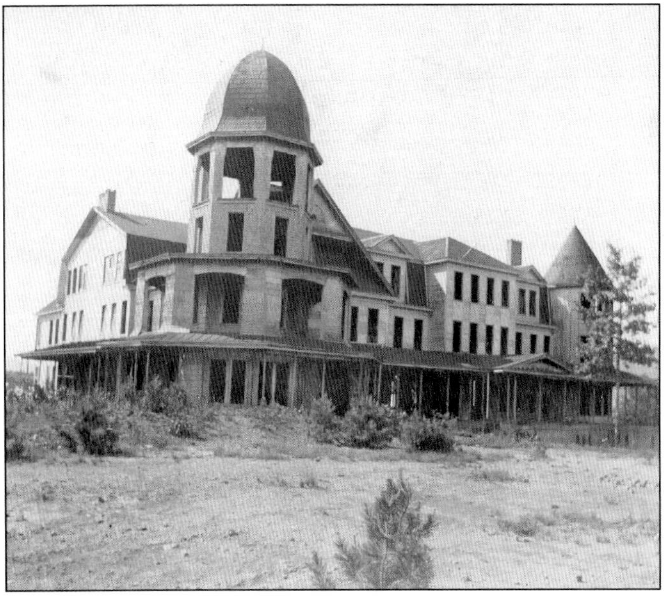

Construction of the Catawba Hotel began on State Street around 1890, and it was envisioned as a profitable resort. Financing dried up, however, and the unfinished building seen here was abandoned. Missionary Mattie Perry purchased it in 1898 and established the Elhanan Bible Training Institute and Orphanage. The building burned in 1928. Marion High School and East McDowell Junior High would later occupy the site. (Courtesy of McDowell County Public Library, Joyce Decker Corbett Collection.)

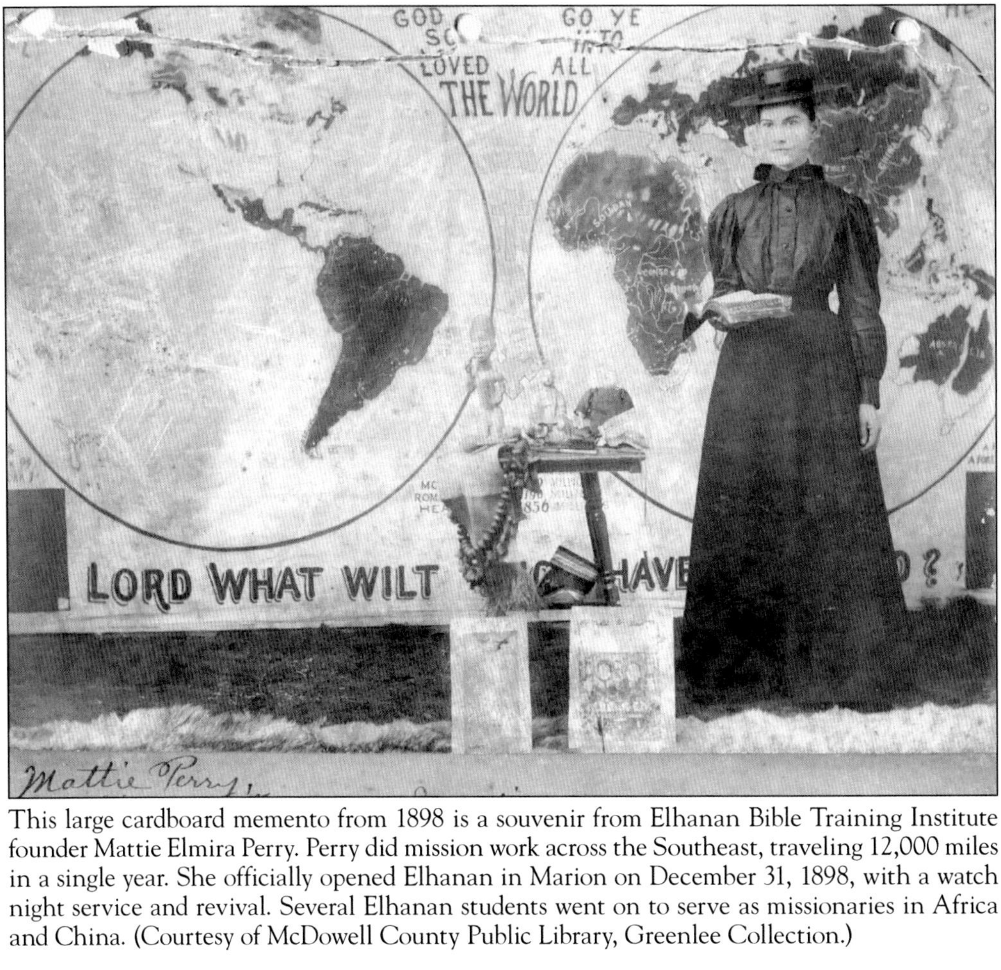

This large cardboard memento from 1898 is a souvenir from Elhanan Bible Training Institute founder Mattie Elmira Perry. Perry did mission work across the Southeast, traveling 12,000 miles in a single year. She officially opened Elhanan in Marion on December 31, 1898, with a watch night service and revival. Several Elhanan students went on to serve as missionaries in Africa and China. (Courtesy of McDowell County Public Library, Greenlee Collection.)

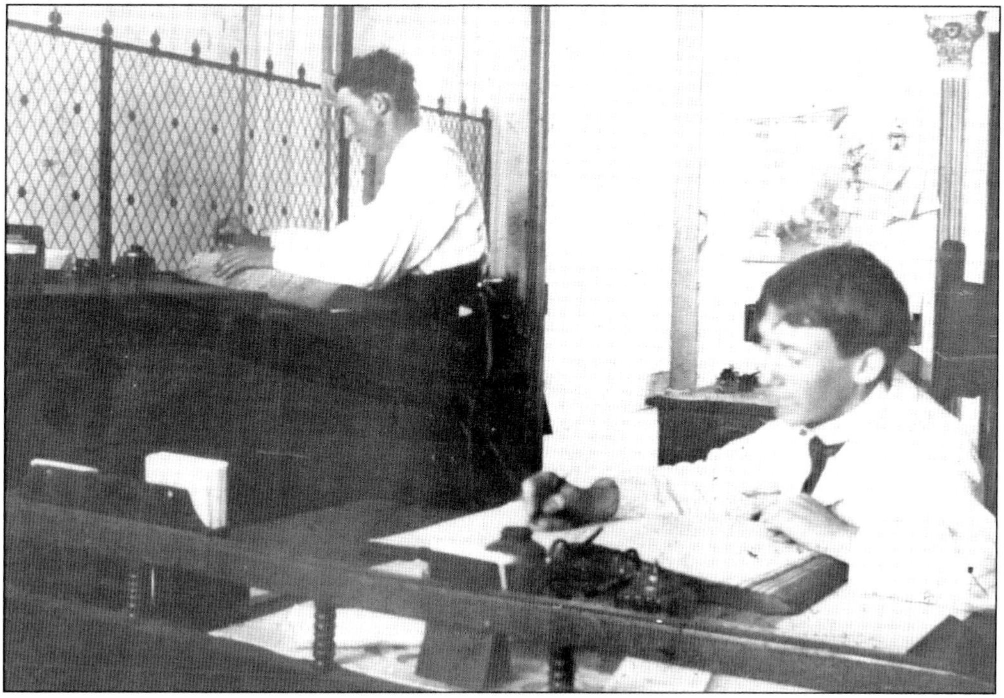

At work in the Commercial Bank of Marion in 1899 are Ernest J. House (seated) and Will Burgin Jr. The Commercial Bank was organized 15 months after the 1894 fire, in part to provide loans for rebuilding and recovery. It became the First National Bank in 1903. House opened the Marion Theatre in 1929. (Courtesy of McDowell County Public Library, Robin Hood Collection.)

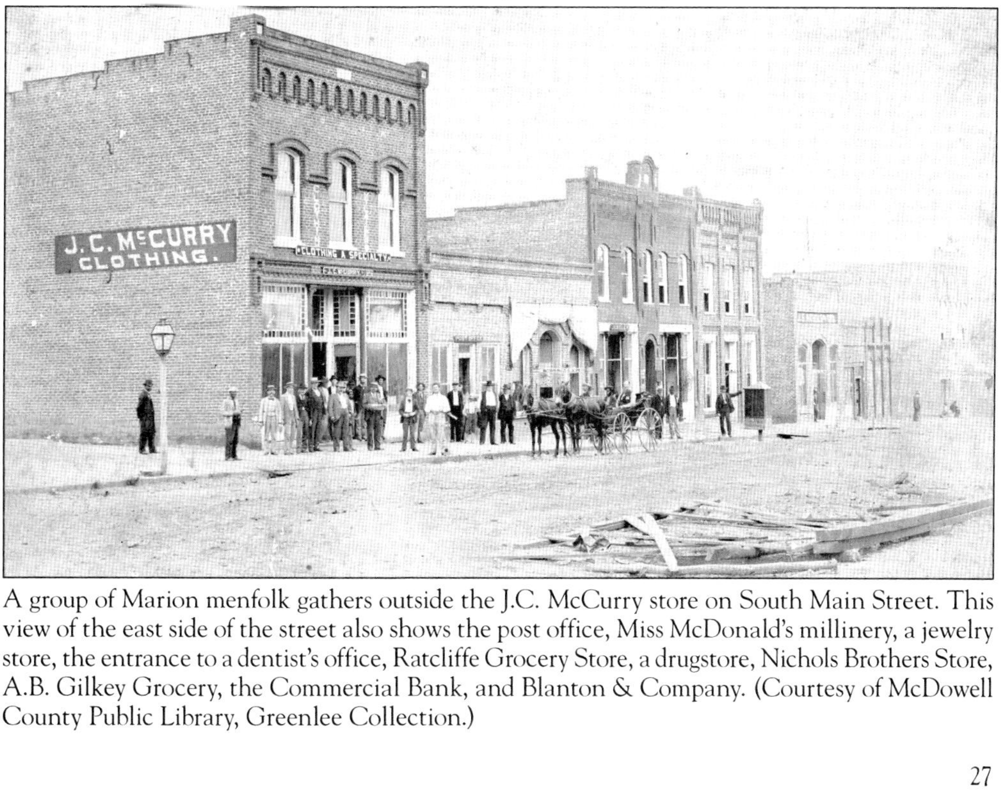

A group of Marion menfolk gathers outside the J.C. McCurry store on South Main Street. This view of the east side of the street also shows the post office, Miss McDonald's millinery, a jewelry store, the entrance to a dentist's office, Ratcliffe Grocery Store, a drugstore, Nichols Brothers Store, A.B. Gilkey Grocery, the Commercial Bank, and Blanton & Company. (Courtesy of McDowell County Public Library, Greenlee Collection.)

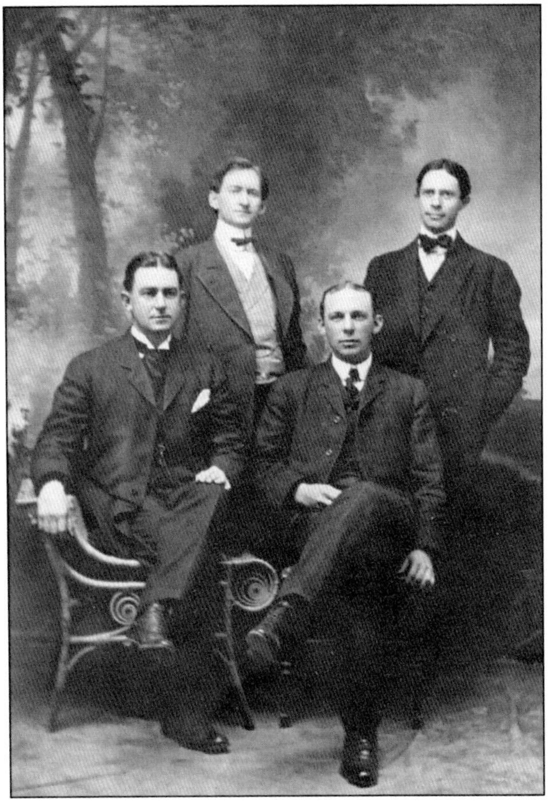

These men were highly influential Marion citizens. From left to right are John Quince Gilkey, James William Pless Sr., William Kelly Marvin Gilkey Sr., and Cy Smith. J.Q. Gilkey was the chairman of city schools and a director of the First National Bank, as was Smith. W.K.M. Gilkey was a city alderman and owner of Marion Veneer Company and Gilkey Hosiery Mill. Pless was one of the most respected civil lawyers in Western North Carolina. (Courtesy of Mountain Gateway Museum, Warren Hobbs Collection.)

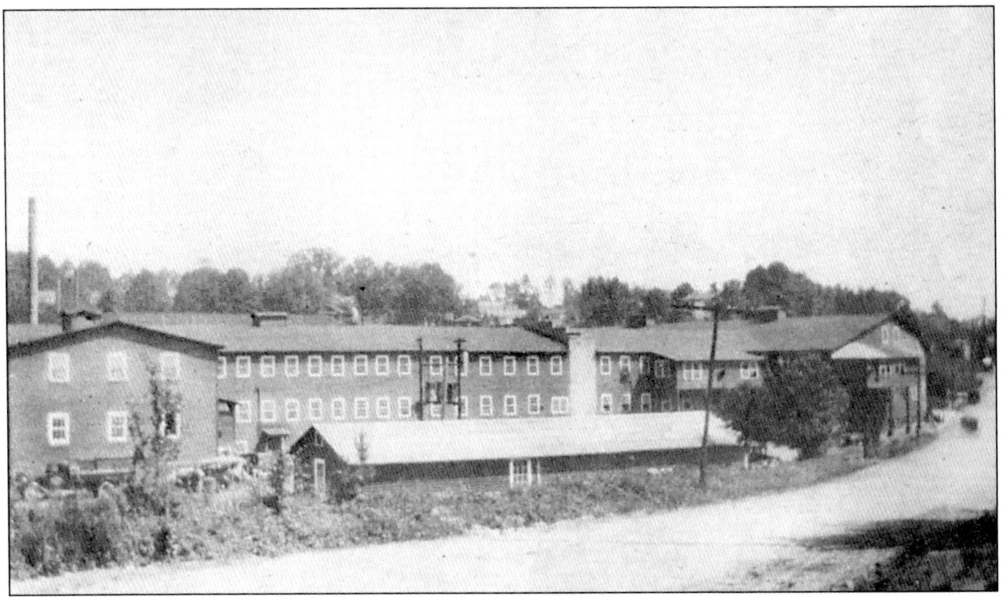

McDowell Furniture Company was established in 1901. By the mid-1930s, the company reported 260 employees and an annual payroll of $250,000. McDowell Furniture manufactured bedroom furniture exclusively, and 90 percent of the lumber used in its operations came from McDowell County forests. This is the only known photograph of the factory. (Courtesy of McDowell County Public Library.)

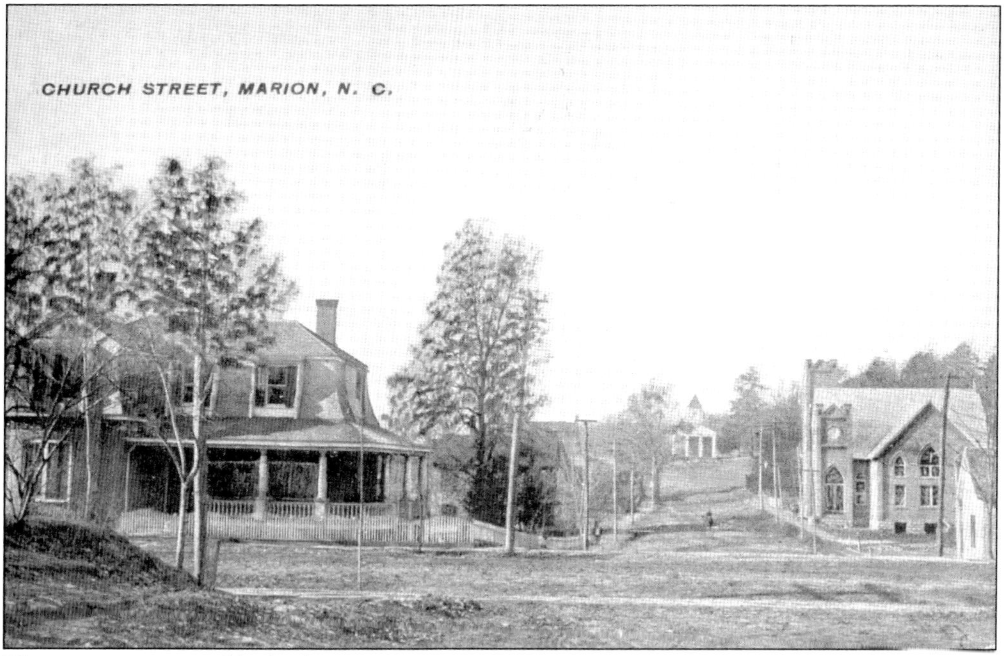

This vintage postcard looks down then Church Street, which would later be renamed Fort Street. Straight ahead is the original First Presbyterian Church building. To the left is the Bennett House, built by distillery owner R.H. Bennett. Clifton McCall would move his funeral home there in 1932. To the right is the third home of the First Methodist Church, built in 1909. (Courtesy of McDowell County Public Library.)

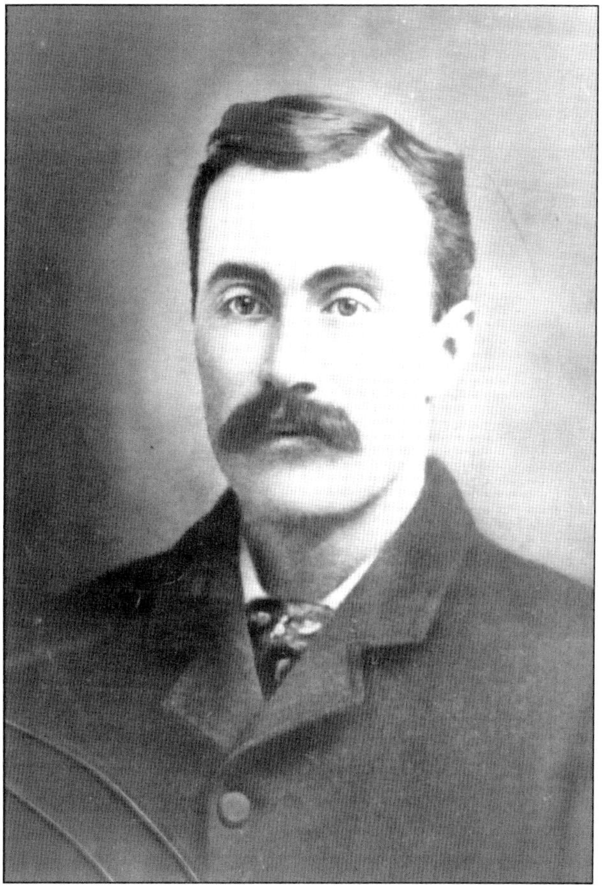

Dr. M.F. Morphew was a druggist, physician, and civic leader. He served as mayor of Marion in 1896 and 1897 when the town was struggling to rebuild after the great fire. He was elected to the North Carolina legislature in 1901 and 1905. He was also on the board of directors of the Commercial Bank of Marion. (Courtesy of Historic Carson House Library.)

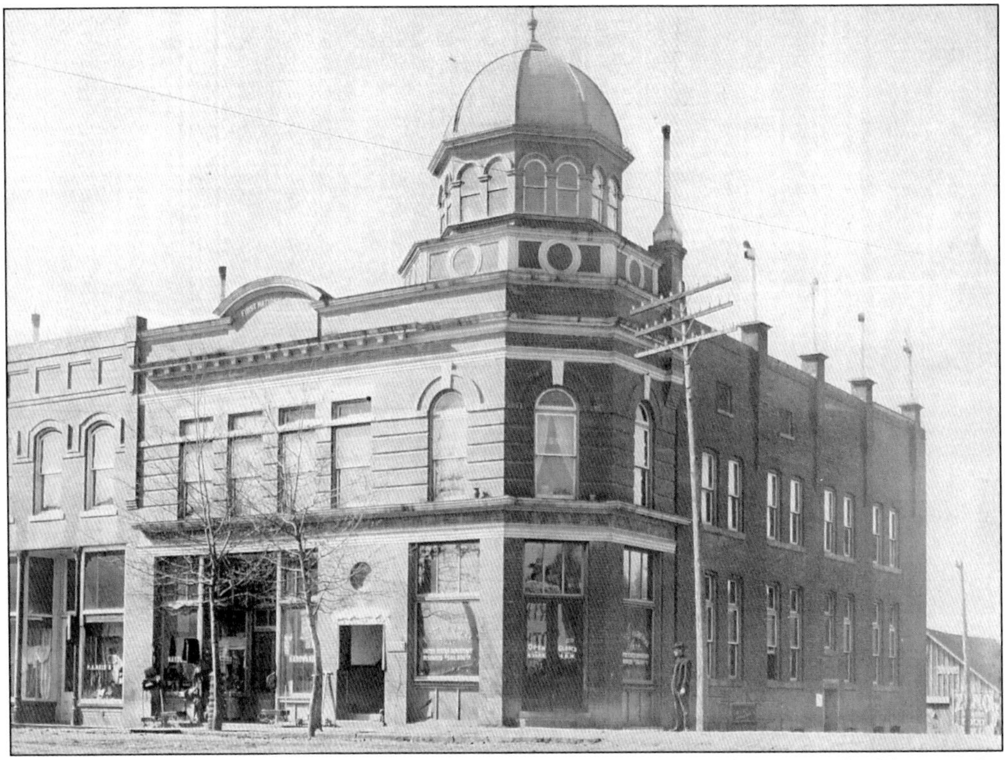

The First National Bank was established in 1902 and moved into this iconic building at the corner of Main and Court Streets a year later. The bank had its roots in the Commercial Bank of Marion, which had been established in 1896. In this c. 1905 photograph, note the meat market in the basement of the bank building and the individual fireplace chimneys. (Courtesy of Mountain Gateway Museum, Warren Hobbs Collection.)

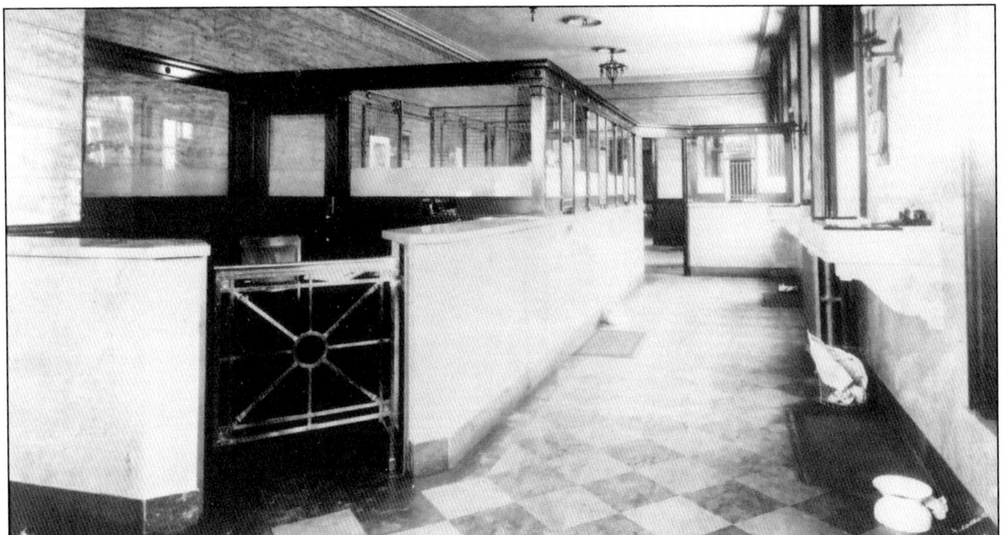

This is a rare peek into the interior of the First National Bank shortly after it was established. It shows how customers saw the bank as they came in through the corner entrance. Note the teller cages on the left, and the spittoon on the lower right. (Courtesy of Historic Carson House Library.)

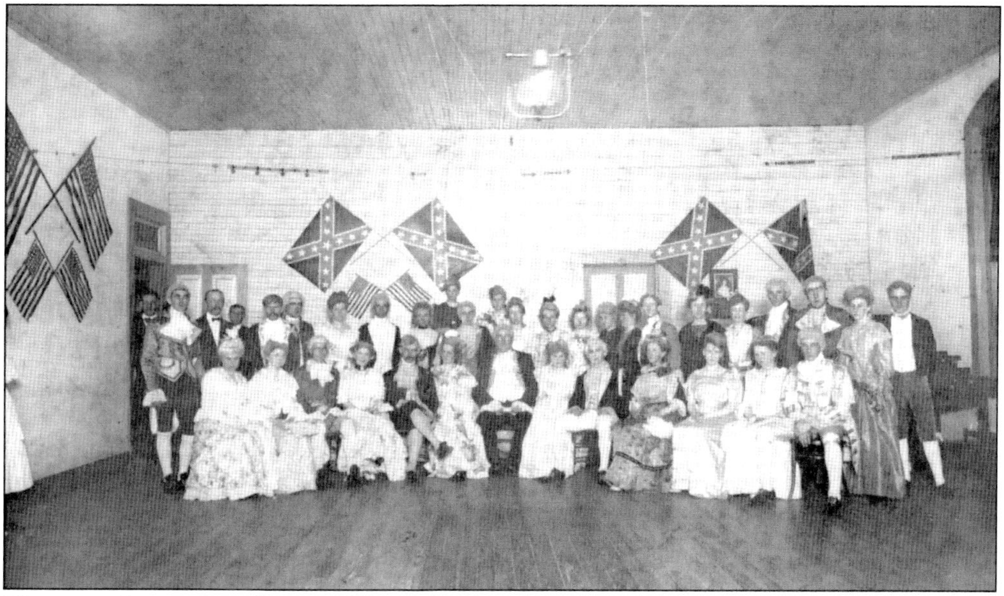

These socialites gathered in 1905 for a masquerade ball are members of the Catawba Club, which met on the second floor of the opera house at South Main and State Streets. The group was later reorganized as the "Manufacturer's Club" to promote Marion's development. The only person in the photograph who can be identified is Robert L. Greenlee, seated fifth from left. (Courtesy of McDowell County Public Library, Warren Hobbs Collection.)

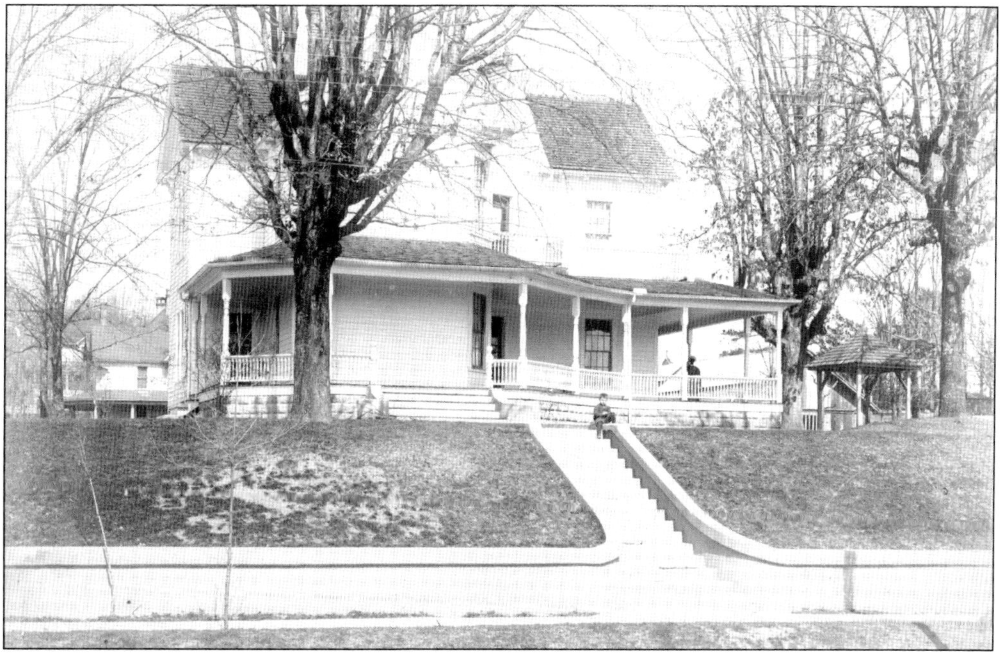

This is the East Court Street home of the A.C. Hewitt family, located on the former site of the Methodist church and future location of an A&P store. Mrs. Hewitt took the photograph in 1906 while son Kenneth sat on the steps and a maid stood on the porch. A.C. came to Marion to start a grocery business, later worked in railroad construction, and established Hewitt Hosiery Mill in 1940. (Courtesy of McDowell County Public Library.)

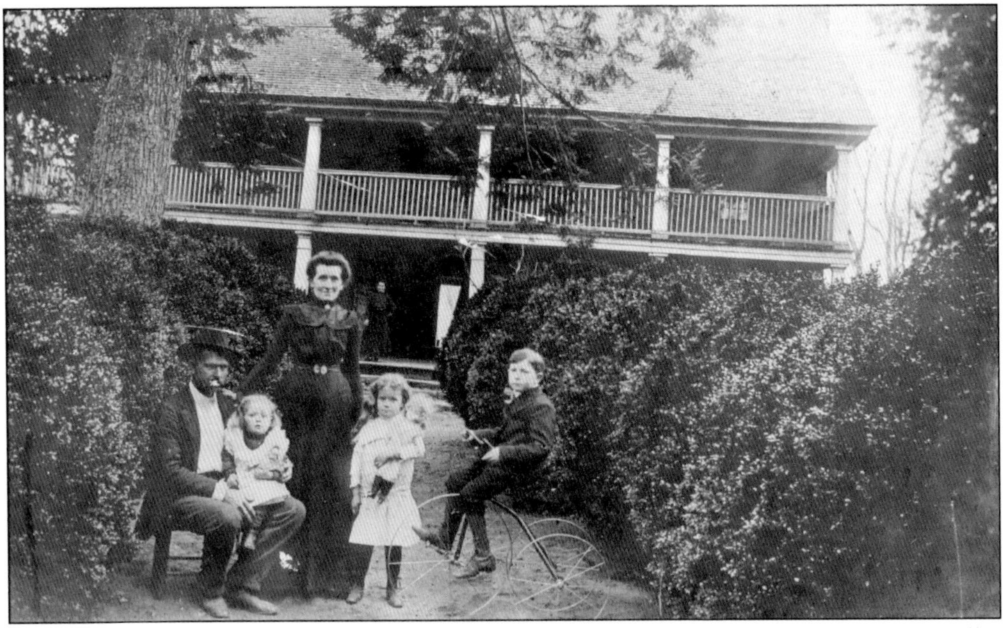

The Brown family gathers in front of the Carson House around 1905, with William E. "Billy" Brown at the far left. Billy's grandfather John Seawell Brown moved into the Carson House after the death of Jonathan Logan Carson and later purchased the house from Carson's widow. J.S. Brown was an original McDowell County commissioner, an officer of the Confederate Home Guard during the Civil War, and a member of the North Carolina legislature. (Courtesy of Historic Carson House Library.)

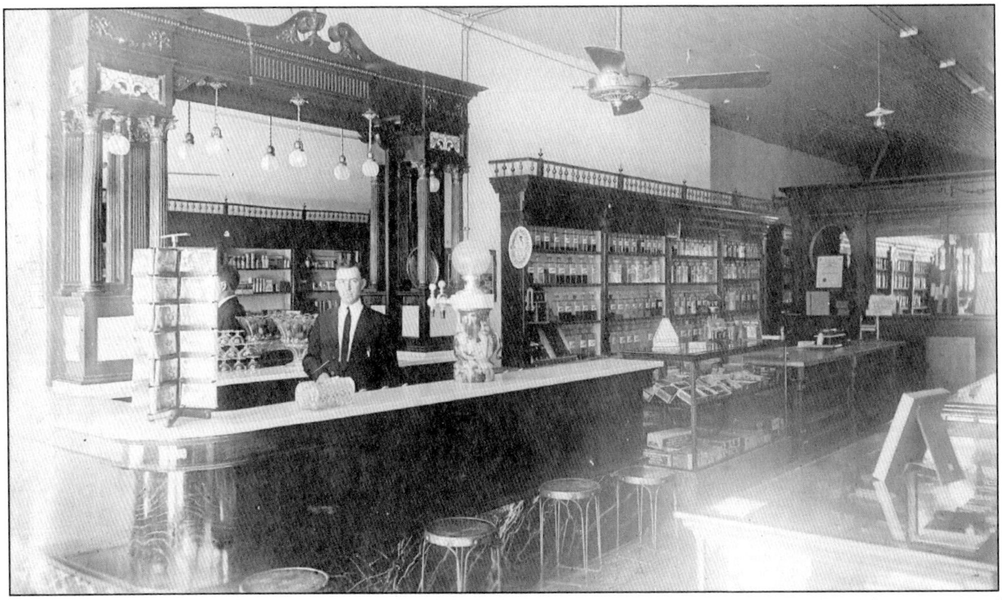

L.C. Griffin stands behind the counter of his newly opened drugstore located at the corner of South Main and Henderson Streets. Griffin moved into the building when previous owner J.W. Streetman relocated across Main Street. A few years later, Dean W. Tainter would purchase the building and continue to operate a drugstore there. (Courtesy of McDowell County Public Library, Joyce Decker Corbett Collection.)

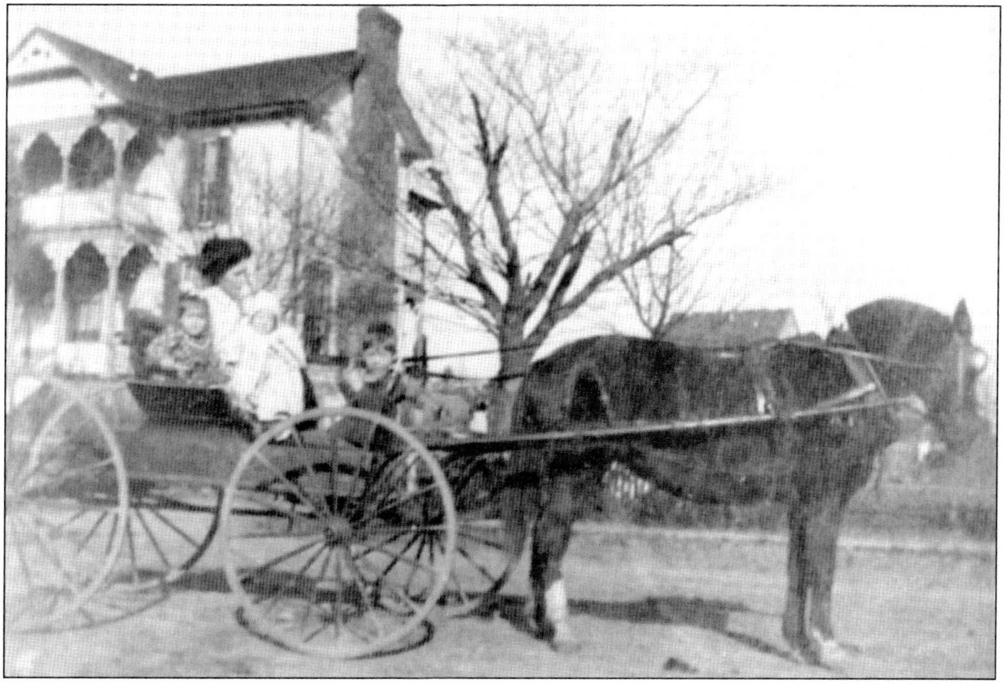

Mrs. John Yancey takes her children for a ride in 1906. Son John Grayson is at the foot of the buggy, Matilda (who would die at age four) is in her mother's arms, and Caroline sits beside Mrs. Yancey. Behind them is the Dr. B.A. Cheek homeplace on North Main Street. (Courtesy of McDowell County Public Library, Robin Hood Collection.)

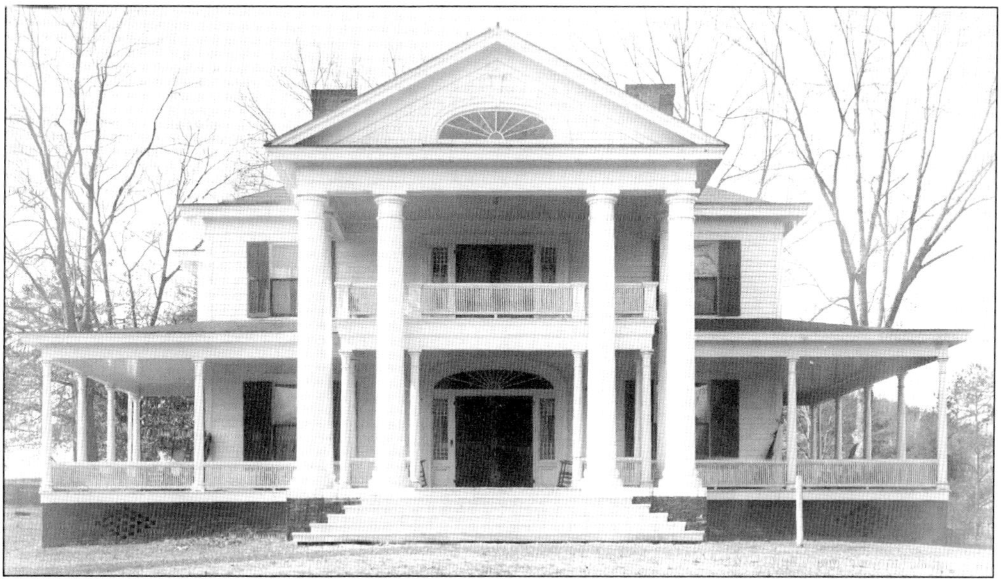

Lone Beech was built in 1905 by Daniel Edward Hudgins and his wife, Josephine Carter Hudgins. Hudgins was a director of the First National Bank, was a charter member of the Building and Loan, was involved in the development of Lake Tahoma, and donated the land for the African American Hudgins School. Lone Beech would later become the restaurant Josephine's, named in Mrs. Hudgins's honor. (Courtesy of McDowell County Public Library.)

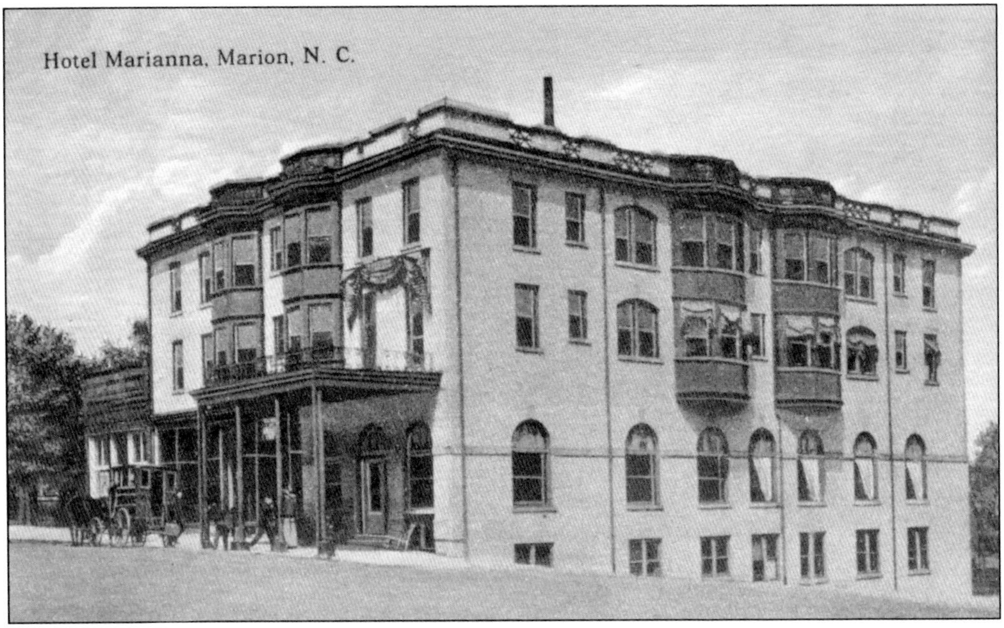

The 48-room Marianna Hotel opened in 1910 after suffering a significant setback when an interior wall collapsed during construction. Several men were injured, and the crash could be heard 10 blocks away. Crawford F. James purchased the hotel in 1931 and added an elevator and other updates. It was then renamed the Hotel James. (Courtesy of Wilson Library, University of North Carolina at Chapel Hill, North Carolina Collection.)

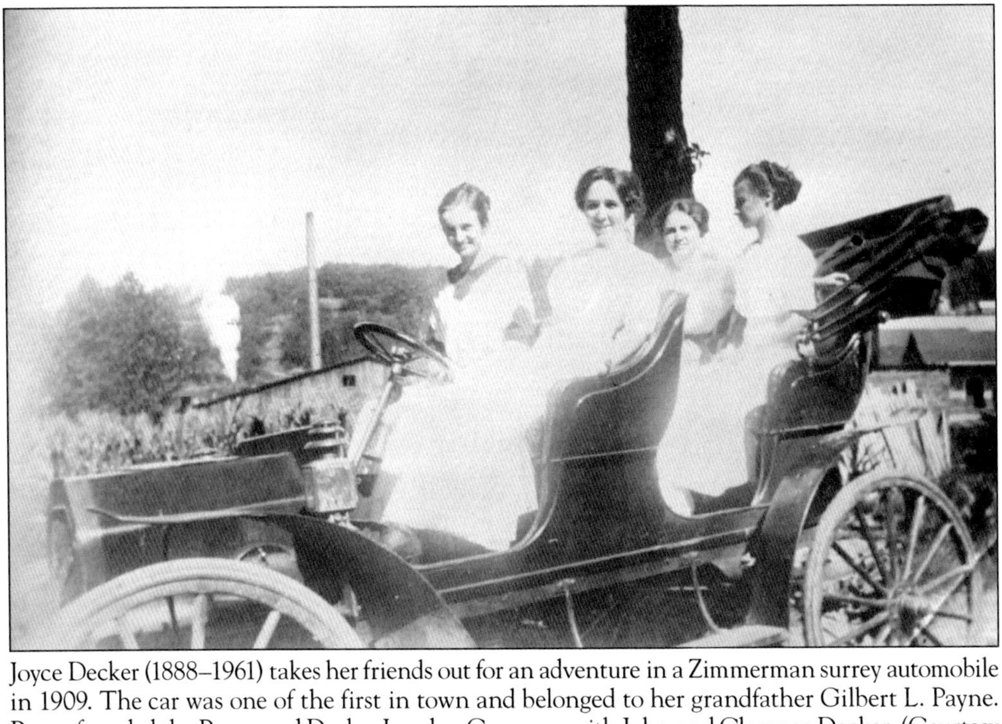

Joyce Decker (1888–1961) takes her friends out for an adventure in a Zimmerman surrey automobile in 1909. The car was one of the first in town and belonged to her grandfather Gilbert L. Payne. Payne founded the Payne and Decker Lumber Company with John and Clarence Decker. (Courtesy of McDowell County Public Library, Warren Hobbs Collection.)

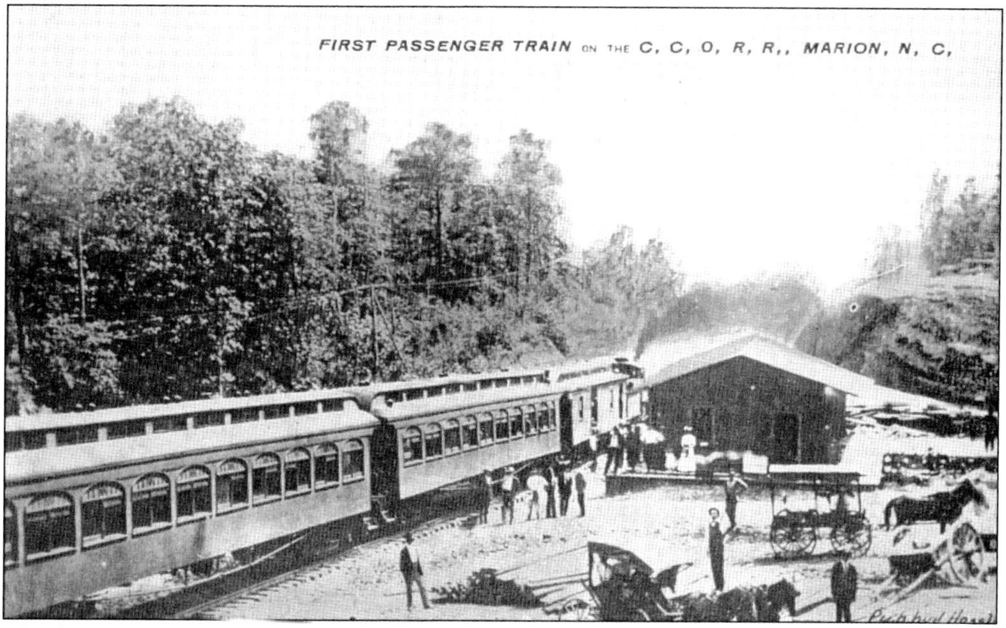

The first passenger train on the line from Altapass arrives at the Carolina, Clinchfield & Ohio Railroad station east of Marion in 1908. The CC&O was more commonly referred to as "the Clinchfield." Its major purpose was to link the coal mines of Kentucky and Virginia to points south. Passenger service on the Clinchfield ceased in 1954, and it was purchased by CSX in 1982. (Courtesy of McDowell County Public Library.)

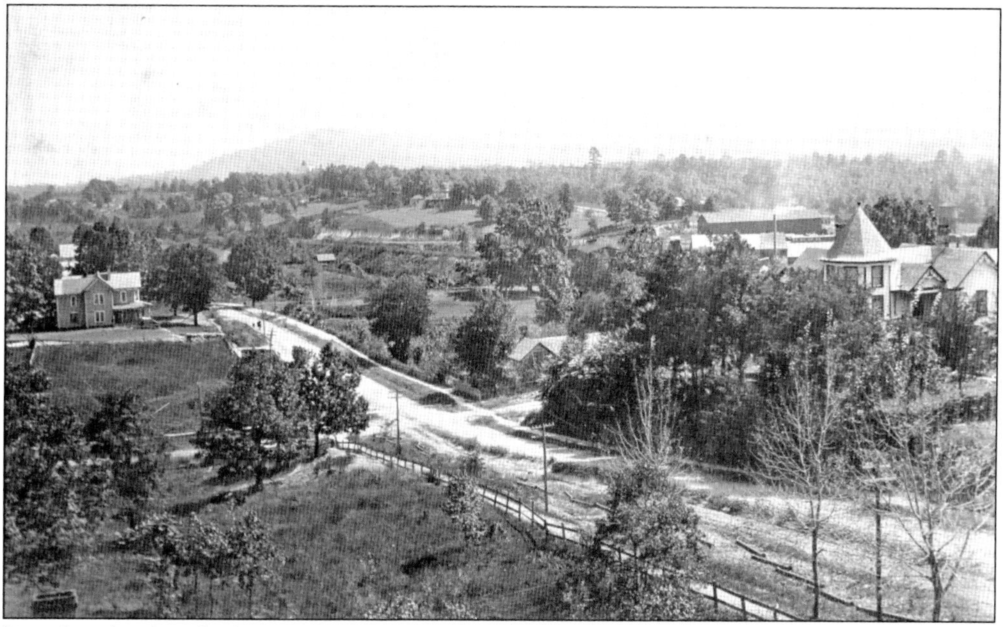

Pipes lined up beside the street indicate that this photograph of East Court Street is from around 1908 when Marion's first water lines were being laid. The near house is the Nichols home, which stood behind the courthouse. The top of the Catawba Furniture Company is visible just beyond. The small house at the bottom of the hill is the Finley home, later the site of the House Theatre. (Courtesy of McDowell County Public Library, Robin Hood Collection.)

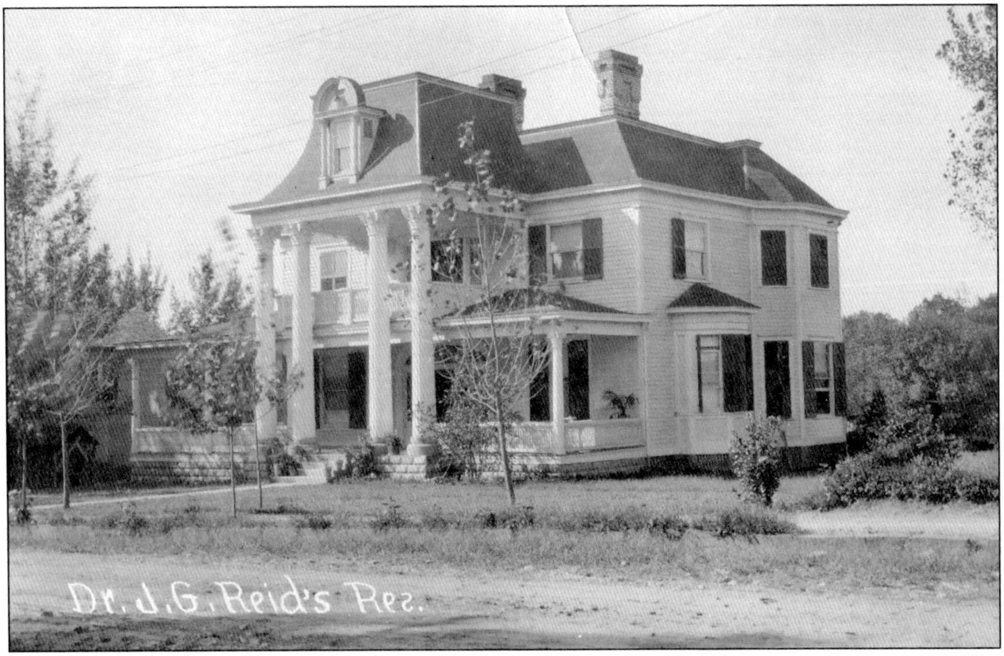

Dr. Joseph Gillespie Reid, a Marion dentist, built this home on South Main Street in 1905. Dr. Reid was highly regarded in his profession and was an advocate of oral hygiene as a preventative measure. He believed that proper dental care could improve the physical, mental, and moral development of children. His house changed hands several times before becoming a funeral home in 1948. (Courtesy of McDowell County Public Library, Warren Hobbs Collection.)

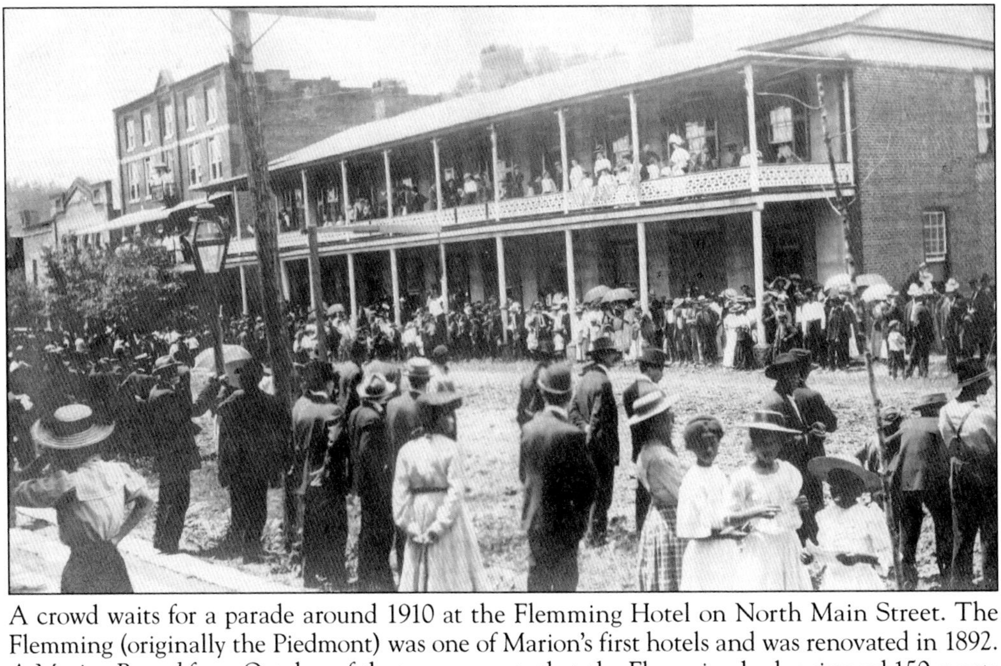

A crowd waits for a parade around 1910 at the Flemming Hotel on North Main Street. The Flemming (originally the Piedmont) was one of Marion's first hotels and was renovated in 1892. A *Marion Record* from October of that year reports that the Flemming had registered 150 guests for the month, "notwithstanding the dull travel." The building would be used as a hospital in the 1920s. (Courtesy of McDowell County Public Library, Greenlee Collection.)

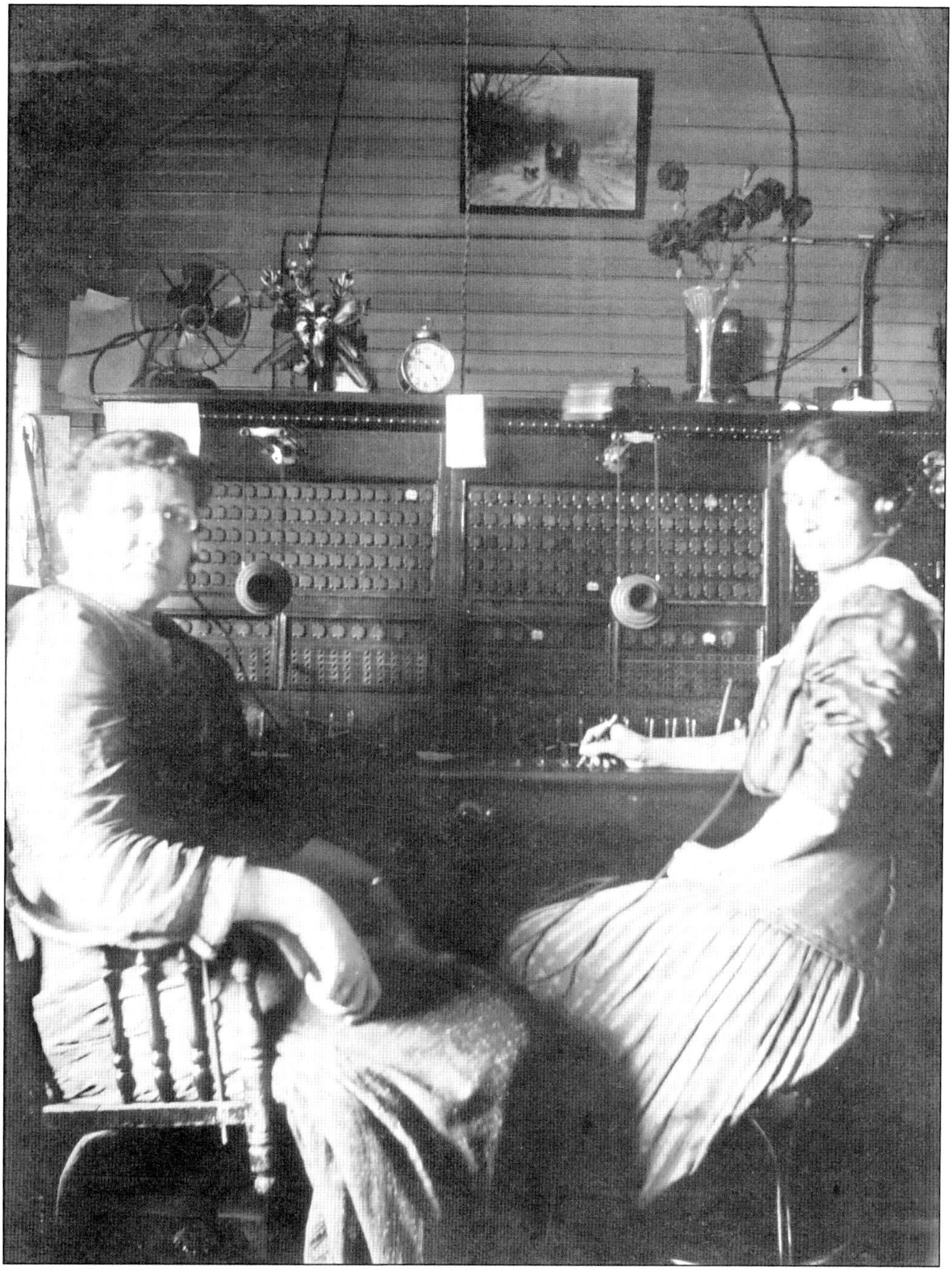

The Marion Telephone Company was established in 1911, a decade after telephones had come to the larger cities of Asheville and Charlotte. It was established by Paul Smith, and "central" was in an upstairs space on Main Street. The Marion operators at the switchboard in this photograph are Nell Shepardson (left) and Joyce Decker. The illuminated jack lamps on the rear panel of the switchboard indicate local subscribers who were "on the line." In addition to routing calls, operators were also expected to be a source of community information. (Courtesy of McDowell County Public Library, Joyce Decker Corbett Collection.)

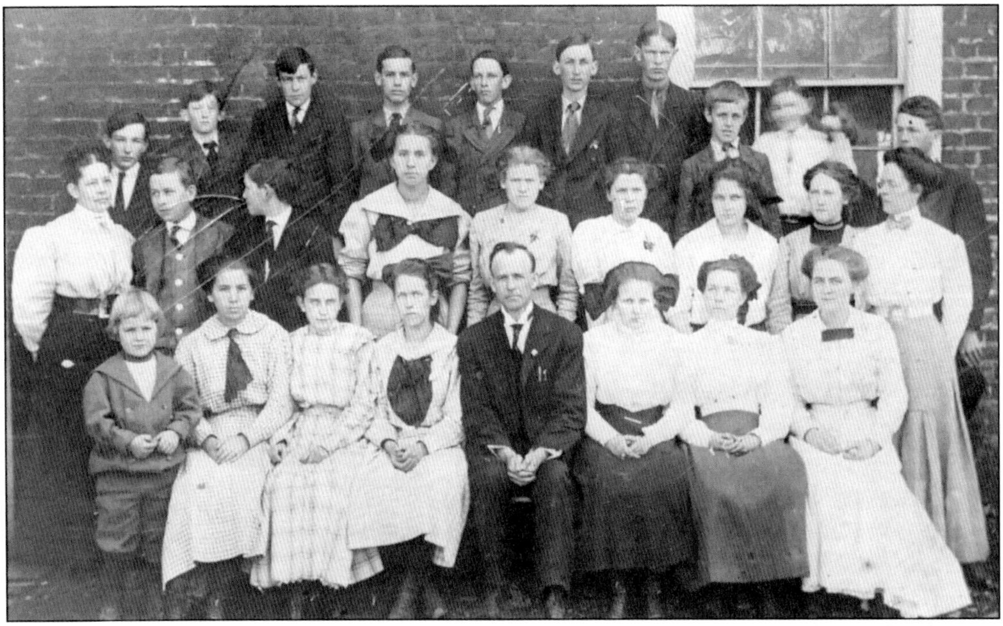

This is the Marion eighth-grade class for school year 1910–1911. Those pictured with the class are mascot Lenoir Byrd (first row, far left), superintendent A.C. Jones (first row, center), teacher Mrs. J.L.C. Byrd (second row, far left), and teacher Nan Guy (second row, far right). These students were among the last to attend classes in the original school building constructed in 1857 on Academy Street. (Courtesy of Mountain Gateway Museum, Warren Hobbs Collection.)

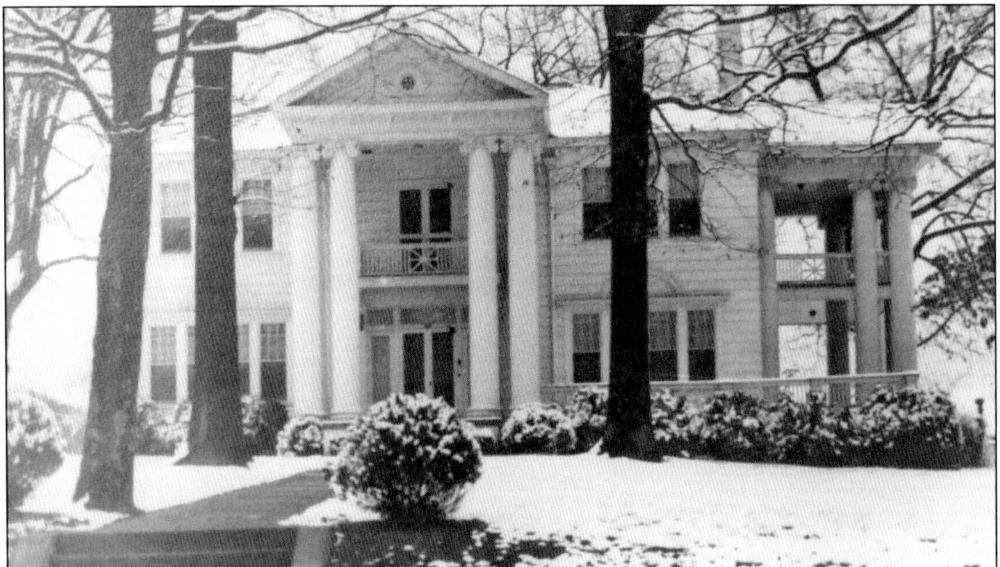

Albert Blanton (1874–1917) was the owner of A. Blanton Wholesale Grocery on Depot Street and commissioned Asheville architect Richard Sharp Smith to design this impressive home. It was constructed on South Main Street in 1915. The house was purchased in the 1920s by W. Lester Morris, who became president of Clinchfield Manufacturing. In later years, the building housed businesses, including the Max Hensley Photography Studio. (Courtesy of Gregg M. Hensley and Hensley Studio.)

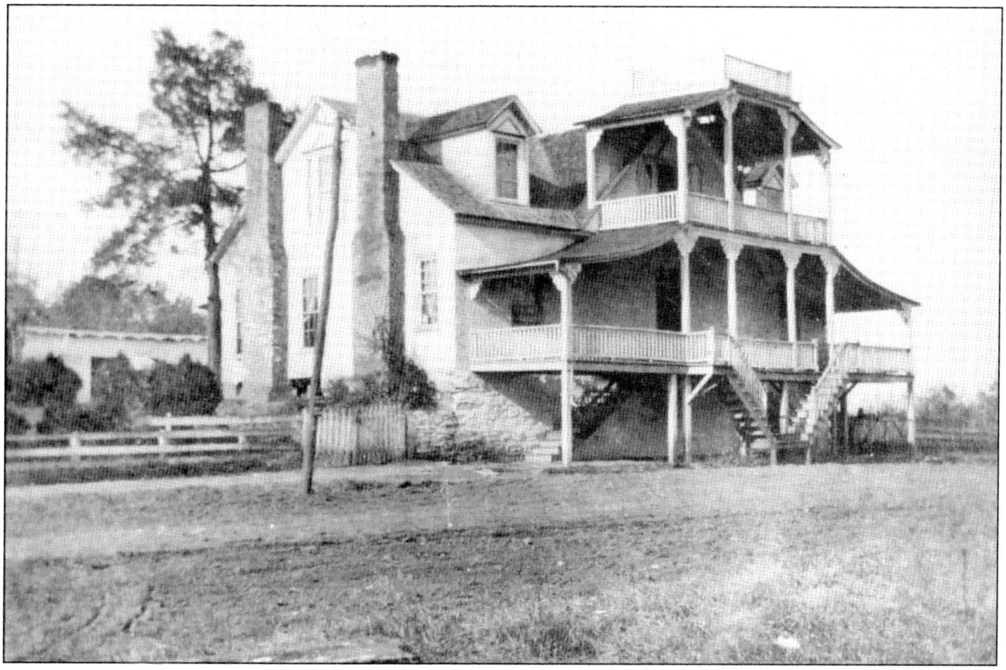

This eccentric house was the John Yancey home on North Main Street. It was originally a two-room structure, and as children were born to the family, Yancey built additions onto the rear. Later, when the town widened and lowered Main Street, the house was left about eight feet above street level. Yancey responded by building an elaborate porch over the sidewalk with steps leading downward. (Courtesy of McDowell County Public Library, Robin Hood Collection.)

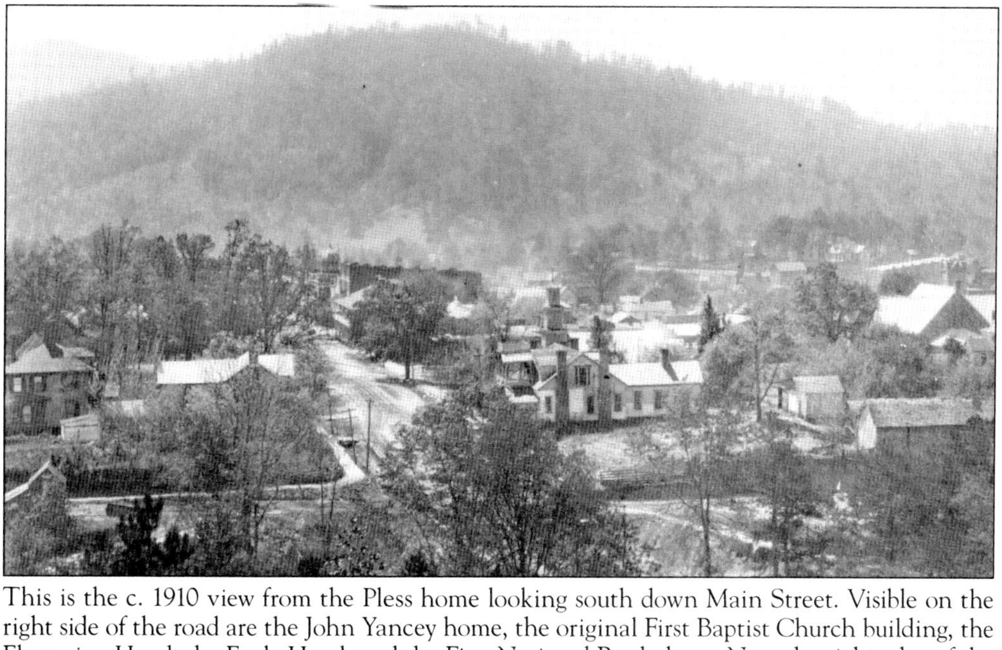

This is the c. 1910 view from the Pless home looking south down Main Street. Visible on the right side of the road are the John Yancey home, the original First Baptist Church building, the Flemming Hotel, the Eagle Hotel, and the First National Bank dome. Near the right edge of the photograph is the second Methodist church building. (Courtesy of McDowell County Public Library, Robin Hood Collection.)

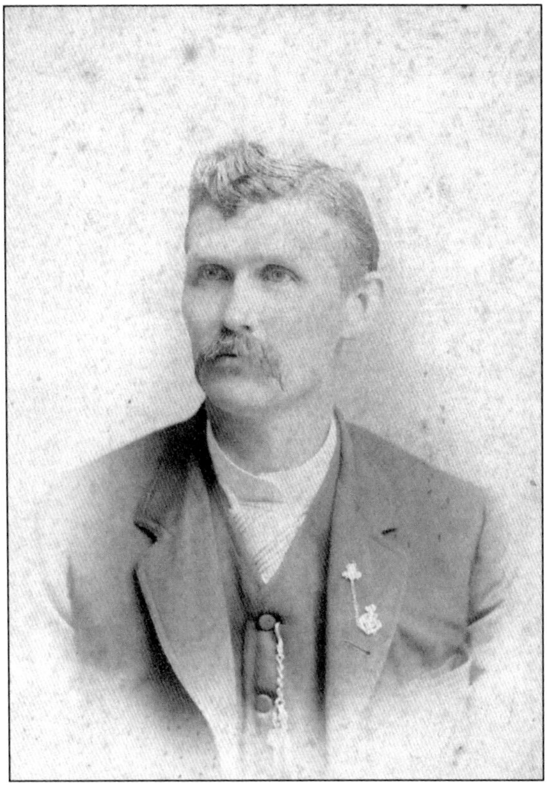

Dr. Robert J. Burgin (1851–1919) was a well-known and respected figure in Marion, where he practiced dentistry for 42 years. His father, Capt. Alney Burgin, served in both houses of the North Carolina legislature and was the second for Samuel Price Carson in the famous Vance-Carson duel. Captain Burgin was also friends with Davy Crockett. Robert's grandfather "Pioneer Ben" Burgin first came to McDowell County around 1770. (Courtesy of McDowell County Public Library, Warren Hobbs Collection.)

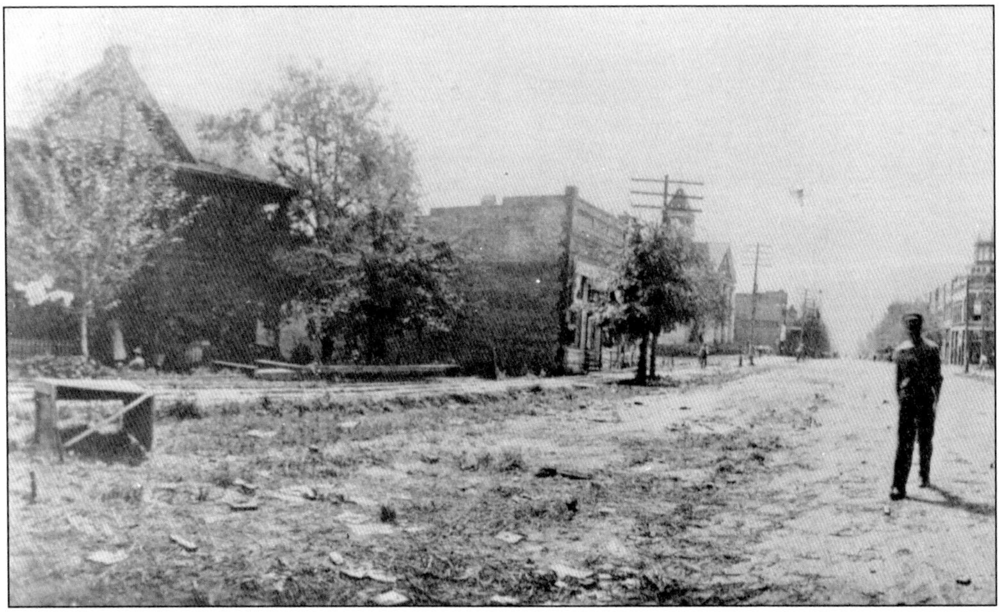

This 1911 image shows a perspective of Main Street that is rarely seen. The house on the left is the R.F. Burton home. Burton was cashier at the Merchants & Farmers Bank, and his wife, Julia, was a music teacher for many years. Older residents remember the sound of her singing and piano-playing drifting out onto the street. (Courtesy of McDowell County Public Library, Robin Hood Collection.)

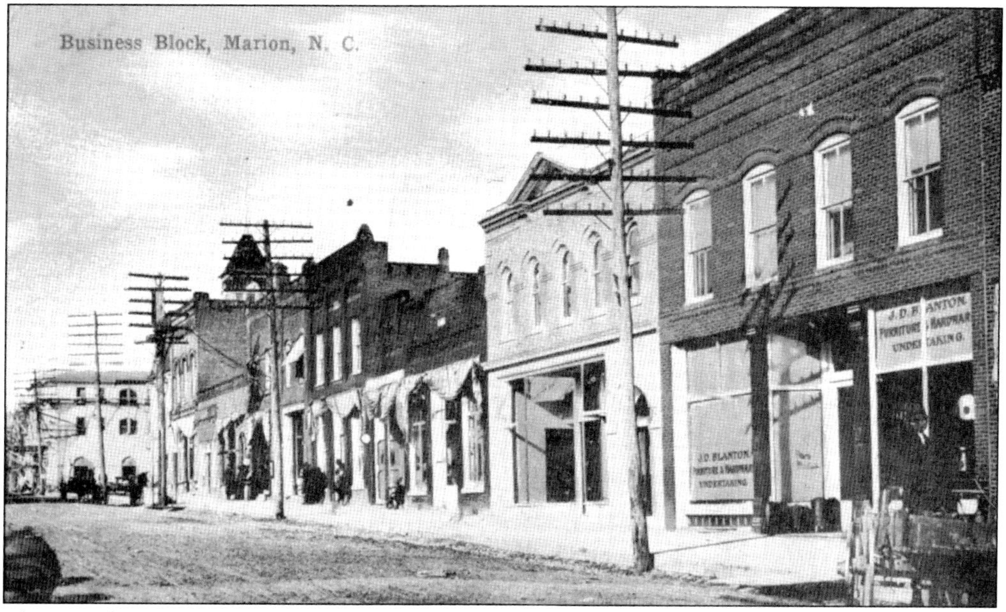

This view looking north on Main Street with J.D. Blanton's store in the foreground is from about 1910. Blanton operated a business on Main Street for 58 years. His original dry goods store business opened around 1900, and he added an adjacent hardware store shortly thereafter. The dry goods side stocked clothing, shoes, domestics, groceries, and textbooks. The telephone number for customers to call in their orders was 8. (Courtesy of Marion Business Association.)

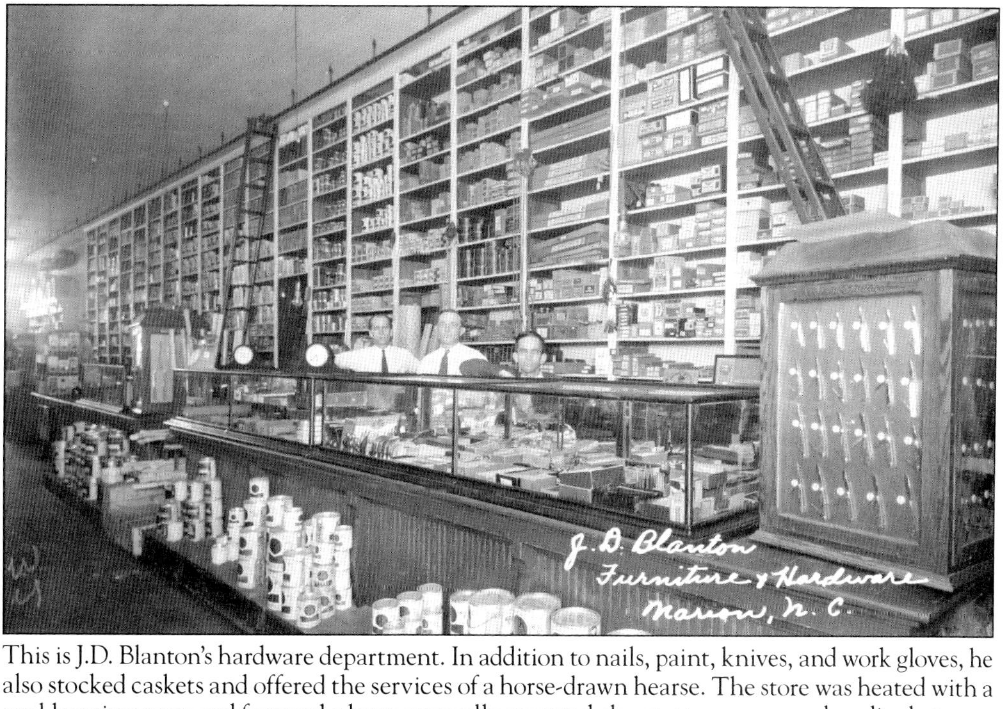

This is J.D. Blanton's hardware department. In addition to nails, paint, knives, and work gloves, he also stocked caskets and offered the services of a horse-drawn hearse. The store was heated with a coal-burning stove and featured a large manually operated elevator to move merchandise between the three floors. Blanton's slogan on his wrapping paper for purchases was "One price to everybody in the same quantity." (Courtesy of Historic Carson House Library, Blanton Collection.)

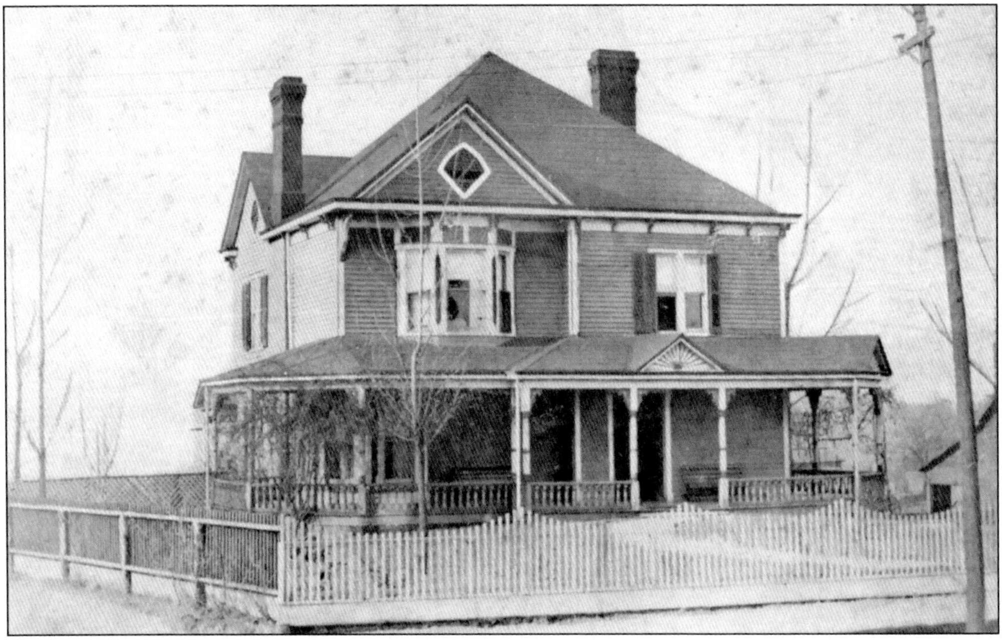

The Dr. B.L. Ashworth residence was located on South Main Street. Ashworth was a member of the staff at Marion General Hospital and a surgeon for the Southern Railway. Mrs. Ashworth was known as a lavish and creative hostess. For a 1916 party, the living room was converted into a flower-laden Japanese grove with attendants outfitted in oriental costume. (Courtesy of McDowell County Public Library.)

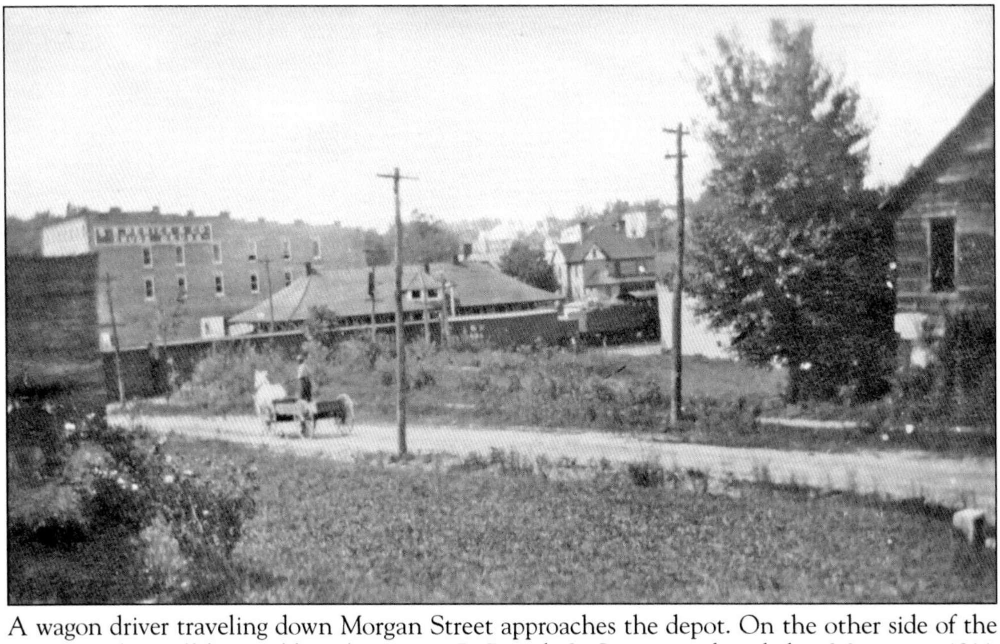

A wagon driver traveling down Morgan Street approaches the depot. On the other side of the station is the Buffaloe Building, housing S.B. Penick & Company, founded in Marion in 1914. Penick was a merchant and miller of local herbs. World War I increased demand for the company's products, prompting relocation to New York. By the 1960s, Penick was a multinational corporation. (Courtesy of McDowell County Public Library, Joyce Decker Corbett Collection.)

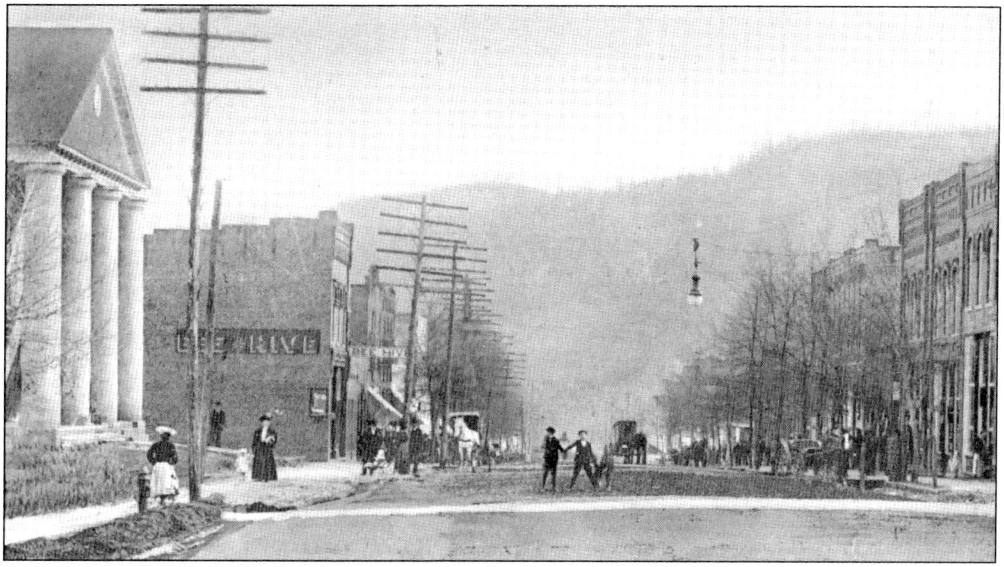

This postcard shows a bustling retail district around 1910. The Bee Hive beside the courthouse was a general store run by J.R. Ledbetter from 1904 to 1913. The Ledbetter family lived upstairs. An early version of an electric streetlight hangs over the middle of the street, and horse drawn carriages and wagons are parked in front of the stores. (Courtesy of Wilson Library, University of North Carolina Library at Chapel Hill, North Carolina Collection.)

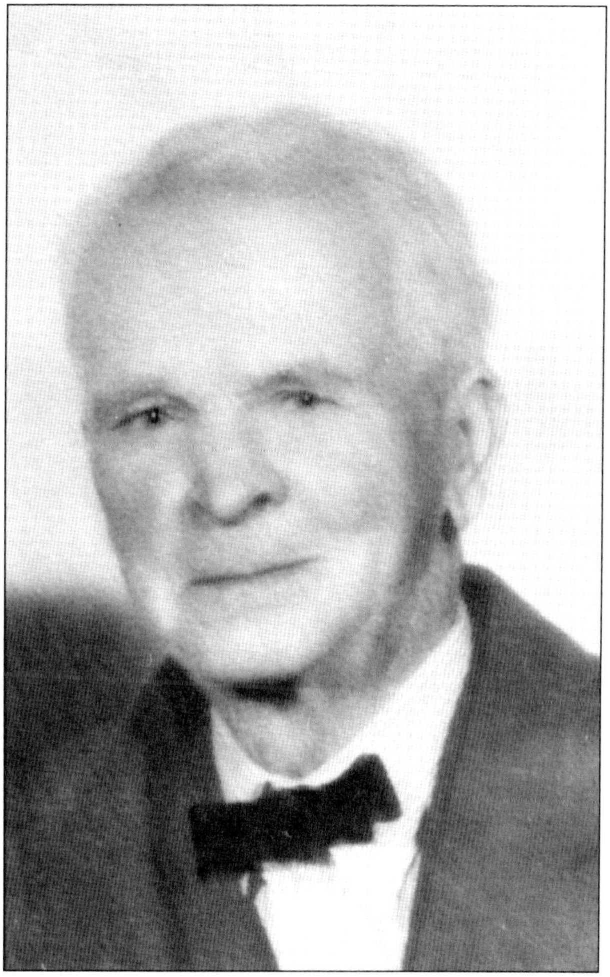

James Lafayette Morgan was one of Marion's most prominent and influential citizens. Early in his career, he was in the tobacco business with J.W. Crawford. With R.H. Bennett, Morgan founded Marion Power and Light and the Blue Ridge Distillery. He was president of the First National Bank and vice president of Clinchfield Manufacturing. When he died in 1938, the *Marion Progress* described him as "the backbone citizen" of the county. (Courtesy of McDowell County Public Library, Warren Hobbs Collection.)

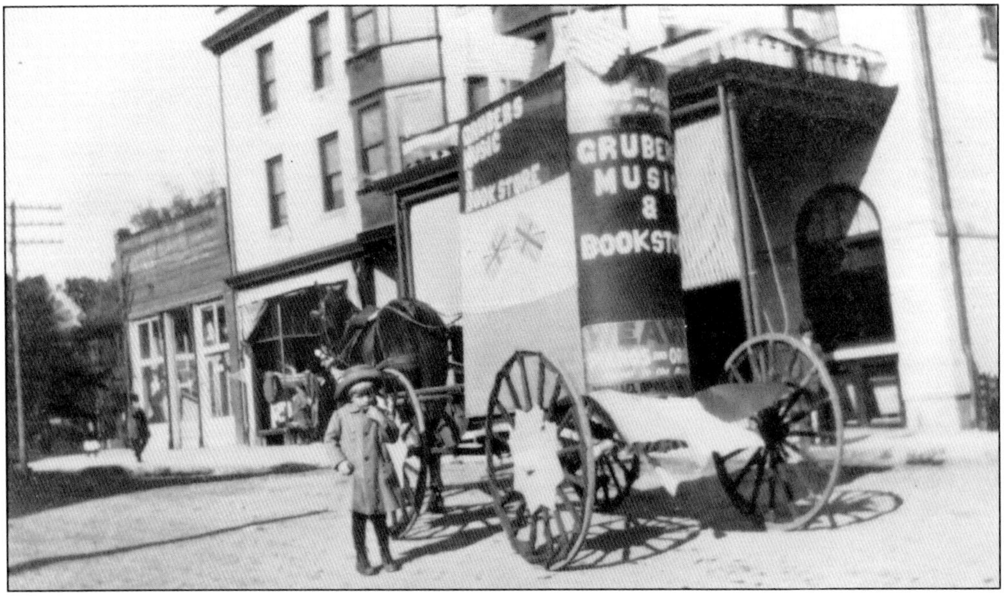

The Gruber's Music and Bookstore float pauses during a 1911 parade. Seven members of the Gruber family had performed together in the 1890s as the Gruber Family Musical Concert Company, led by Prof. Stephen Frederick Gruber. They performed in opera houses throughout the South and Northeast and in Marion at the Flemming and Eagle Hotels. The music and bookstore was operated by William R. Gruber, Professor Gruber's son. (Courtesy of Marion Business Association.)

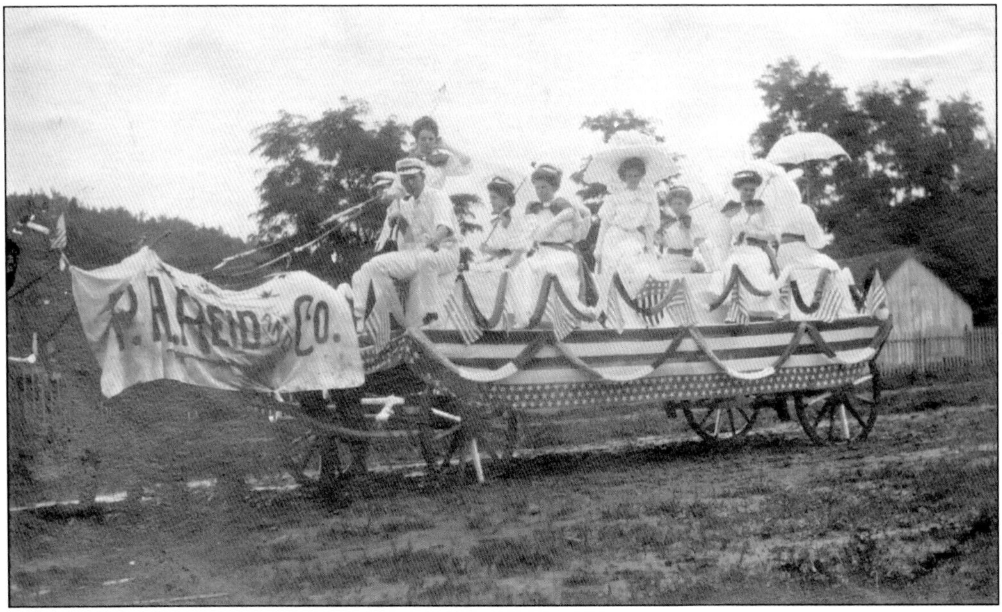

This is merchant P.A. Reid's entry in an early downtown parade. Reid carried silk thread, pearl buttons, ginghams, parasols, notions, and clothing. To promote the store's line of James A. Banister shoes for men, Reid's slogan was "Any policeman can walk our beat, but no policeman can beat our shoes." (Courtesy of McDowell County Public Library, Greenlee Collection.)

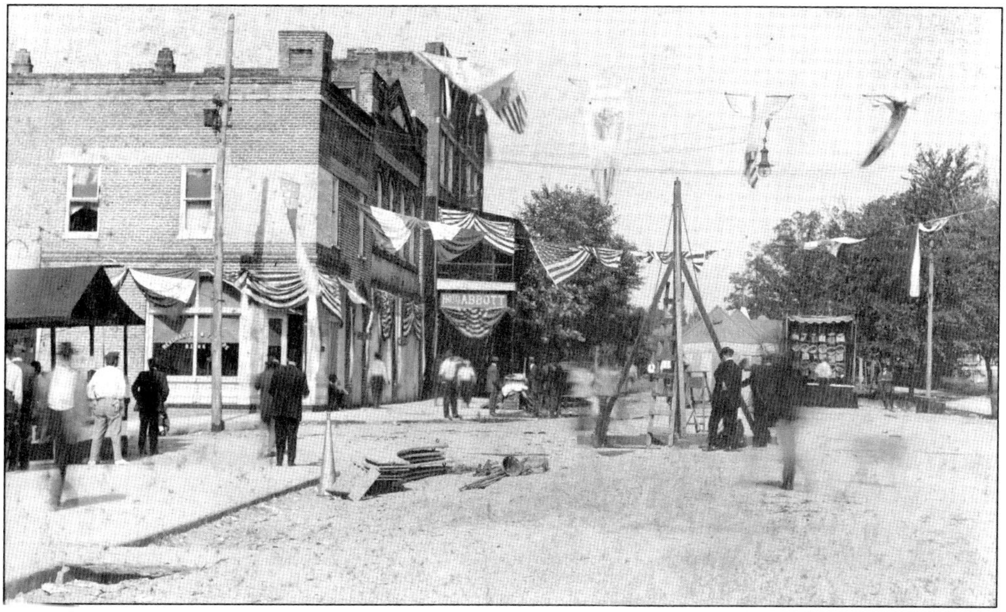

The fair comes to Marion in 1914. The view is looking north on Main Street at the intersection with Court Street. To the left are the Merchants & Farmers Bank, the Bobbitt Building, and the Hotel Abbott. Exhibits were located inside the Bobbitt Building, and the "wine room" over the bank was open for celebration. The point and the name atop the Bobbitt Building were later removed during remodeling. (Courtesy of McDowell County Public Library, Greenlee Collection.)

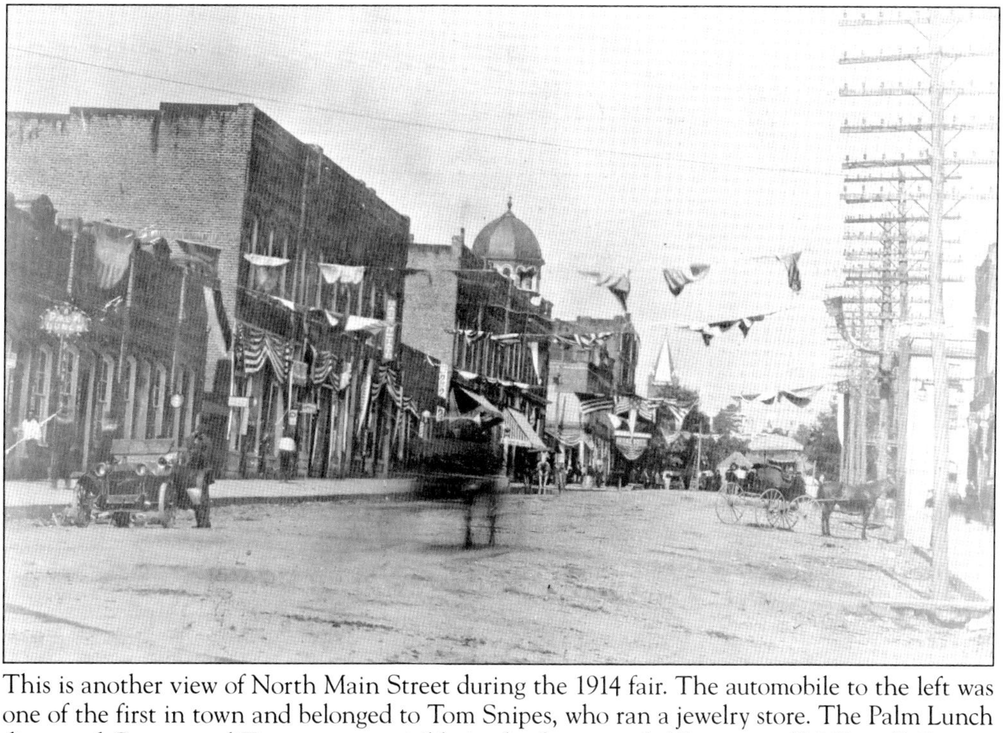

This is another view of North Main Street during the 1914 fair. The automobile to the left was one of the first in town and belonged to Tom Snipes, who ran a jewelry store. The Palm Lunch diner and Gaston and Tate store are visible in the foreground. (Courtesy of McDowell County Public Library, Robin Hood Collection.)

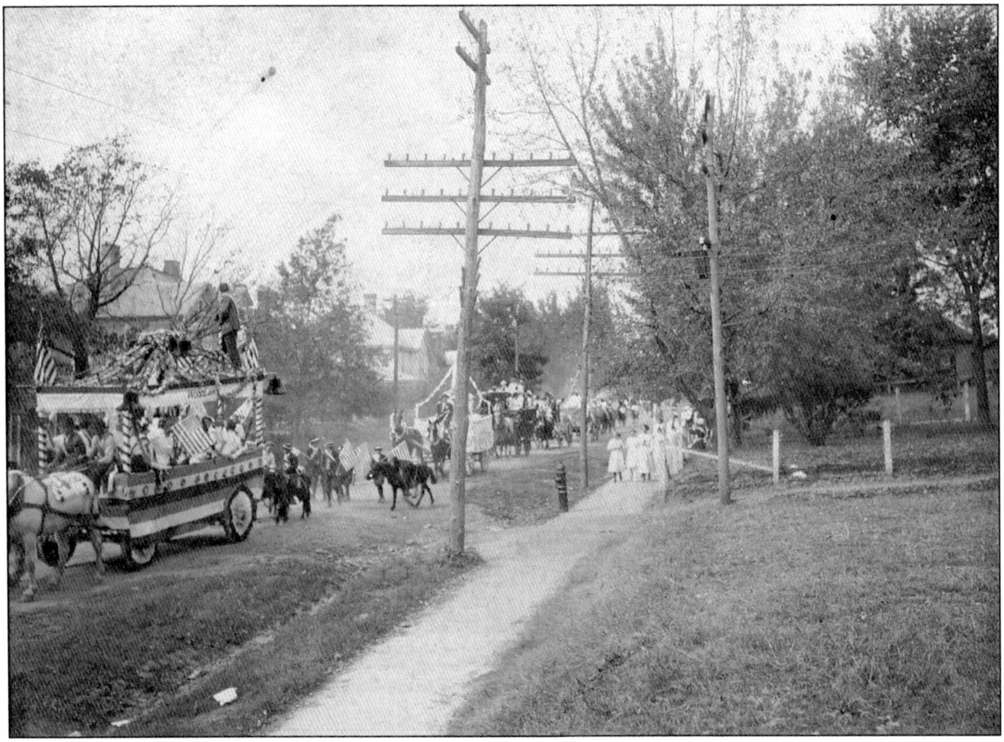

A group from Woodlawn is in the foreground of this photograph of a parade traveling down South Main Street. Marion parades were generally organized on Academy Street and proceeded on Fort Street to Main Street, and then concluded at the end of South Main Street. Carnivals and other celebrations sometimes took place at the end of South Main Street at the foot of Mount Ida. (Courtesy of McDowell County Public Library, Greenlee Collection.)

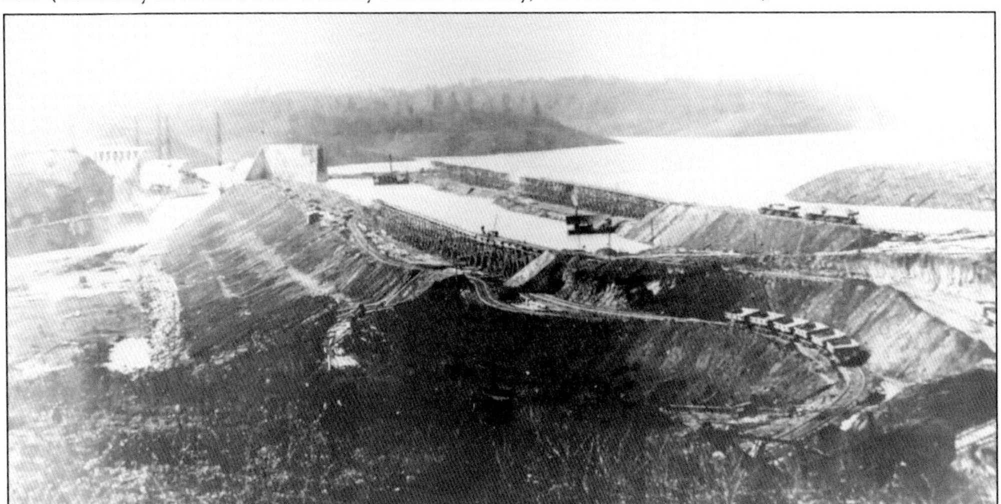

Lake James was built between 1916 and 1923 by damming the waters of the Catawba River, the Linville River, and Paddy's Creek. Entire communities were relocated, and a self-contained railroad was built within the site to move supplies, rock, and dirt. At the time of its completion, this was one of the largest earthen dams in the world. (Courtesy of Gregg M. Hensley and Hensley Studio.)

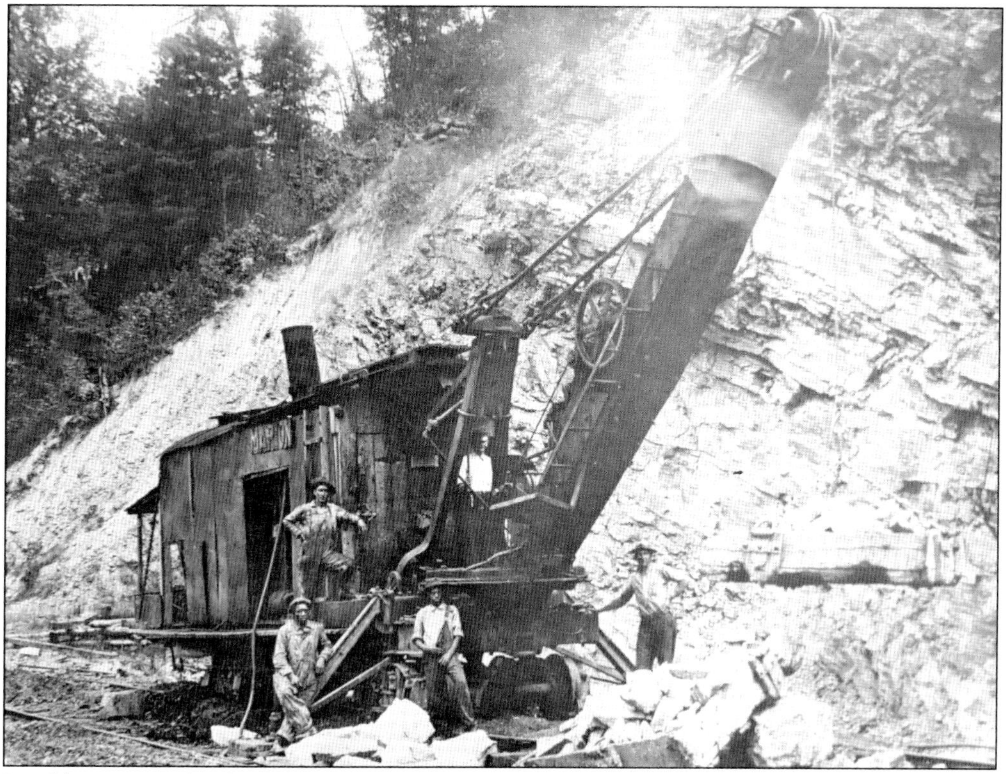

In addition to mules, horses, and steam shovels, a tremendous amount of manpower was required for the Lake James project. Work was available for any local man who wanted it, convicts were used, and laborers were brought in from South Carolina, Georgia, and Alabama. The name Marion on the steam shovel in this 1917 photograph is coincidental. It was the name of the steam shovel manufacturer. (Courtesy of McDowell County Public Library.)

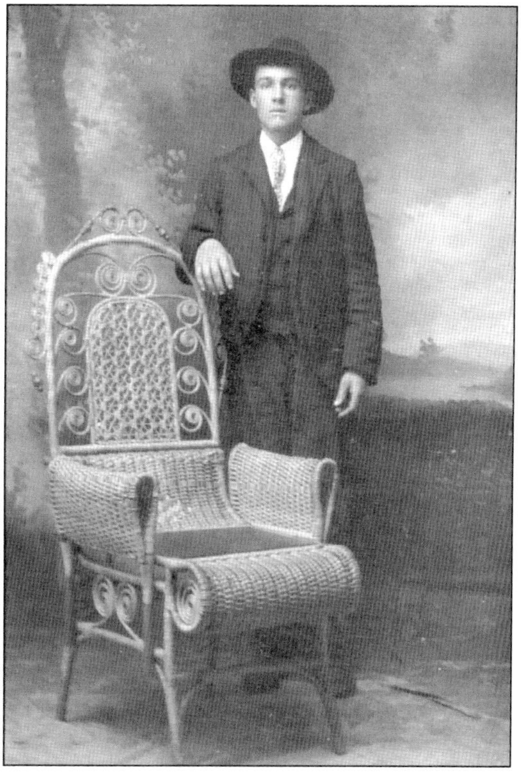

Thomas W. Solomon was one of the many men who lost their lives while working on the construction of Lake James. The Buncombe County native was killed when he was struck by the dipper of a steam shovel in December 1917. A carpenter by trade, Solomon was working on the form for the dam when the accident occurred. He was 24 years old. (Courtesy of David Vess.)

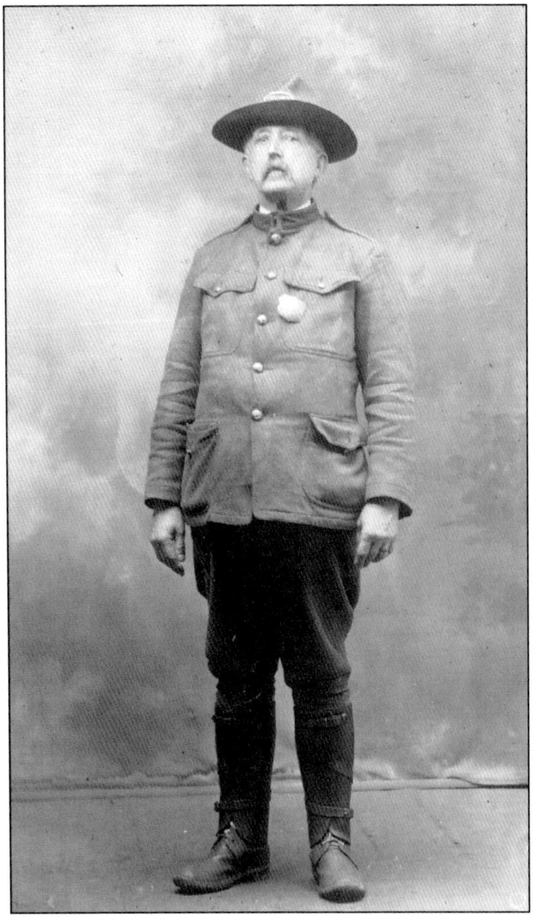

Seagle W. Halliburton from Marion was one of nearly 500 McDowell residents who saw action abroad during World War I. Halliburton was wounded and then returned home to manage the business of his grandfather George Halliburton, a Confederate veteran. (Courtesy of McDowell County Public Library, Warren Hobbs Collection.)

Red Cross nurses take part in a patriotic parade on May 10, 1919. It was Confederate Memorial Day, and World War I had ended just months before. The procession marched south to the crossroads of South Main, Morgan Street, and Rutherford Road. There, the McDowell County National Guardsmen fired their rifles across a cornfield toward Mount Ida. (Courtesy of McDowell County Public Library, Robin Hood Collection.)

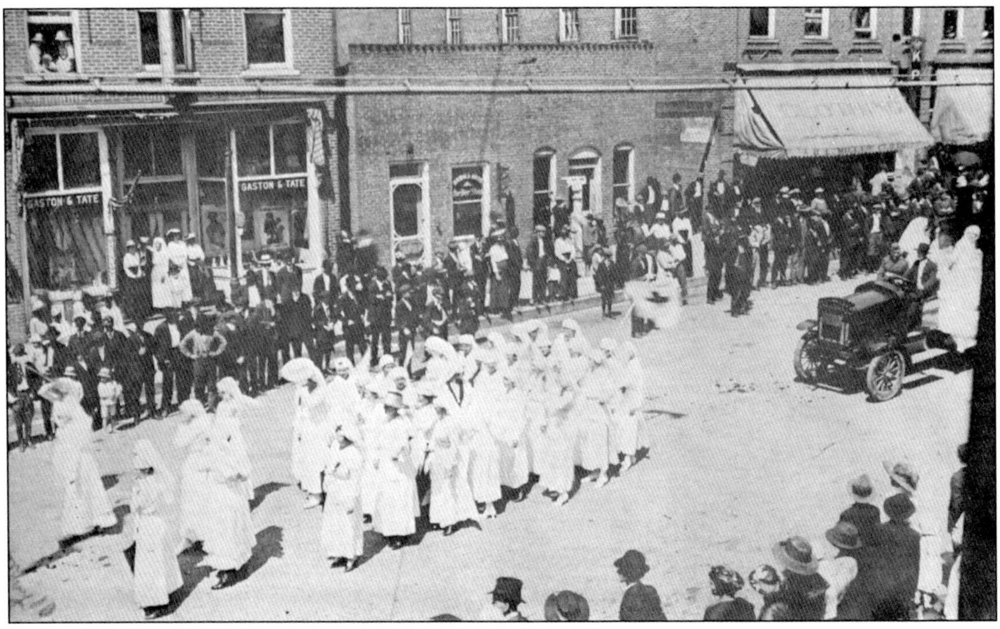

Three

Between the Wars

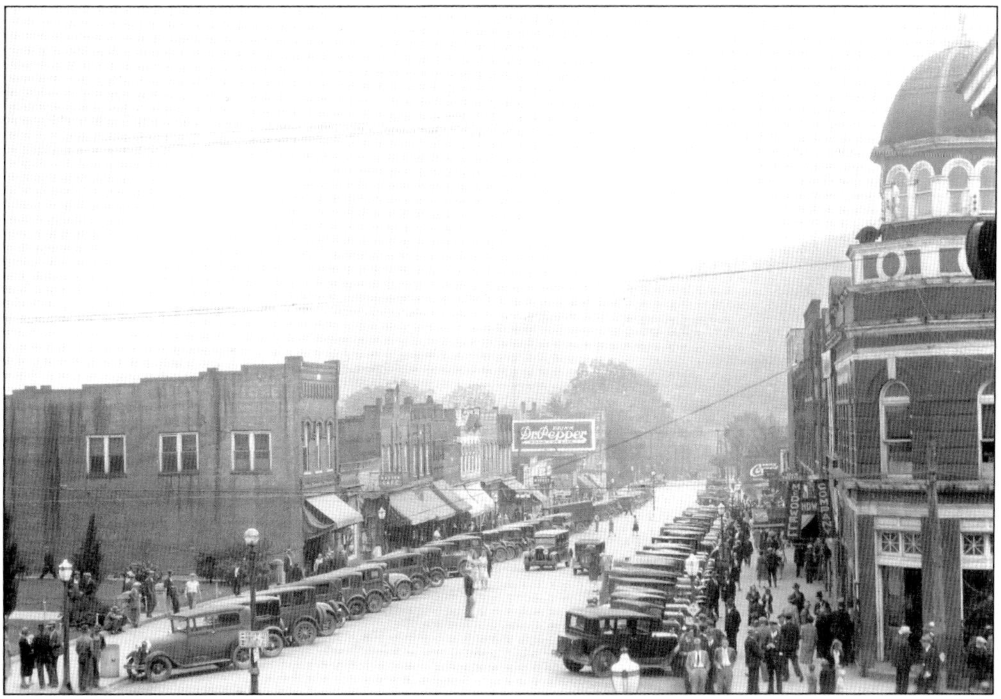

Even though the stock market had crashed two years before, this 1931 image of downtown Marion shows a vibrant and lively town. At the time this photograph was made, Herbert Hoover was president, the Empire State Building had just opened, *Dick Tracy* had recently debuted in the comics section, and *Little Orphan Annie* was a new radio serial. The electric razor, nylon, and aerosol cans were new inventions. (Courtesy of Gregg M. Hensley and Hensley Studio.)

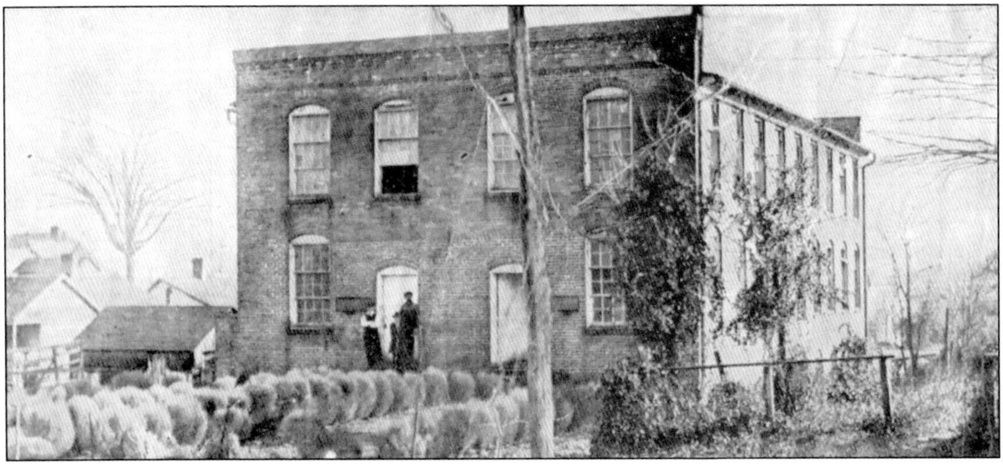

This photograph of Marion Knitting Mills was made in 1919. A relatively small-scale operation located near the business district, the plant employed less than 100 people and touted the fact that its employees lived in town instead of in a mill village. Superintendent J.A. Ruth, B.P. Webster, and R.H. Bomar are seen at the front entrance. (Courtesy of McDowell County Public Library, Greenlee Collection.)

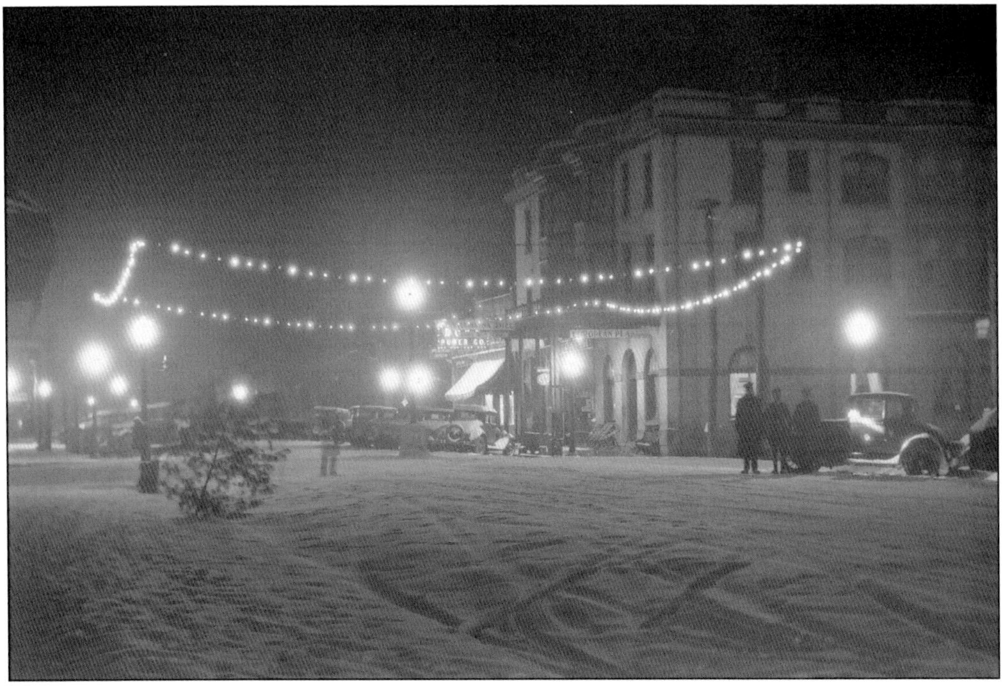

The Marianna Hotel dominates the town square on a snowy evening during a holiday season in the 1920s. The "European Plan" advertised at the hotel entrance refers to a lodging package that excluded full meals. Evening dances were often held at the Marianna on special occasions, with the Charles LaFell Dance Orchestra a perennial favorite. (Courtesy of Gregg M. Hensley and Hensley Studio.)

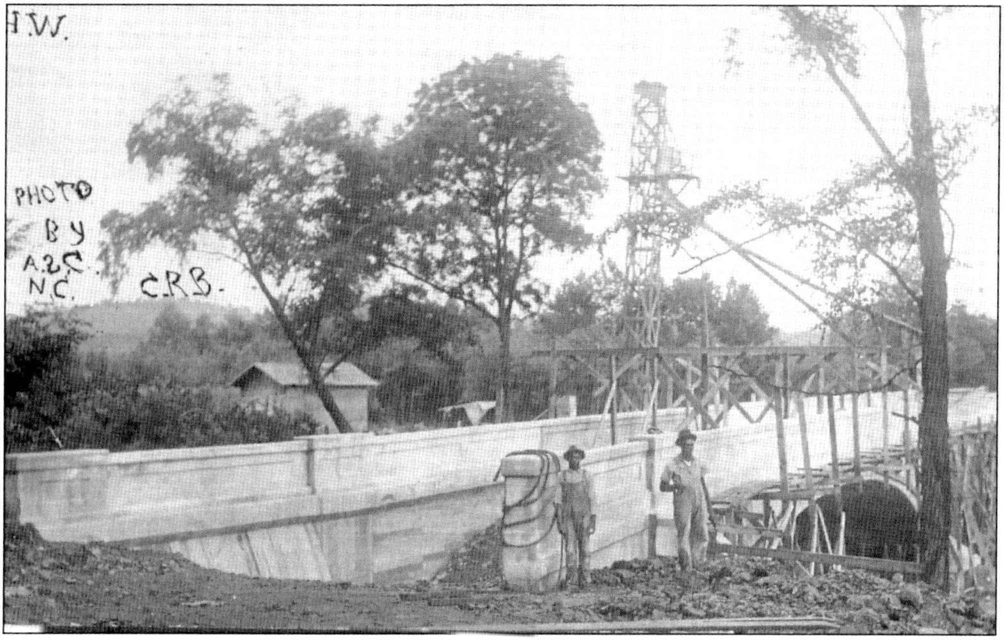

Workers pause in the early 1920s during construction of a bridge over the Catawba River just north of Marion, near the McDowell House. The growing popularity of the automobile had created demand for sturdier bridges and better roads across the region. The 1921 "Good Roads" program passed by the North Carolina legislature helped pay for the improvements. (Courtesy of David Padgett.)

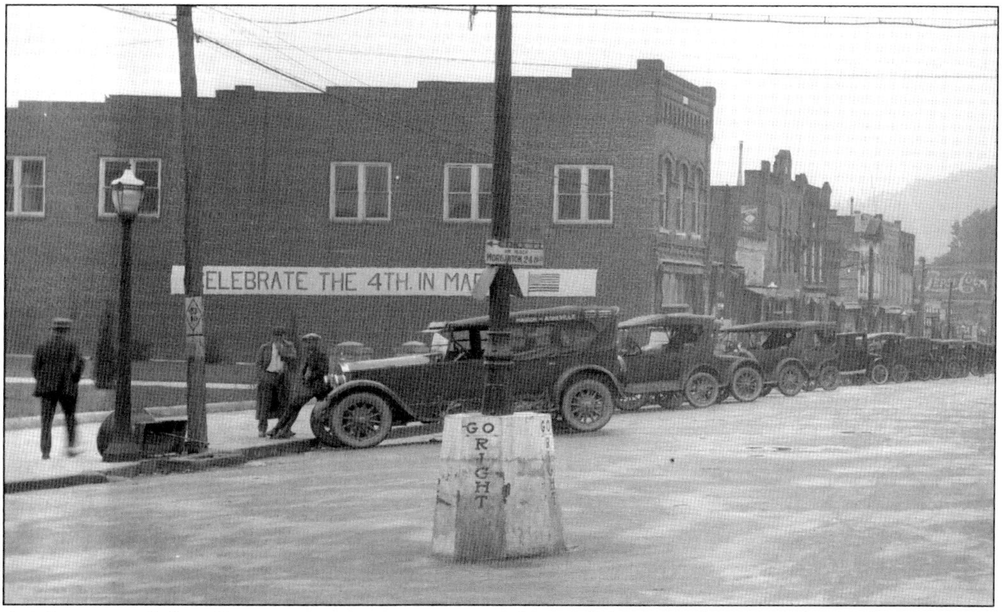

A Marion-to-Asheville taxi awaits passengers in front of the courthouse in the mid-1920s. The rudimentary traffic circle in the intersection of Main and Court Streets was referred to by some drivers as "the go-right" for obvious reasons. The large number of cars parked on this side of Main Street suggests that court is in session. (Courtesy of D.H. Ramsey Library Special Collections, University of North Carolina at Asheville, E.M. Ball Collection.)

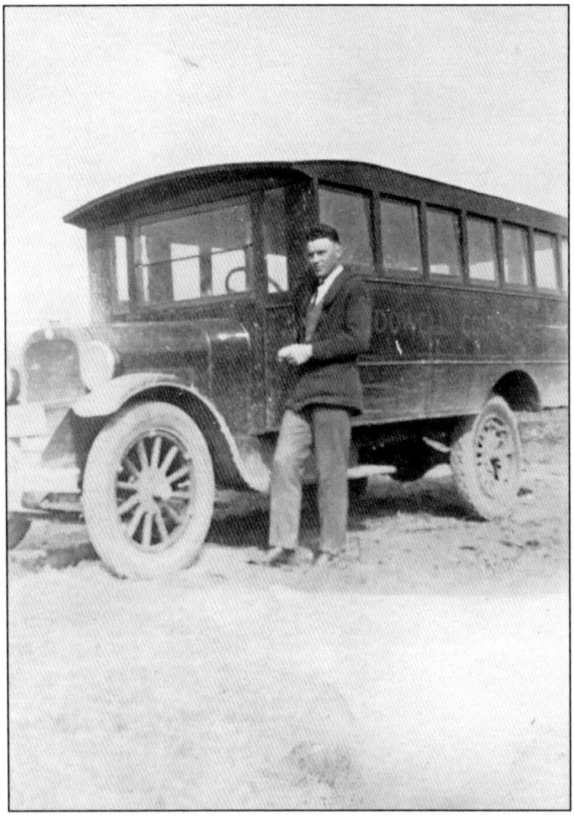

The first McDowell County school bus was purchased in 1921 and was assigned to Stroudtown (West Marion). In 1922, buses were appropriated for North Cove, Glenwood, and Nebo. The vehicle shown here covered a Pleasant Gardens route and was driven by Elmer Greenlee, who is standing beside it. (Courtesy of McDowell County Public Library, Greenlee Collection.)

This is the only known photograph of the interior of the Marion Candy Company, which was in operation in the mid-1930s. An article in the *Marion Progress* reports that the firm was "rapidly winning the popular favor with its extensive lines of candy and confectionaries." (Courtesy of McDowell County Public Library, Warren Hobbs Collection.)

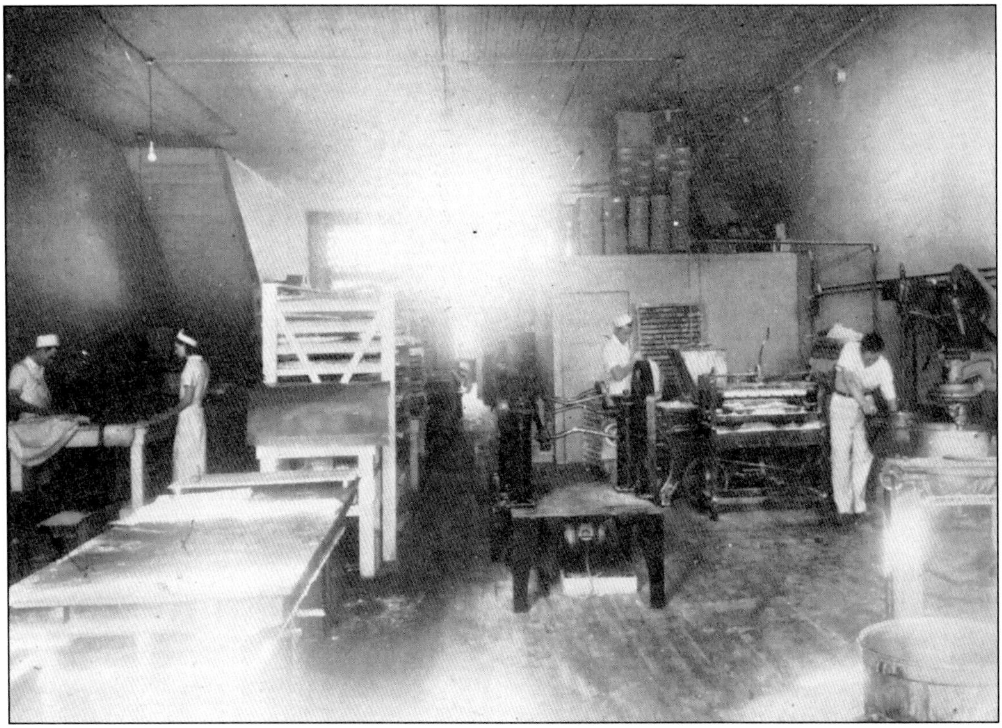

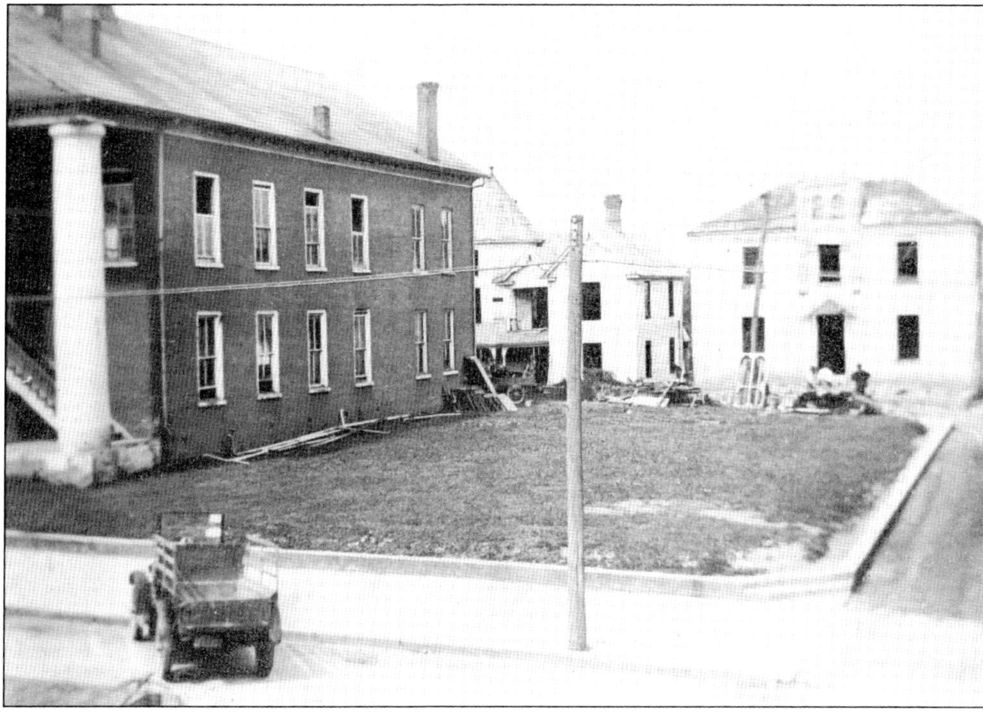

Preparations to demolish the county jail and the R.L. Nichols home behind the courthouse are evident in this image from 1922. A new courthouse would soon be built on the site and would open its doors the next year. The original courthouse had been built in 1845 and remodeled in 1902. (Courtesy of McDowell County Public Library, Warren Hobbs Collection.)

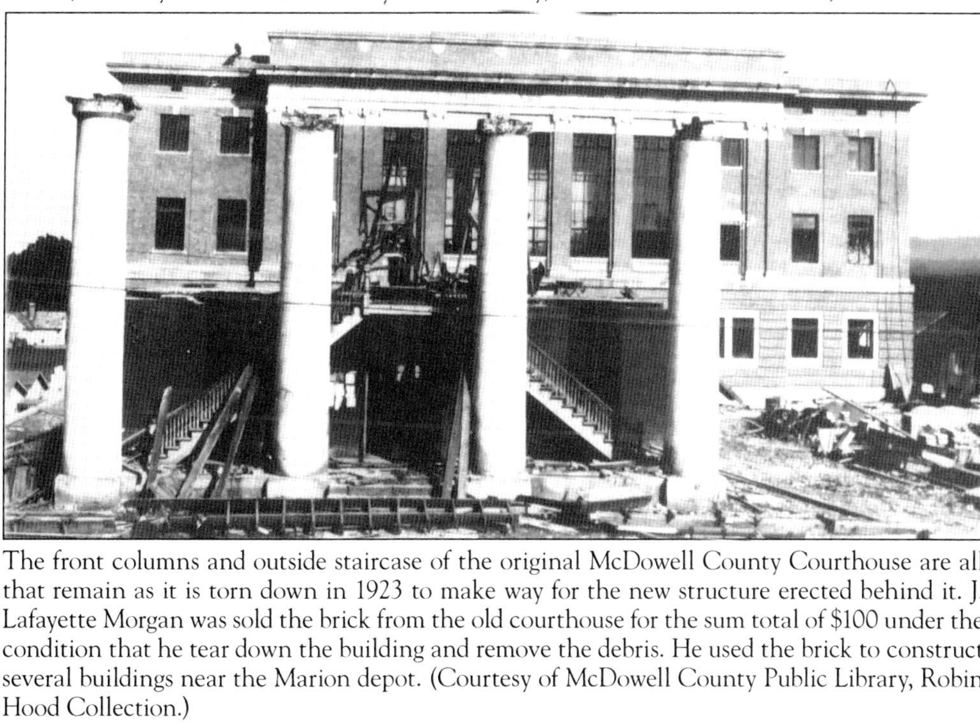

The front columns and outside staircase of the original McDowell County Courthouse are all that remain as it is torn down in 1923 to make way for the new structure erected behind it. J. Lafayette Morgan was sold the brick from the old courthouse for the sum total of $100 under the condition that he tear down the building and remove the debris. He used the brick to construct several buildings near the Marion depot. (Courtesy of McDowell County Public Library, Robin Hood Collection.)

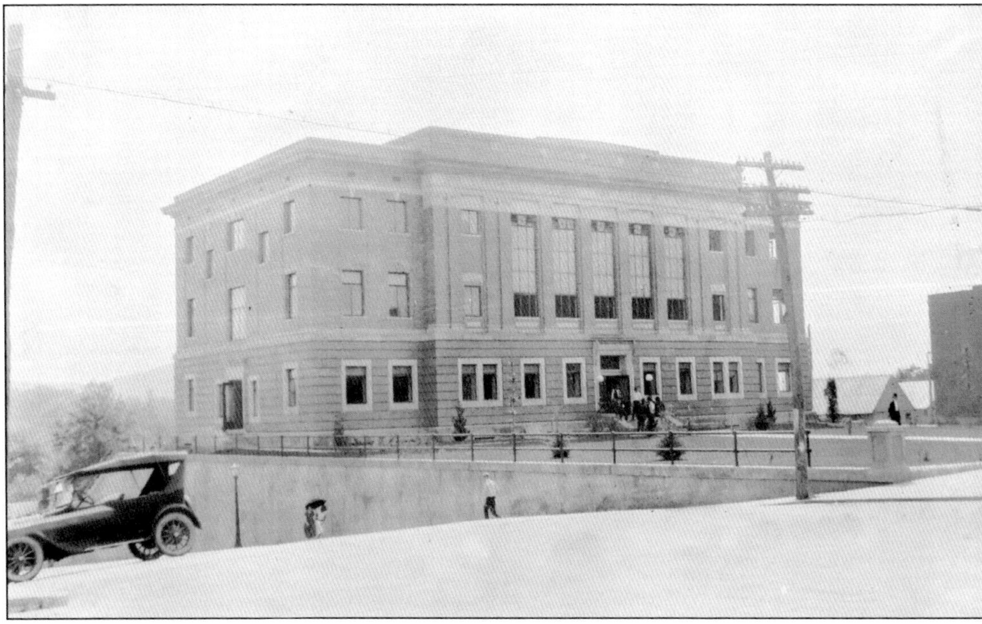

This is the new McDowell County Courthouse as it appeared shortly after being brought into service in 1923. The McDowell County sheriff at the time was J.L. Nichols, and the board of commissioners consisted of J.L. Lackey, E.E. English, and J.L. Wilson. (Courtesy of McDowell County Public Library, Warren Hobbs Collection.)

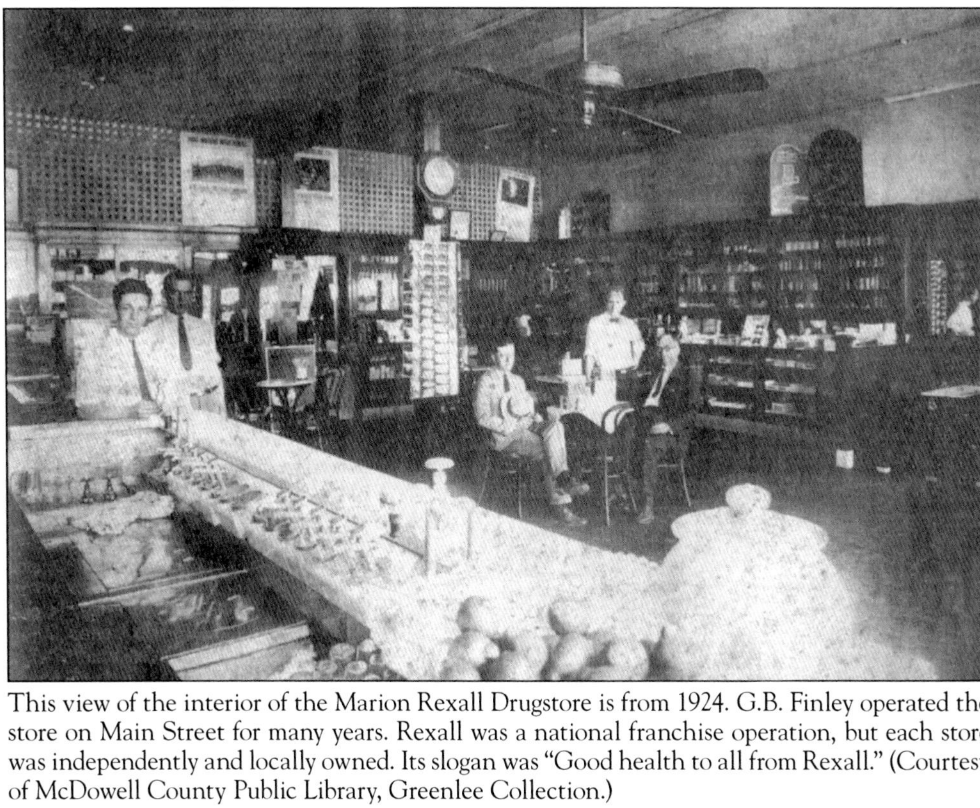

This view of the interior of the Marion Rexall Drugstore is from 1924. G.B. Finley operated the store on Main Street for many years. Rexall was a national franchise operation, but each store was independently and locally owned. Its slogan was "Good health to all from Rexall." (Courtesy of McDowell County Public Library, Greenlee Collection.)

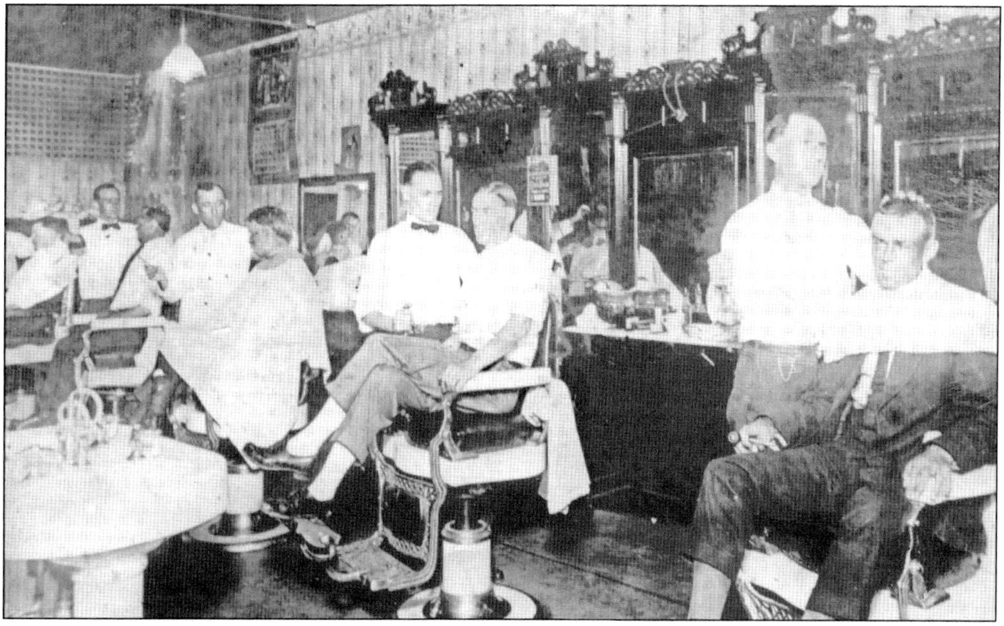

The chairs are full in 1924 at City Barbershop, which was established in the very early 1900s. For decades, customers had their shoes shined by Willie "Rhythm" Shade, whose cadenced snapping of his shoeshine rag earned him the nickname. Jack Harris ran the business for many years, and his son Tommy was still operating City Barbershop in 2012 in its original location. (Courtesy of Tommy Harris.)

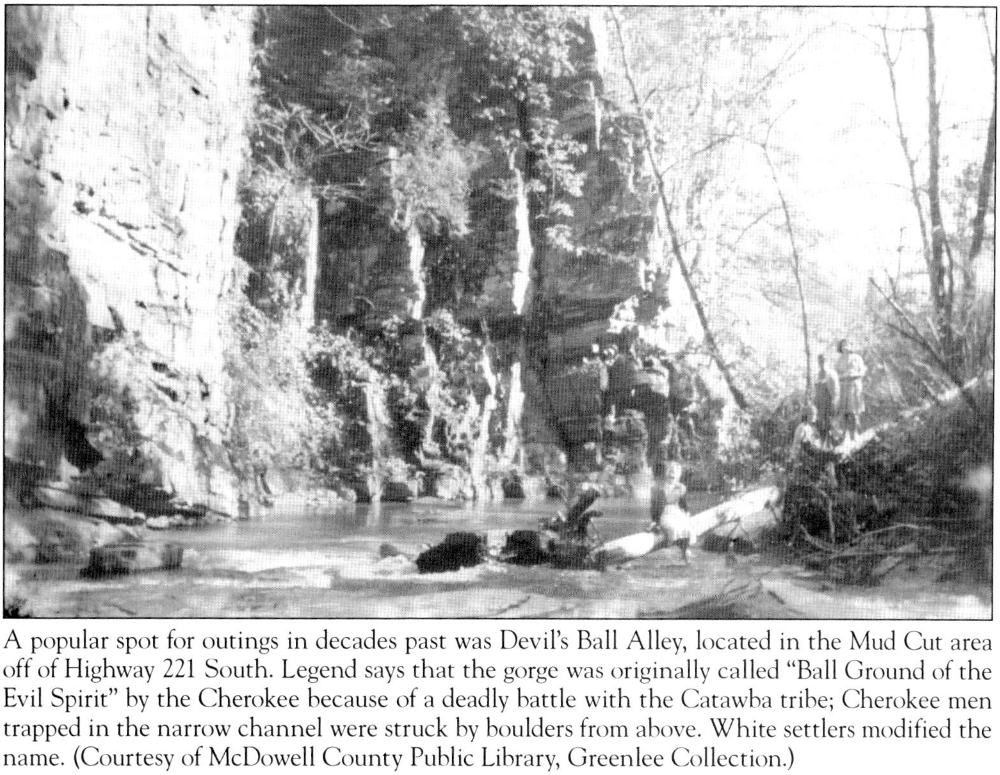

A popular spot for outings in decades past was Devil's Ball Alley, located in the Mud Cut area off of Highway 221 South. Legend says that the gorge was originally called "Ball Ground of the Evil Spirit" by the Cherokee because of a deadly battle with the Catawba tribe; Cherokee men trapped in the narrow channel were struck by boulders from above. White settlers modified the name. (Courtesy of McDowell County Public Library, Greenlee Collection.)

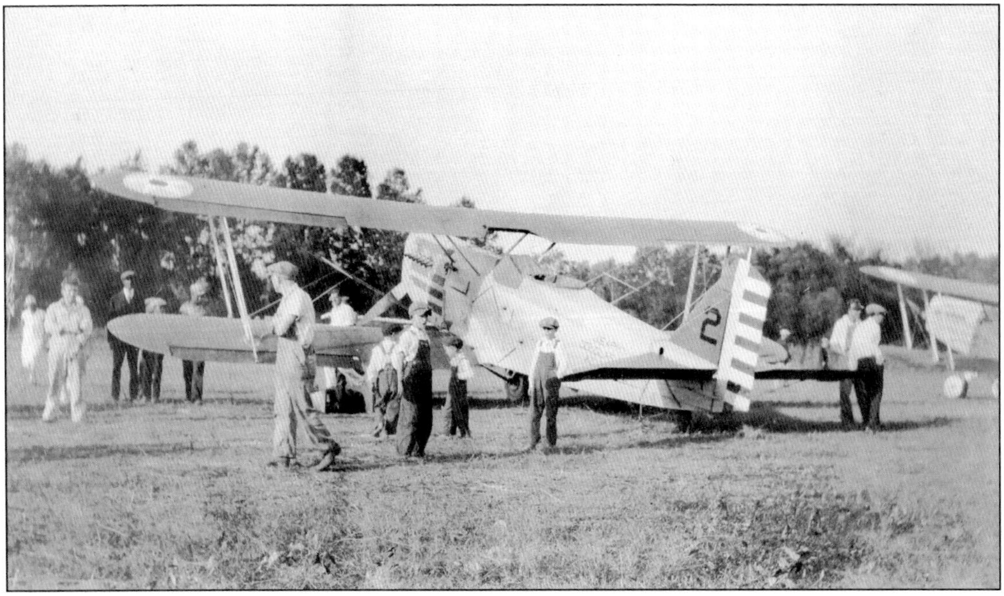

Marion's airport, originally called Francis Marion Field, opened on September 22, 1928. Earlier that year, the chamber of commerce had appointed W.S. Shiflet to form a committee to study the feasibility of an airfield in Marion and to identify possible locations. Eight prospective sites were considered, with the committee choosing a 227-acre tract just north of town owned by Duke Power, J.H. Tate, and A.H. Giles. For the opening, four Army planes offered rides. Ruth Greenlee took these photographs and wrote, "I had a dandy ride in number 2 with Lieutenant Arnold." The name of the airport was later changed to Shiflet Field. (Both, courtesy of McDowell County Public Library, Greenlee Collection.)

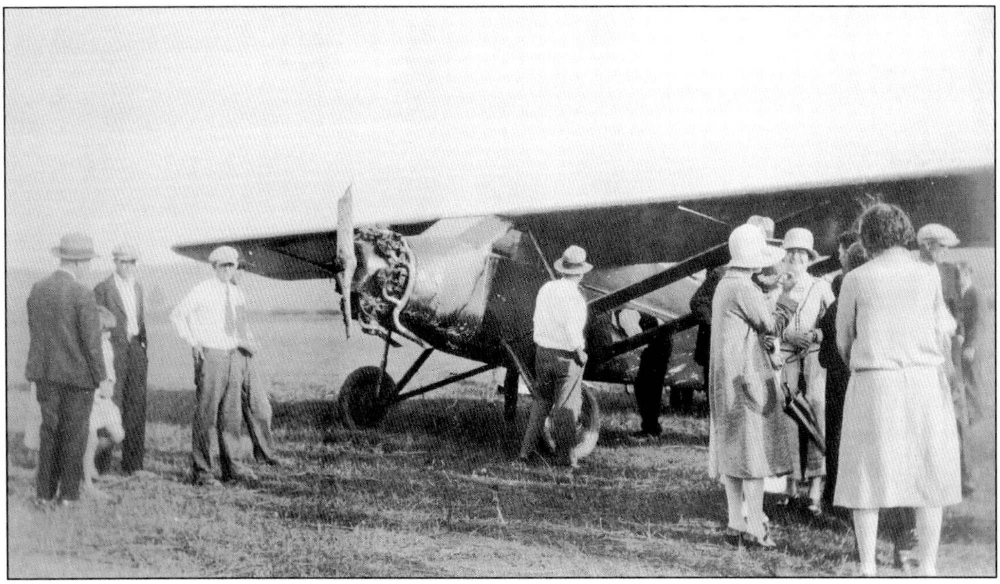

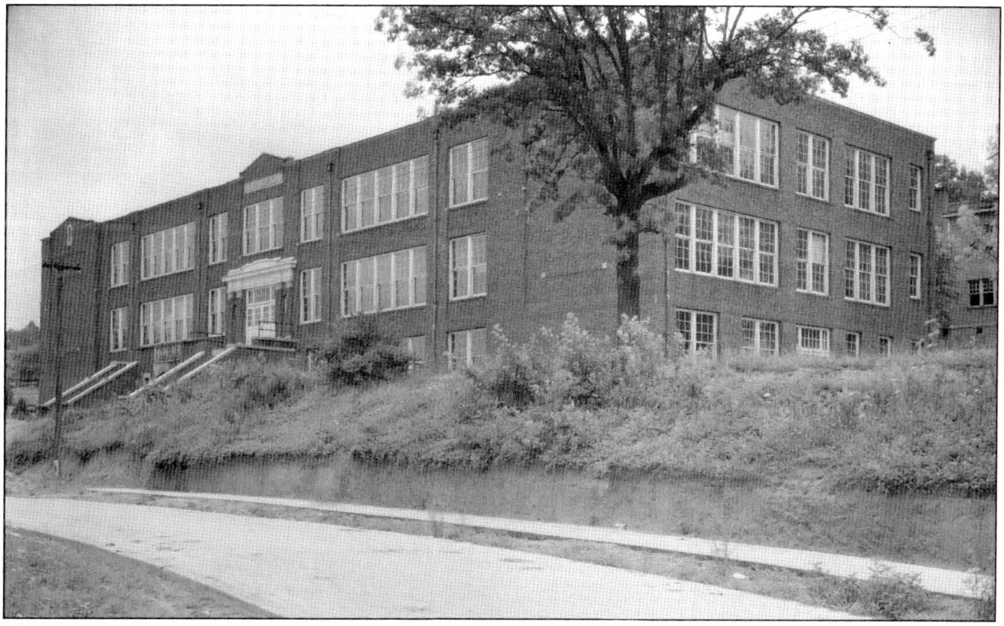

The Marion High School building was constructed in 1923 on West Court Street. Up to that time, the high school had been in the old Marion Graded School building around the corner on Academy Street. The structure seen here was in use until 1955. The last class to graduate from this building numbered 116 students. (Courtesy of D.H. Ramsey Library Special Collections, University of North Carolina at Asheville, E.M. Ball Collection.)

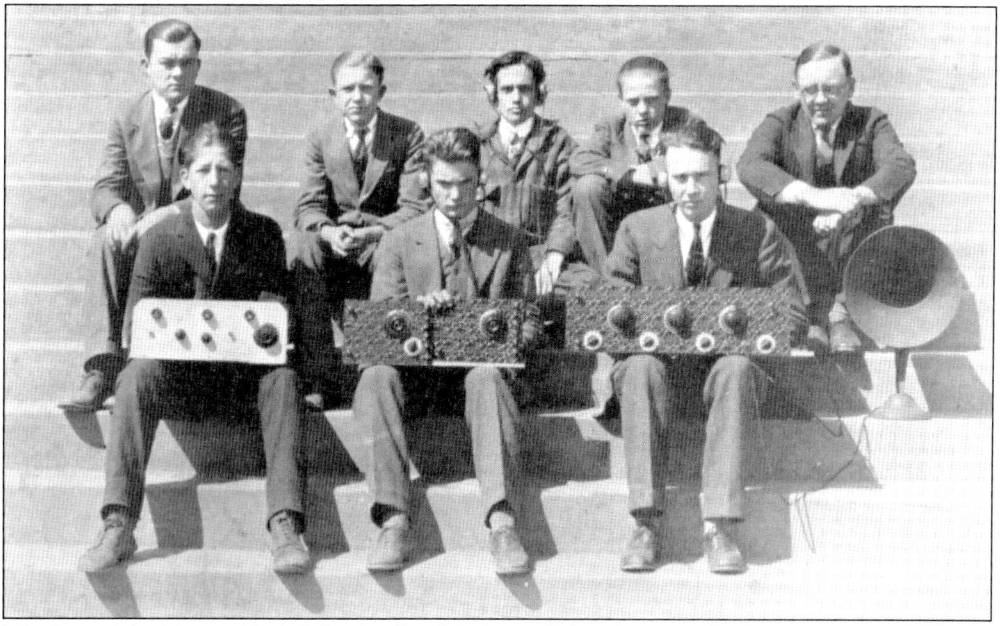

Members of the Marion High School radio club show off their homemade sets in 1925. Manufactured radios did not become widely available until the late 1920s, so most early enthusiasts built their own from kits or from blueprints. Radio broadcasting was in its infancy, but these students could tune in programming from WBT Charlotte, WSM Nashville, WSB Atlanta, and KDKA Pittsburgh among a few others. (Courtesy of McDowell County Public Library.)

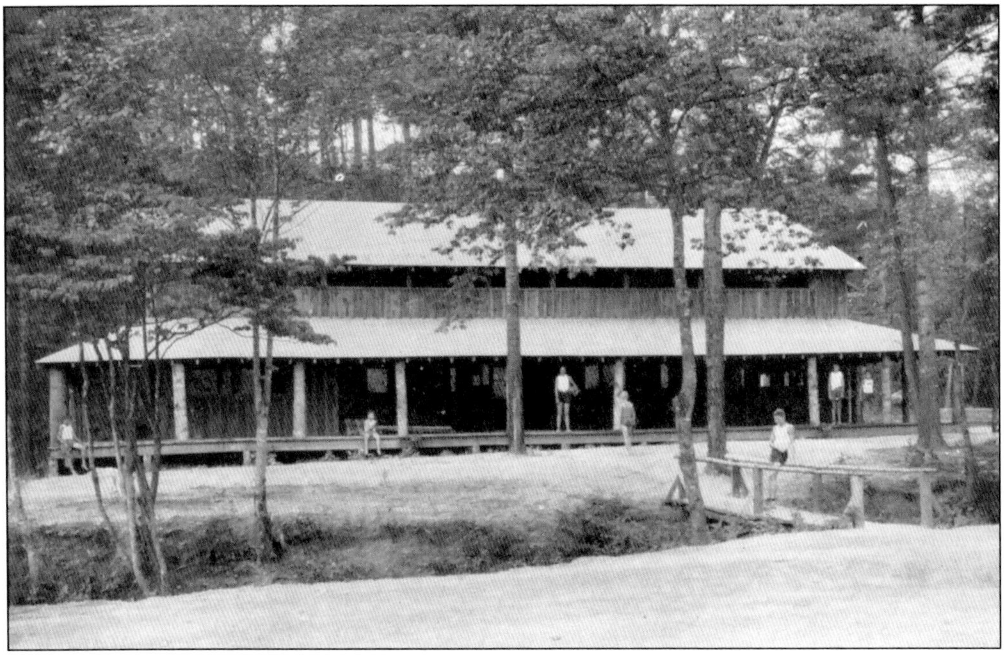

Black Bear Camp for boys was established near Lake James in 1926 by a group of educators from across North Carolina. In its first year, the 430-acre camp was managed by Prof. Macon Reed of Hampden-Sydney College in Virginia. The gymnasium pictured here offered basketball games, movies, lectures, and minstrel shows. The camp closed for several years but reopened in 1939 with future state governor Terry Sanford as associate director. (Courtesy of McDowell County Public Library.)

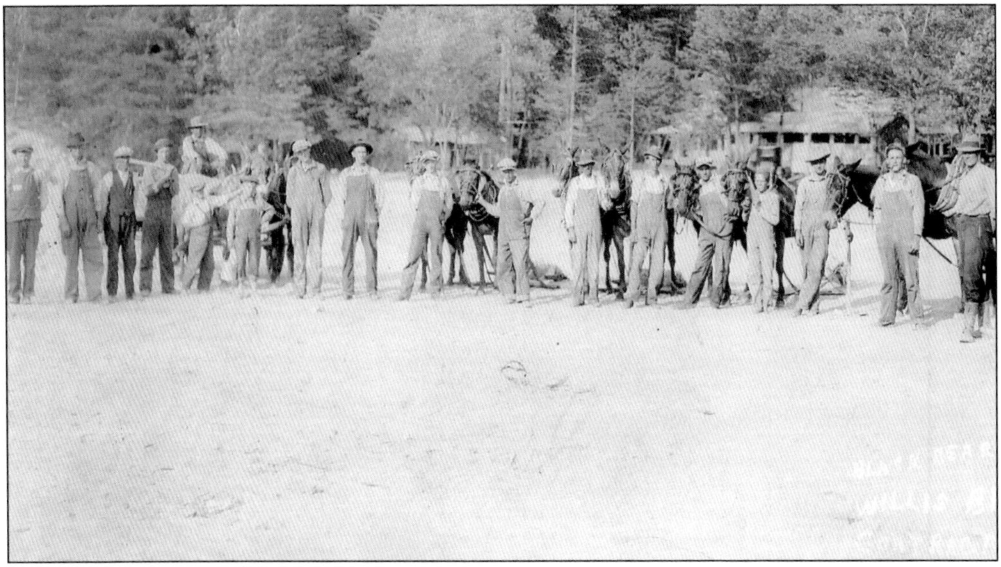

These men of Willis Building and Construction played a large role in building Black Bear Camp. Behind them are some of the structures of the then new facility. Standing with their mules in 1925 are, from left to right, unidentified, Lurm Willis, Walter Willis, two unidentified people, Paul Willis, Roy Willis, ? Owenby, two unidentified people, Baxter Lewis, unidentified, Elk Duncan, three unidentified people, Ernest Duncan, and Sam Duncan. (Courtesy of Harold Willis.)

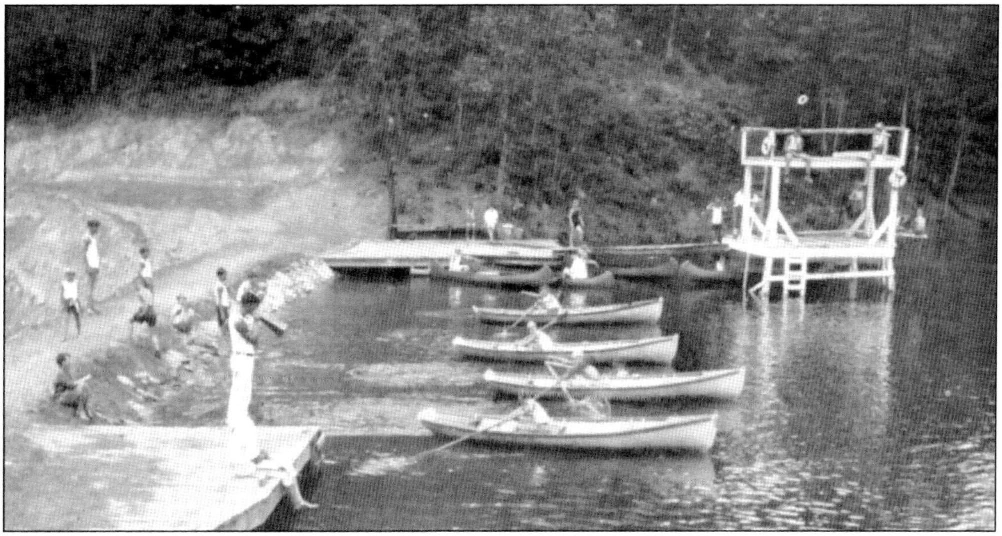

Campers at Black Bear spent much of their time in the water. Each morning started at 7:45 with a dip, and an hour was allotted for swimming before lunch. Other water sports, such as canoe racing, were also favorites of the boys. These activities did not take place in the waters of Lake James, however. The smaller Lake Jimmy on the grounds of the camp was used. (Courtesy of McDowell County Public Library.)

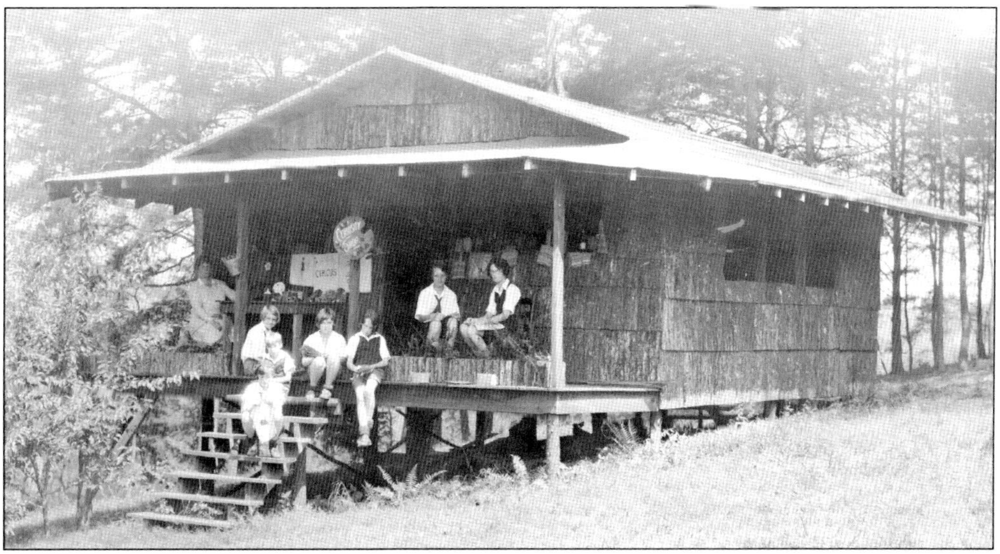

Summer campers relax in front of the "Curiosity Shop" at Camp Terra Alta. Located two miles from Marion near Lake James, the camp for girls attracted attendees from eight states in the 1920s and 1930s. Enrollment was limited to 40, and there was a counselor for every three girls. Campers rode their horses on a network of trails that dated back to the early 1800s. (Courtesy of McDowell County Public Library.)

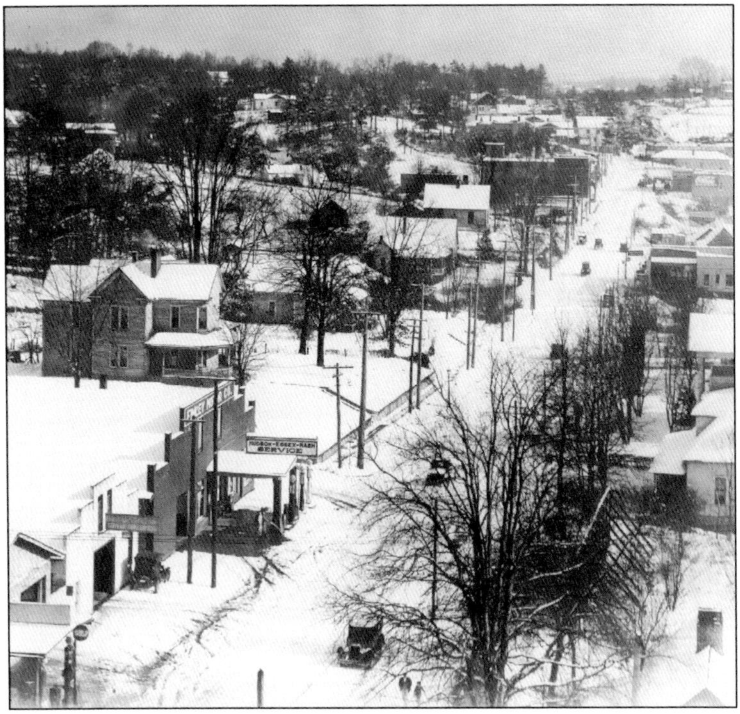

This view of East Court Street dates to the 1920s. Finley Motor Company, a dealer of Hudson, Essex, and Nash automobiles, is in the foreground, just past the Garden Street intersection. The A.C. Hewitt home is next on the left. The large brick building on the left side of the street just before the curve is the Coca-Cola Bottling Company. (Courtesy of Gregg M. Hensley and Hensley Studio.)

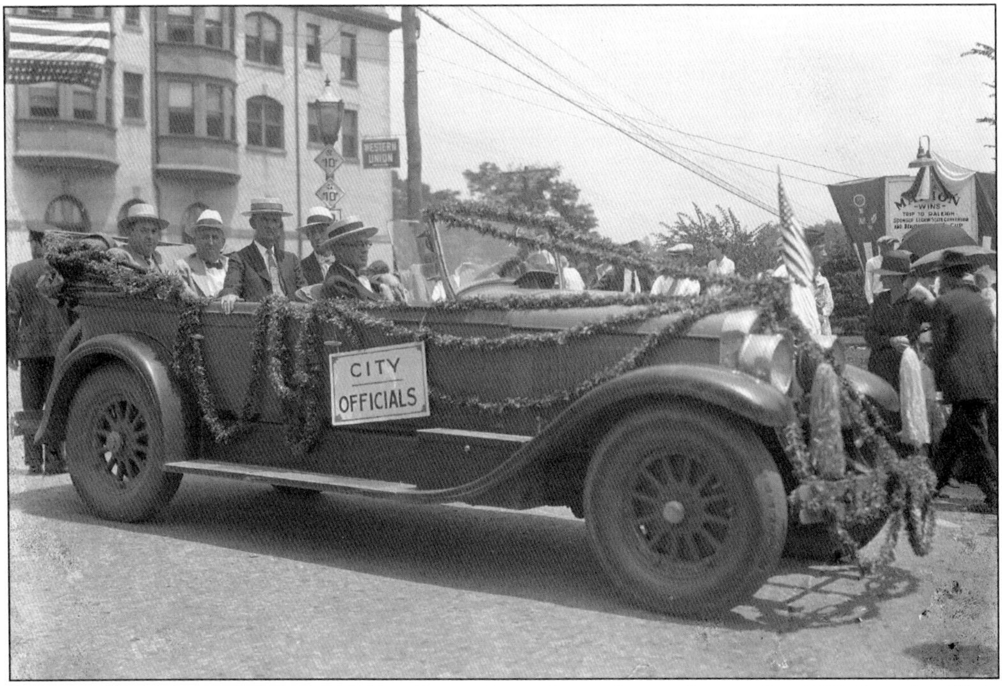

Marion officials turn south onto Main Street from Court Street during the 1929 Fourth of July Parade. On the courthouse lawn is an American Legion booth promoting a Miss Marion contest, with a trip to Raleigh as first prize. Other holiday activities included music by the Charlotte Drum and Bugle Corps, boxing matches, and a singing and dancing revue at the Oasis Theatre. (Courtesy of Gregg M. Hensley and Hensley Studio.)

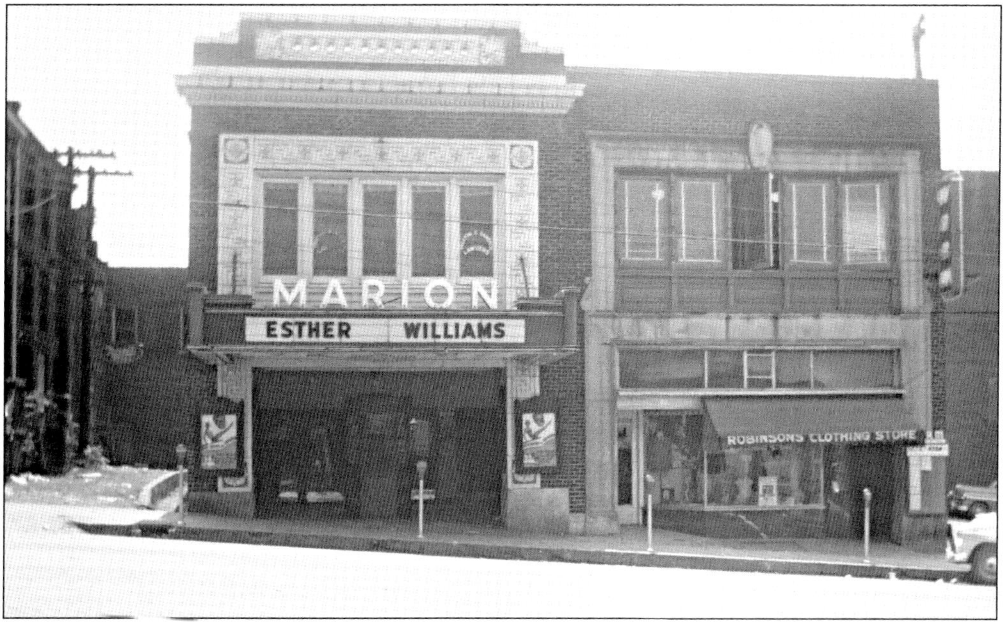

The Marion Theatre was opened in July 1929 on West Court Street by Ernest J. House. It seated over 600 and is described in the *Marion Progress* as "attractively modern and commodious with courteous attendants awaiting the pleasure of its patrons." In addition to first-run films, the Marion Theatre also brought musical and theatrical groups to its stage. (Photograph by Eckenrod Studio.)

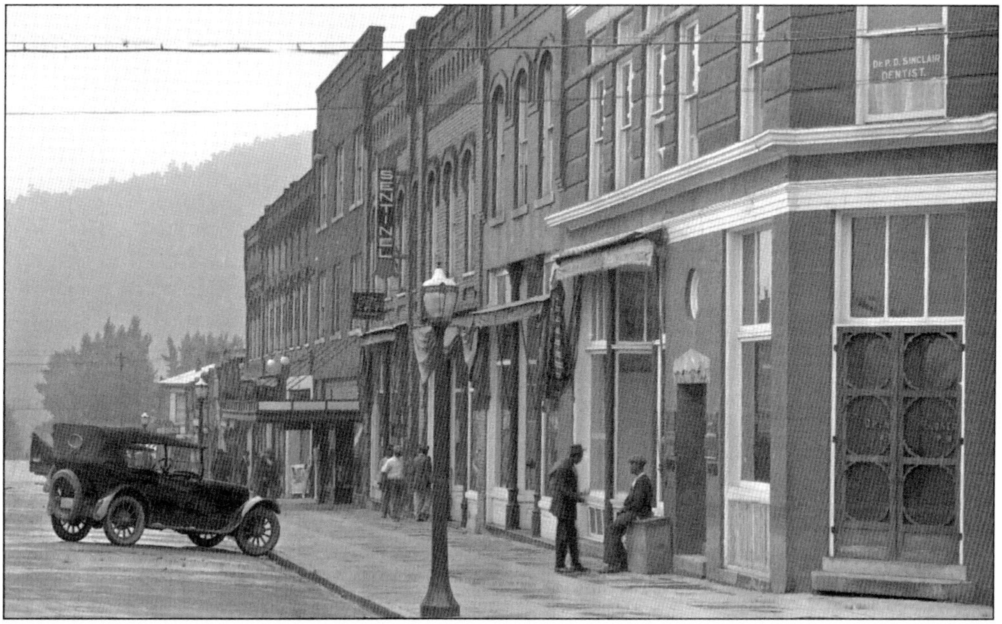

Men await the start of the workday in this early-morning scene on the west side of Main Street in the 1920s. Down the street are the Oasis Theatre and the offices of the short-lived newspaper the *McDowell Sentinel*. Also visible is a sign for the Mount Ida chapter of the Knights of Pythias (KP), a fraternal organization. (Courtesy of D.H. Ramsey Library Special Collections, University of North Carolina at Asheville, E.M. Ball Collection.)

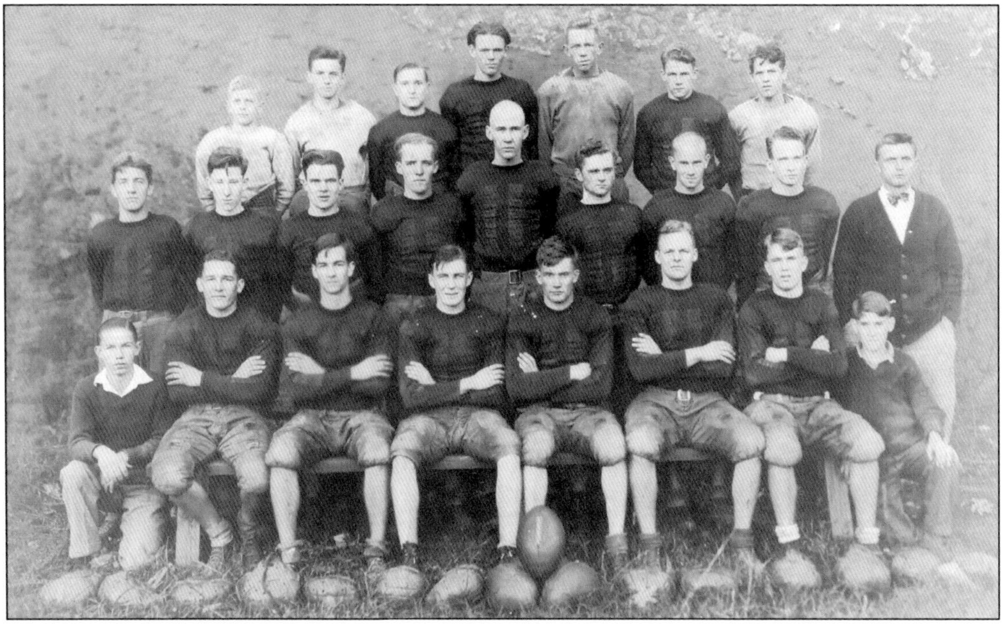

This is the 1929 Marion High School football team, with Coach Hawn at far right in bow tie. The team won its opener against Swannanoa 50-0. Other teams on the schedule that year were Salisbury, Lenoir, Canton, Biltmore, Black Mountain, Forest City, and Hendersonville. (Courtesy of McDowell County Public Library.)

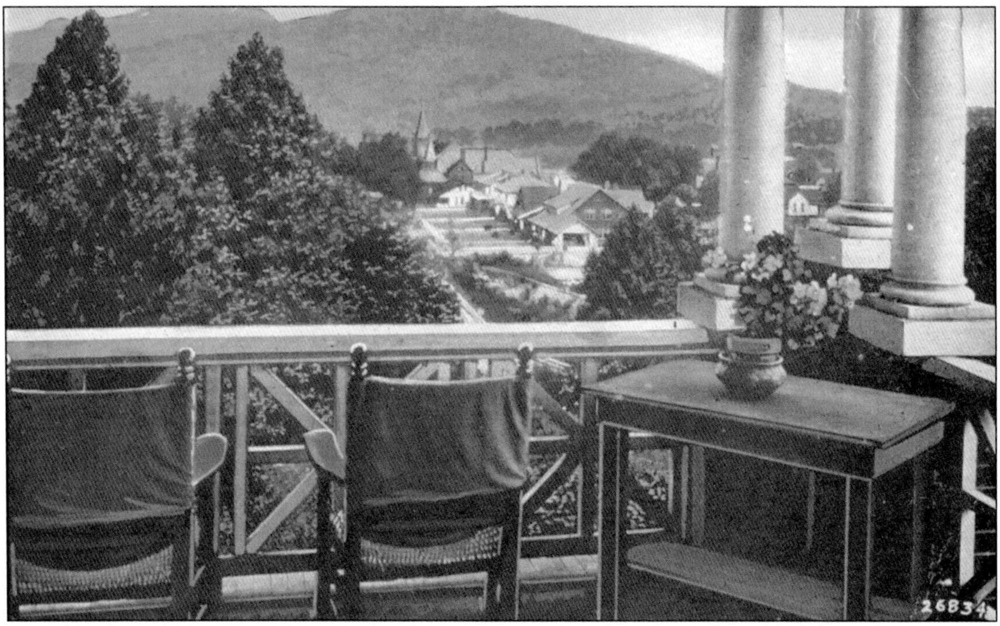

This postcard view shows the vantage point from Pless Hill, the home of Judge J.W. Pless and Annie Miller, located on the north end of Marion. Mount Ida rises in the distance. The peak was named for the daughter of Capt. James Moore Neal, McDowell County sheriff and Confederate officer. For obvious reasons, the Pless property was also referred to as "View Point" and "Heavenly Heights." (Courtesy of Wilson Library, University of North Carolina Library at Chapel Hill, North Carolina Collection.)

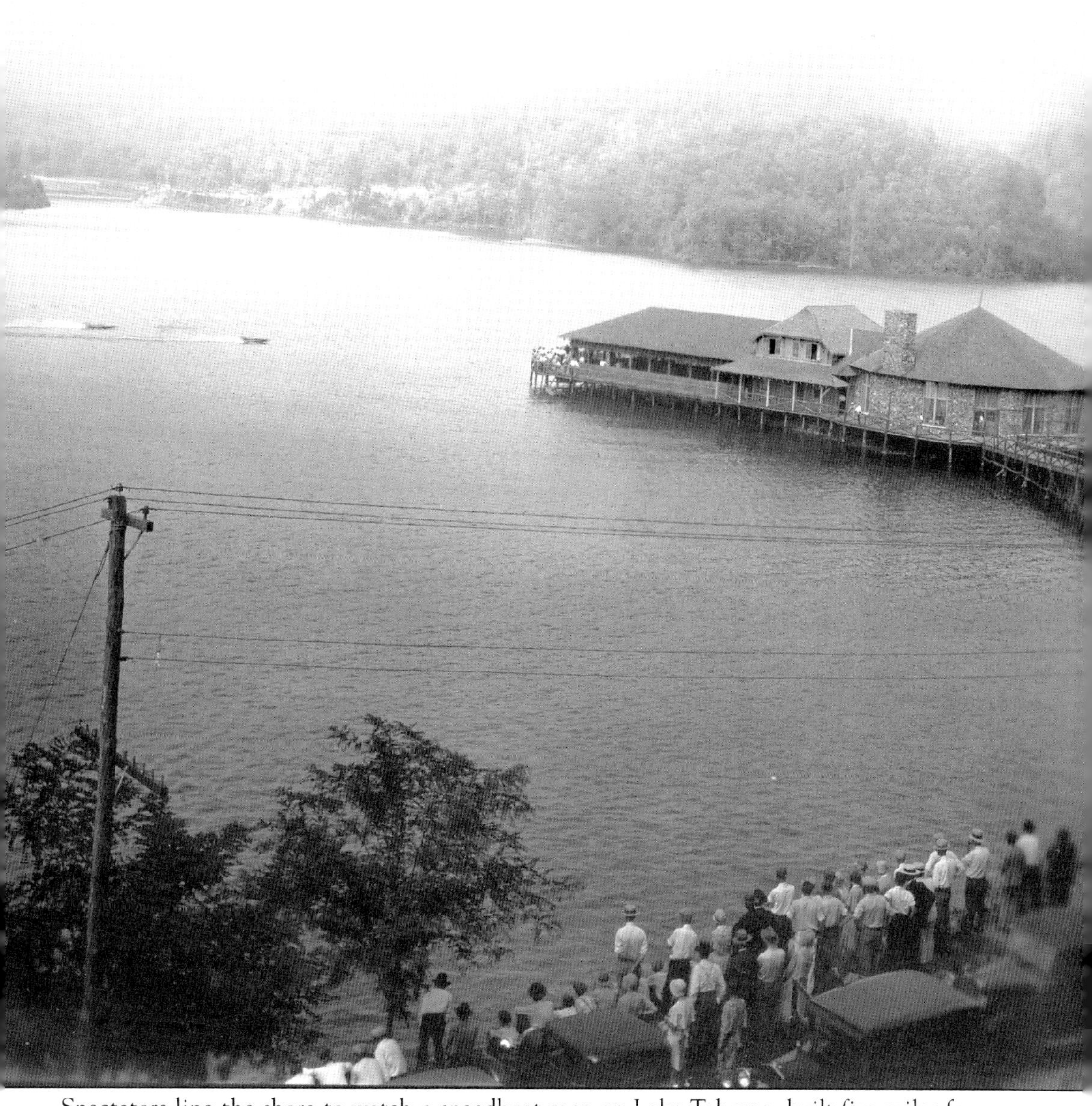

Spectators line the shore to watch a speedboat race on Lake Tahoma, built five miles from Marion in 1924. The clubhouse seen here hosted big-name dance bands, such as Kay Kyser, Hal Kemp, and Jan Garber. Construction of a 40-room hotel advanced to the point that plumbing equipment was being installed, but it was halted by the Great Depression. The entire property was eventually foreclosed, and it became a private community following World War II. The name Tahoma was the winning submission in a "name the lake" contest. (Courtesy of Gregg M. Hensley and Hensley Studio.)

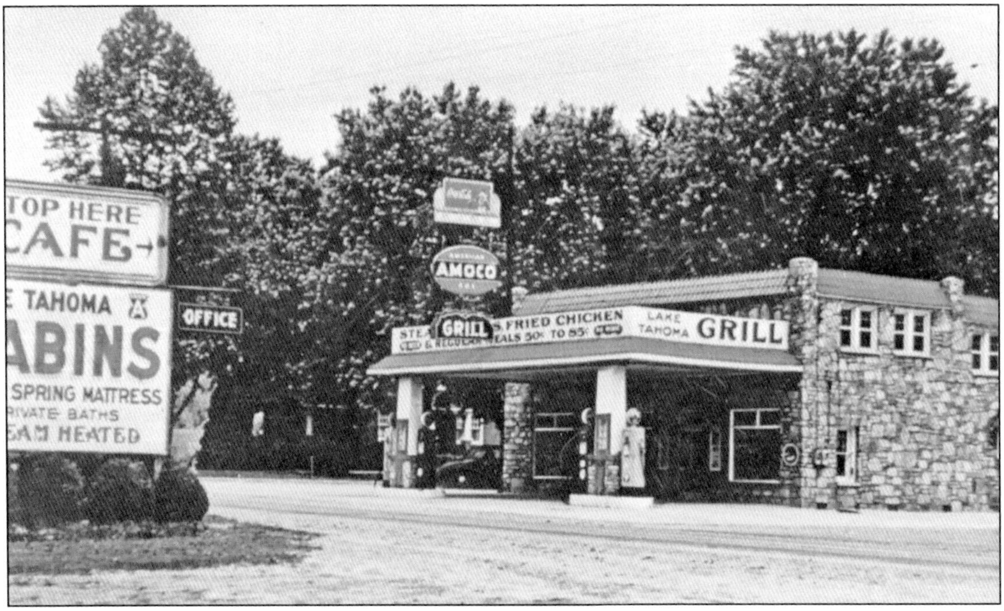

The Lake Tahoma Grill began as a filling station operated by W.B. Gibbs around 1930 at the junction of US 70 and NC 80. Gibbs expanded the station to sell a variety of goods to travelers on their way to Asheville or Mount Mitchell and later remodeled the business to serve food. In 1945, Gibbs tore down the Lake Tahoma Grill and replaced it with the larger Lake Tahoma Steakhouse. (Courtesy of Pete Gibbs.)

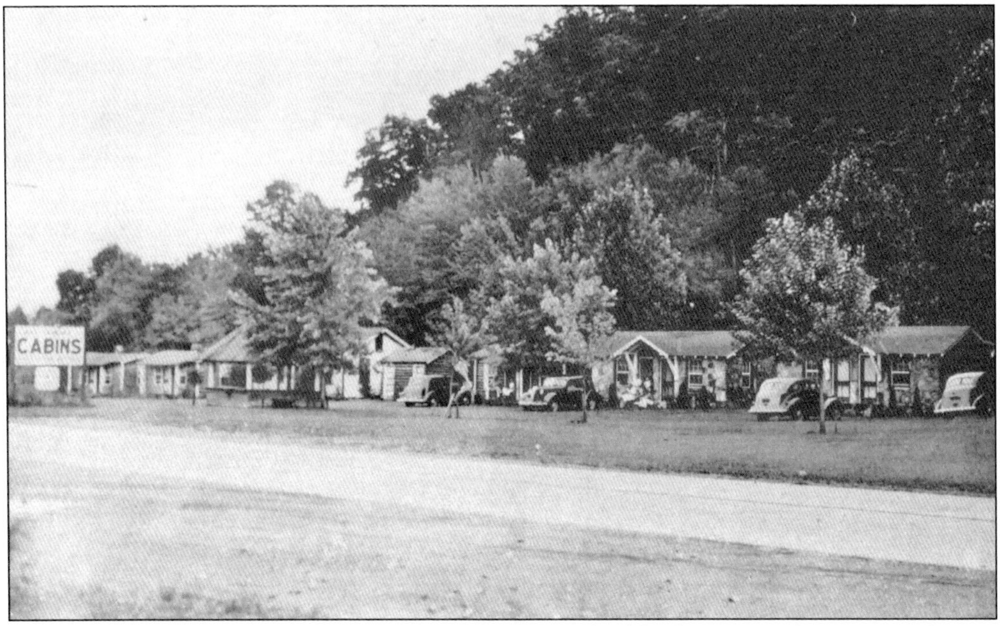

The heavy automobile traffic through the area convinced Gibbs that overnight accommodations were needed. He purchased eight acres across the highway from the grill and built a row of log cabins. Later, the log cabins were razed in favor of rock cottages. This photograph shows log cabins on the left and the structures that were replacing them on the right. (Courtesy of Wilson Library, University of North Carolina Library at Chapel Hill, North Carolina Collection.)

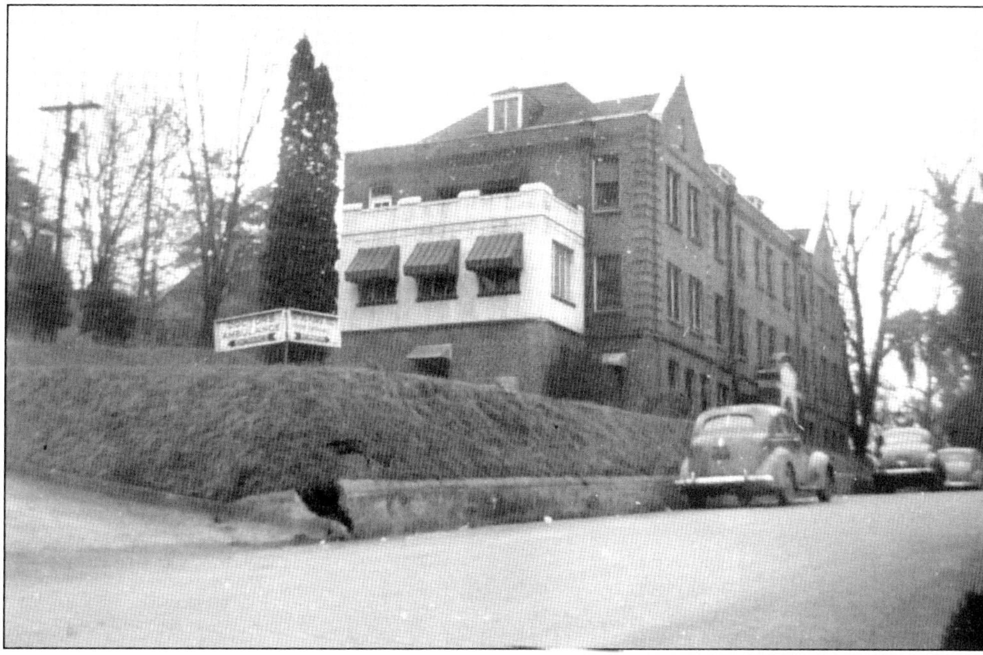

Marion General Hospital was built on James Avenue in 1930 after it became obvious that the community needed a larger and better-equipped facility than the one being run in the old Flemming Hotel. J. Lafayette Morgan spearheaded a fundraising drive, and the Duke Endowment assisted in financing. This structure was closed in 1952 and sold to W. Ray Smith, who converted it into apartments. (Courtesy of McDowell County Public Library, Robin Hood Collection.)

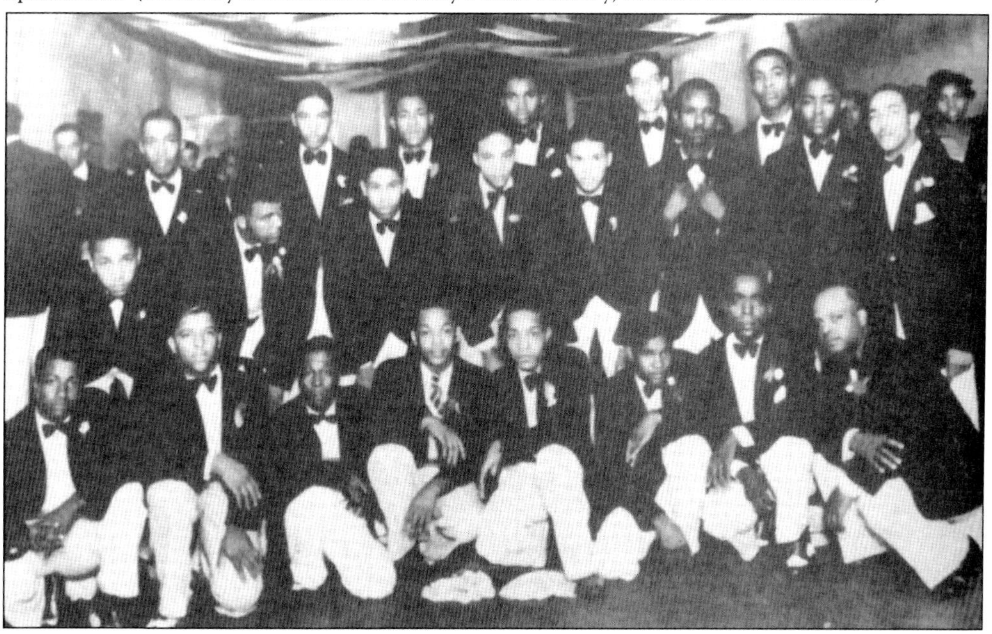

The Marionite Club was a prestigious African American men's club organized in 1929. The civic and social group sponsored dances that drew large crowds of both blacks and whites in the 1930s. Performers at the dances included the OK Babies and Bill Lacey and His Band, who hailed from Florida. (Courtesy of McDowell County Public Library, Warren Hobbs Collection.)

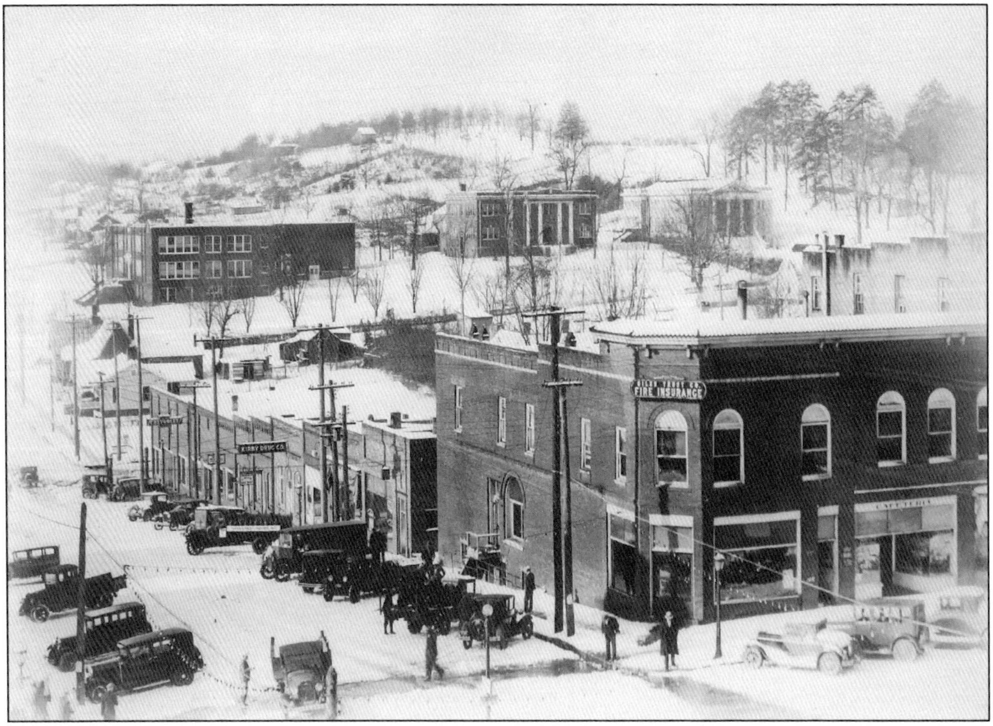

This view is looking west on Court Street in the early 1930s. Marion High School, Marion Elementary School (formerly Marion Graded School), and the Presbyterian church are visible along Academy Street in the background of the photograph. The small white house at the bottom of the image would soon be torn down to make way for the post office. (Courtesy of Gregg M. Hensley and Hensley Studio.)

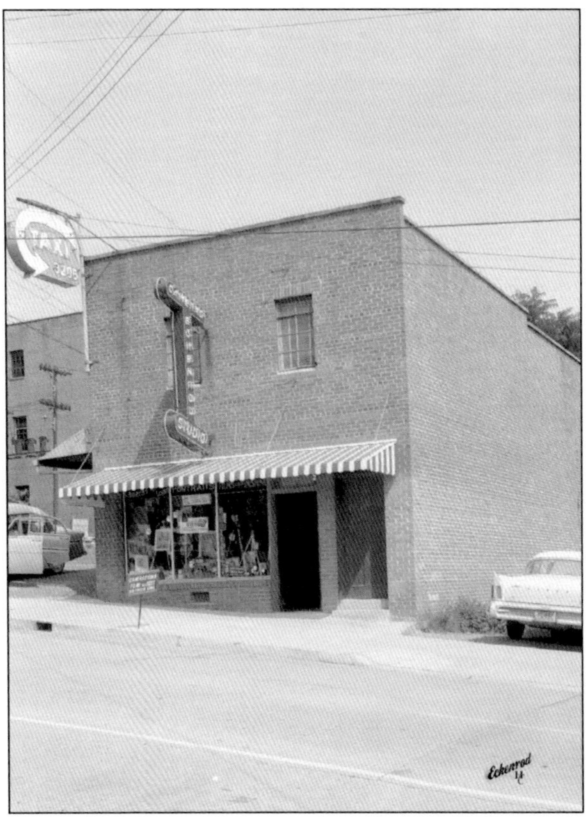

Eckenrod Studio opened for business in Marion in 1930, first located in an upstairs space on Main Street and then moving to Court Street behind the Hotel James in 1949. Originally, Eckenrod's business was primarily portraiture and camera sales. At this writing, Eckenrod is still operating on Court Street and is a repository of thousands of vintage photographs of Marion, with many being for sale to the public. (Photograph by Eckenrod Studio.)

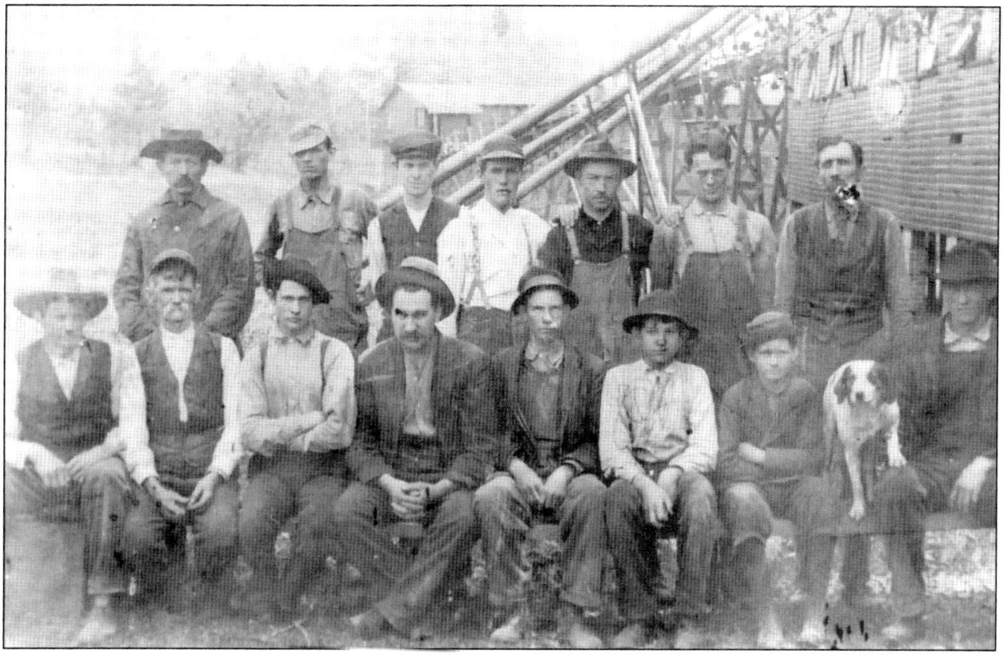

These men were employees of the Catawba Furniture Company in the early 1930s. Established around the start of the 20th century, it was the first furniture factory in Marion and occupied several acres on State and Garden Streets. The company specialized in bedroom suites, wardrobes, and dressers. (Courtesy of Louis Wall.)

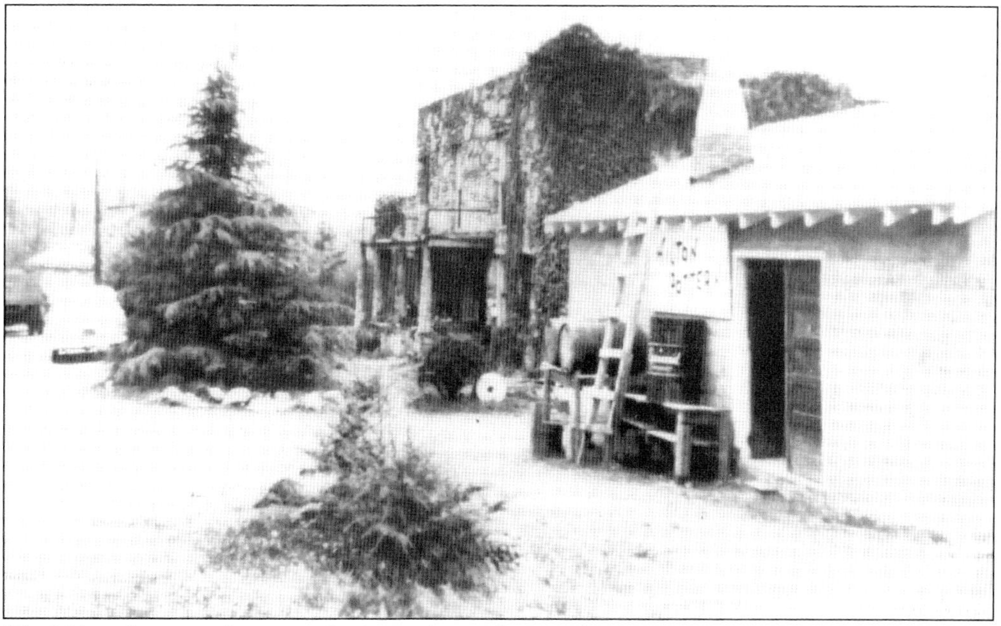

The Hilton home and pottery shed were located on Highway 70 just outside Marion in Pleasant Gardens. Ernest Auburn Hilton and his wife, Clara Maude, moved the family pottery business from Catawba County to this site on the banks of the Catawba River in 1935. Known for its "blue edge" and raised dogwood pattern, Hilton Pottery was prized by collectors all over the United States. (Courtesy of McDowell County Public Library, Warren Hobbs Collection.)

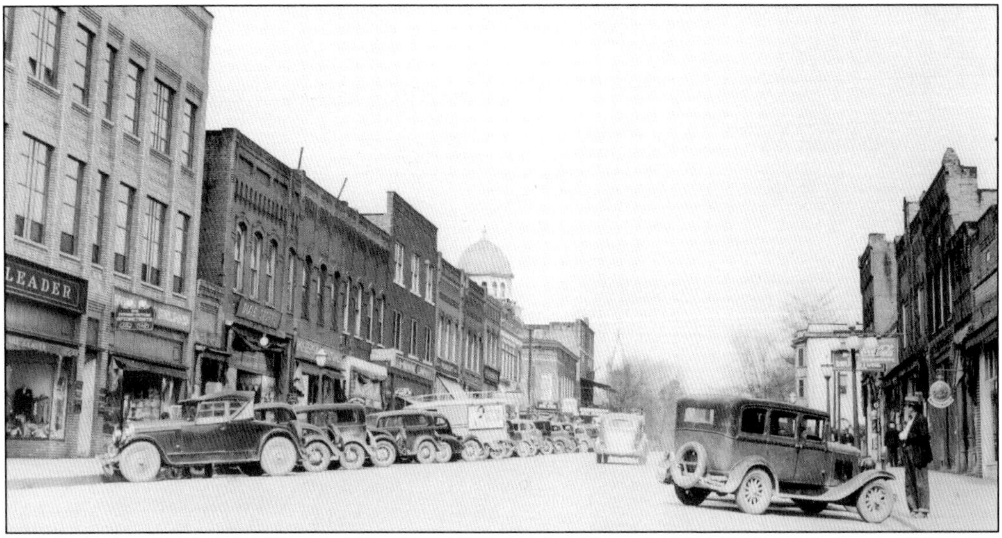

A pedestrian walking south on Main Street pauses to talk with a child in a nearby car. Just over the gentleman's shoulder is a sign for watchmaker L.D. Greene. In addition to making and selling watches, Greene was the official watch inspector for the railroad, making sure that railroad employees' timepieces were precise. Among the businesses across the street is the Dixie Store, which was the precursor to Winn-Dixie grocery store. (Courtesy of Louis Wall.)

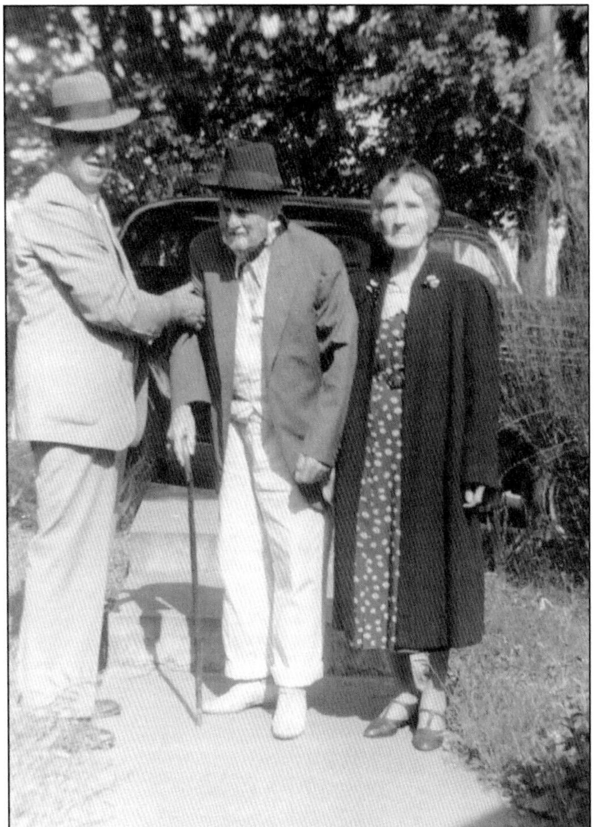

C.Y. Banning lends assistance to James Morris in this photograph from the late 1930s. Morris was McDowell's last surviving Confederate veteran and had served as mayor of Marion from 1892–1895. With Morris is his wife, "Miss Mamie." The couple was married in 1879 in the original Methodist church on East Court Street. It was the first church wedding in Marion. Morris died in 1941. (Courtesy of Mountain Gateway Museum.)

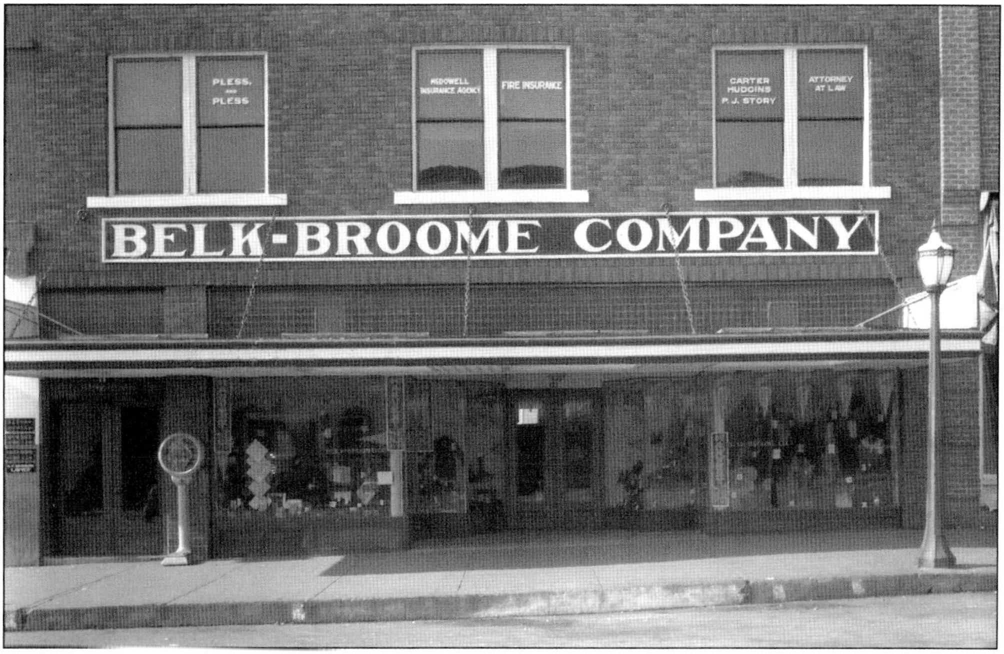

Belk-Broome was a mainstay in downtown Marion for over 50 years. This "Harvest Days" promotion took place shortly after the store first opened in September 1931. Note the penny fortune scale to the left. Attorneys Pless and Pless, Carter Hudgins, P.J. Story, Roy W. Davis, and G.F. Washburn had offices upstairs. (Courtesy of Gregg M. Hensley and Hensley Studio.)

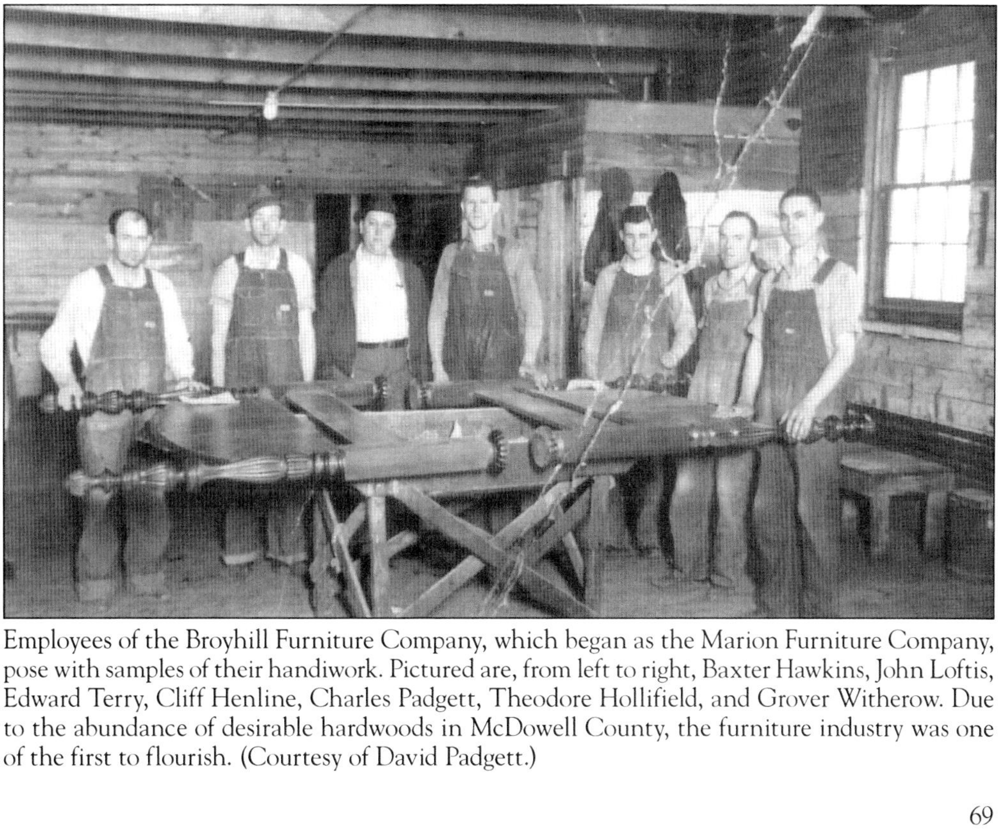

Employees of the Broyhill Furniture Company, which began as the Marion Furniture Company, pose with samples of their handiwork. Pictured are, from left to right, Baxter Hawkins, John Loftis, Edward Terry, Cliff Henline, Charles Padgett, Theodore Hollifield, and Grover Witherow. Due to the abundance of desirable hardwoods in McDowell County, the furniture industry was one of the first to flourish. (Courtesy of David Padgett.)

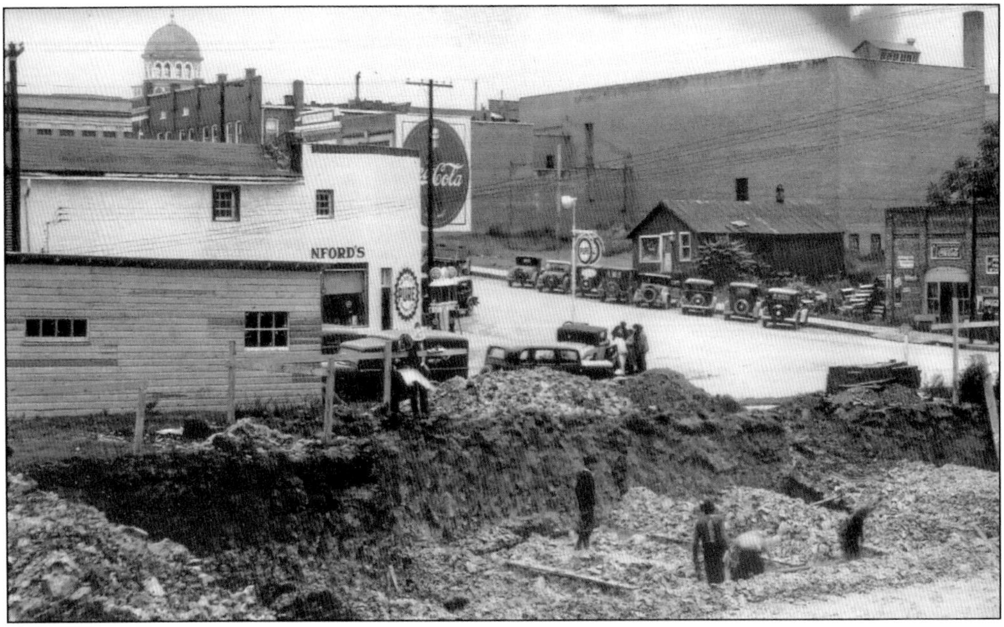

Workers prepare to lay the foundation of the new post office on West Court Street. To the left is the former C.C. Bolch Pure service station and car dealership. Across the street in the small brick building is Penland's Fruit Stand, which sold oranges, apples, soft drinks, and snacks. Penland's was a favorite stop for students from the nearby Marion Elementary and Marion High schools. (Courtesy of Louis Wall.)

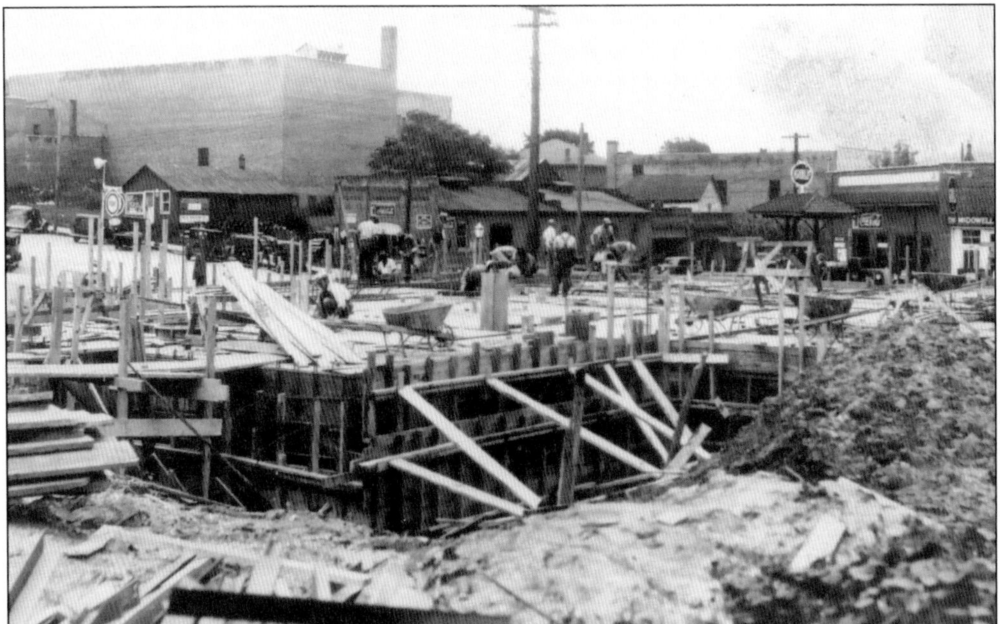

Here is a later phase of construction of the post office. This view also shows the Gulf station across the street on West Court and the offices of the *McDowell News*. The newspaper would move into a larger facility in the early 1950s. (Courtesy of McDowell County Public Library, Robin Hood Collection.)

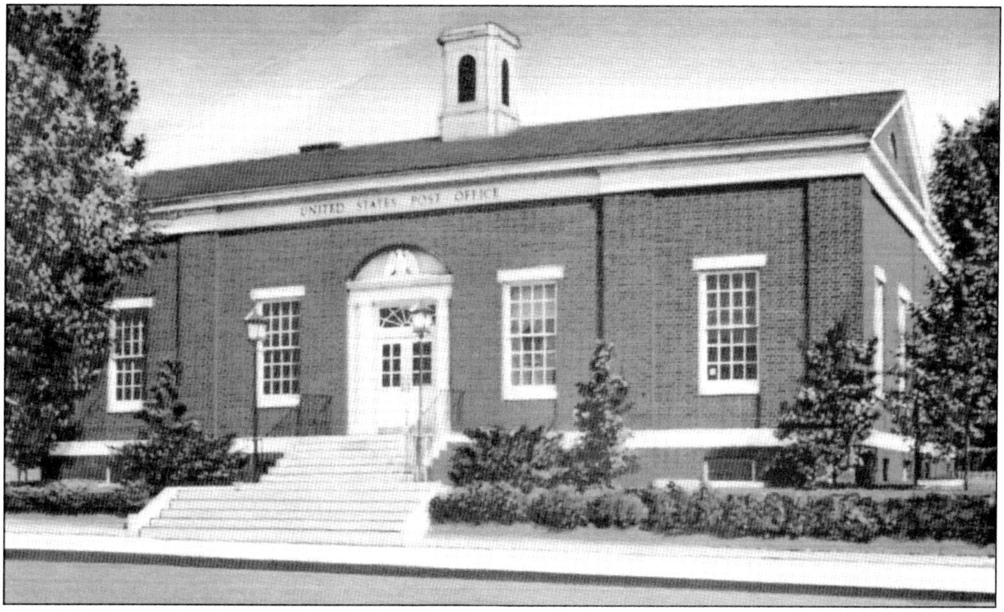

The Marion Post Office opened in this building on West Court Street in 1935. The first post office in McDowell County had been located in Pleasant Gardens and was operated by the Carsons and McDowells. When the city of Marion was established, the central postal service moved into town. Locations included a small building on West Henderson Street in 1867 and on South Main in the early 1900s. (Courtesy of Marion Business Association.)

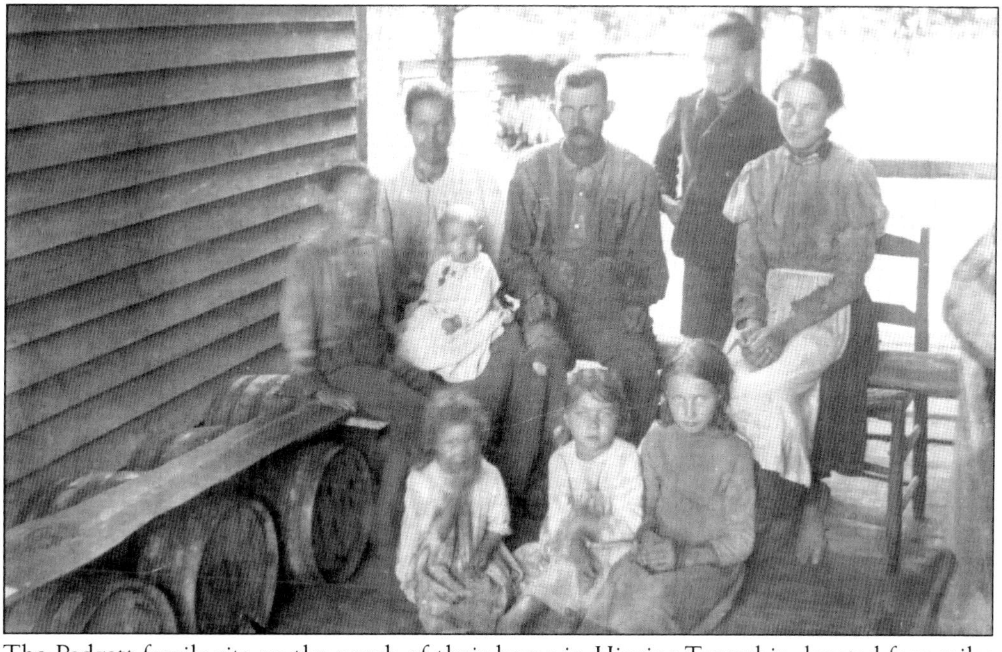

The Padgett family sits on the porch of their home in Higgins Township, located four miles southeast of Marion. Note that one of the children is sitting over a row of whiskey barrels. Making "corn liquor" was one of the few ways that those in rural McDowell County could earn enough cash to bring into town to buy goods that they could not produce themselves. (Courtesy of David Padgett.)

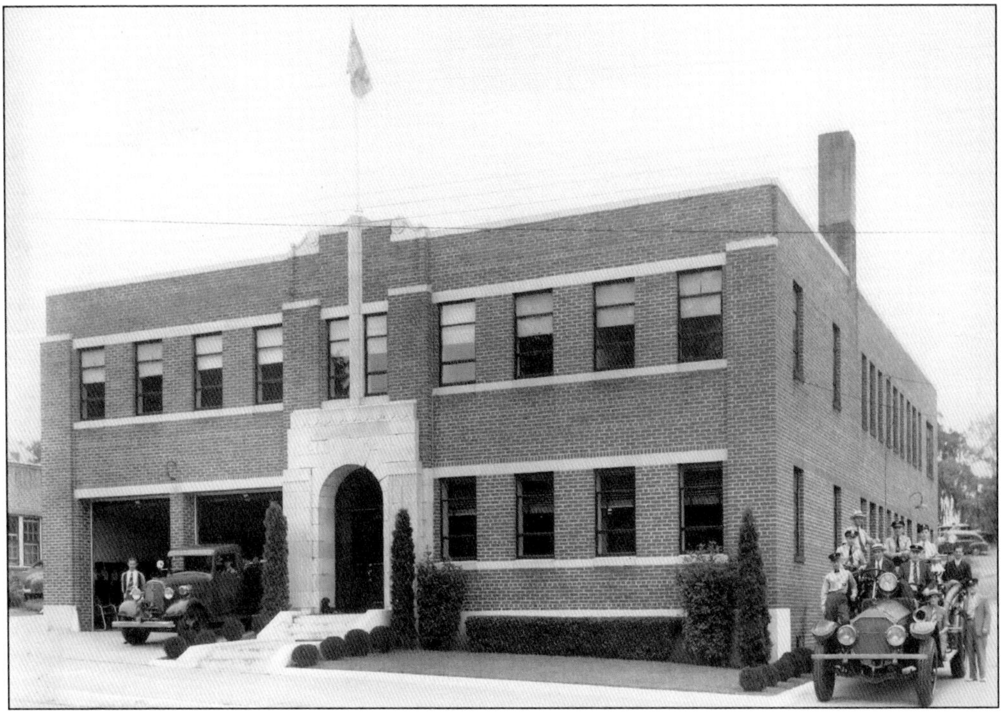

This city hall building was erected in 1937 on the former site of the Frank Hall home on Logan Street. The police department, fire department, and city offices were all housed here. Marion City Hall and the Marion Fire Department faced Logan Street, while the Marion Police Department faced Brown Street. The building also housed a jail with five cells. (Courtesy of McDowell County Public Library, Warren Hobbs Collection.)

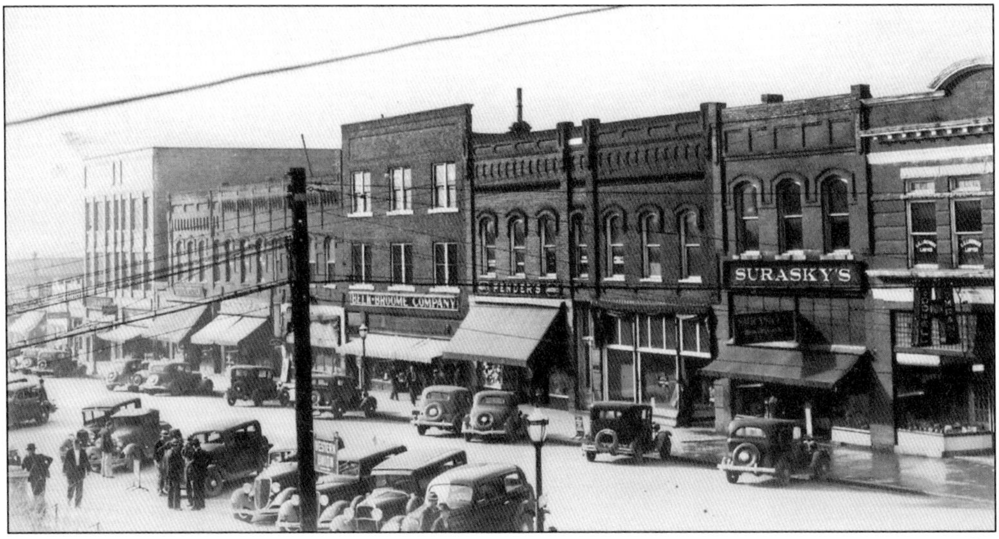

Most prominent in this Main Street scene from the 1930s is Surasky's Department Store. The business was one of several opened in Marion by Jewish immigrants from Germany shortly before World War II. The Surasky family also owned a store in nearby Morganton. Their home was at the intersection of Fleming Avenue and North Garden Street. Most immigrant merchants left Marion after the war. (Courtesy of Louis Wall.)

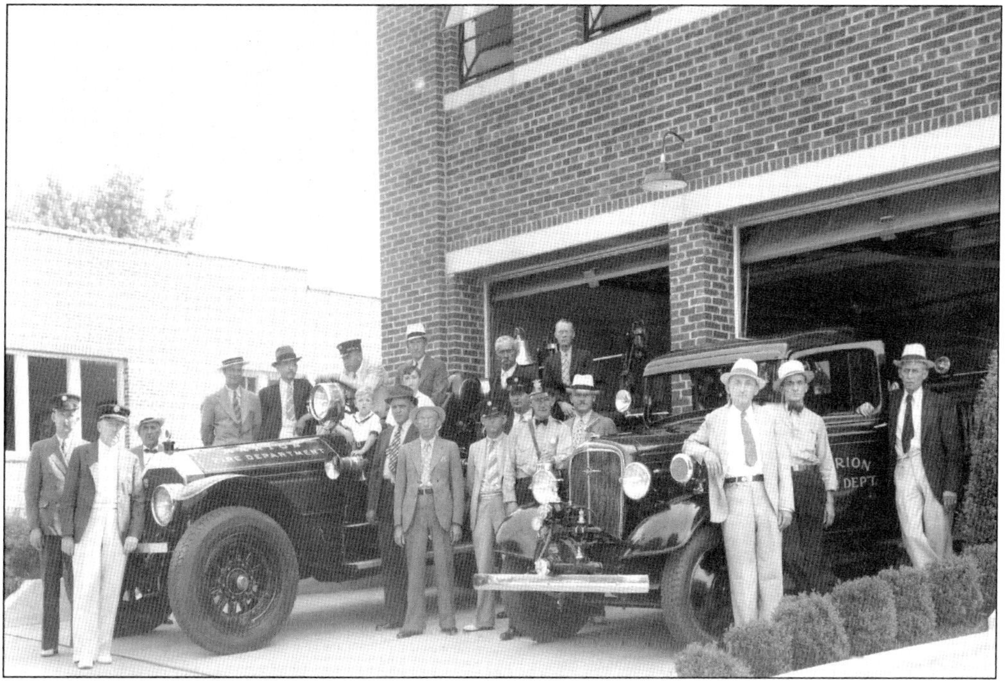

Members of the Marion Fire Department show off their new 1935 model truck (right) and its faithful predecessor. Two lucky boys were allowed to join the group: the dark-haired boy in the 1924 American La France to the left is Michael McCall, with his father, Clifton R. McCall, in the white hat; and the blond boy is John Mack Laughridge, seated beside his father, Morris Laughridge. (Courtesy of Dr. Michael McCall.)

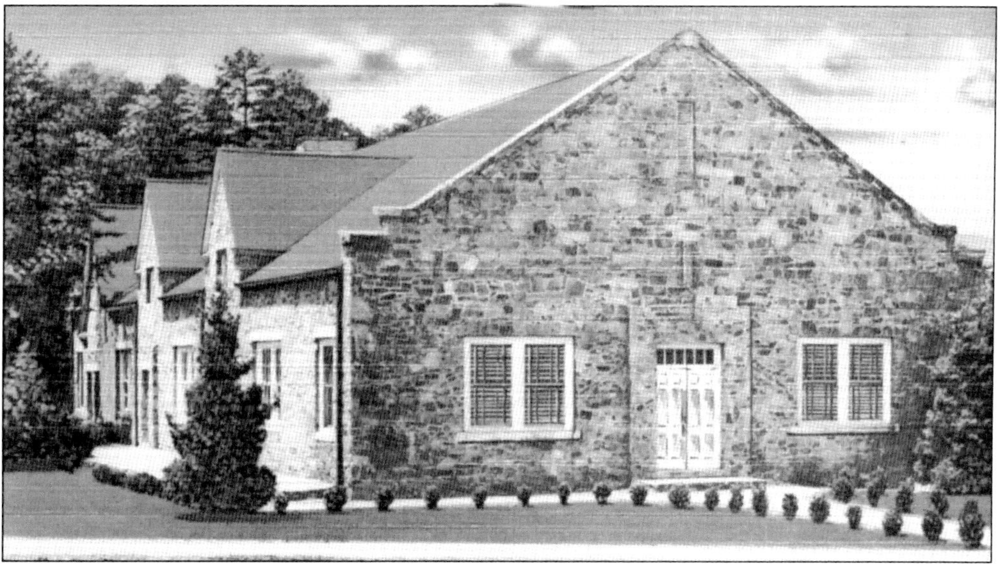

The Marion Community Building was constructed on North Main Street in 1938 by the New Deal–era Works Progress Administration. The county library was housed there briefly after the building opened, with WPA workers checking out books for patrons and performing other duties. The WPA also built other public structures in the county, including several schools and Mountain Gateway Museum. (Courtesy of Marion Business Association.)

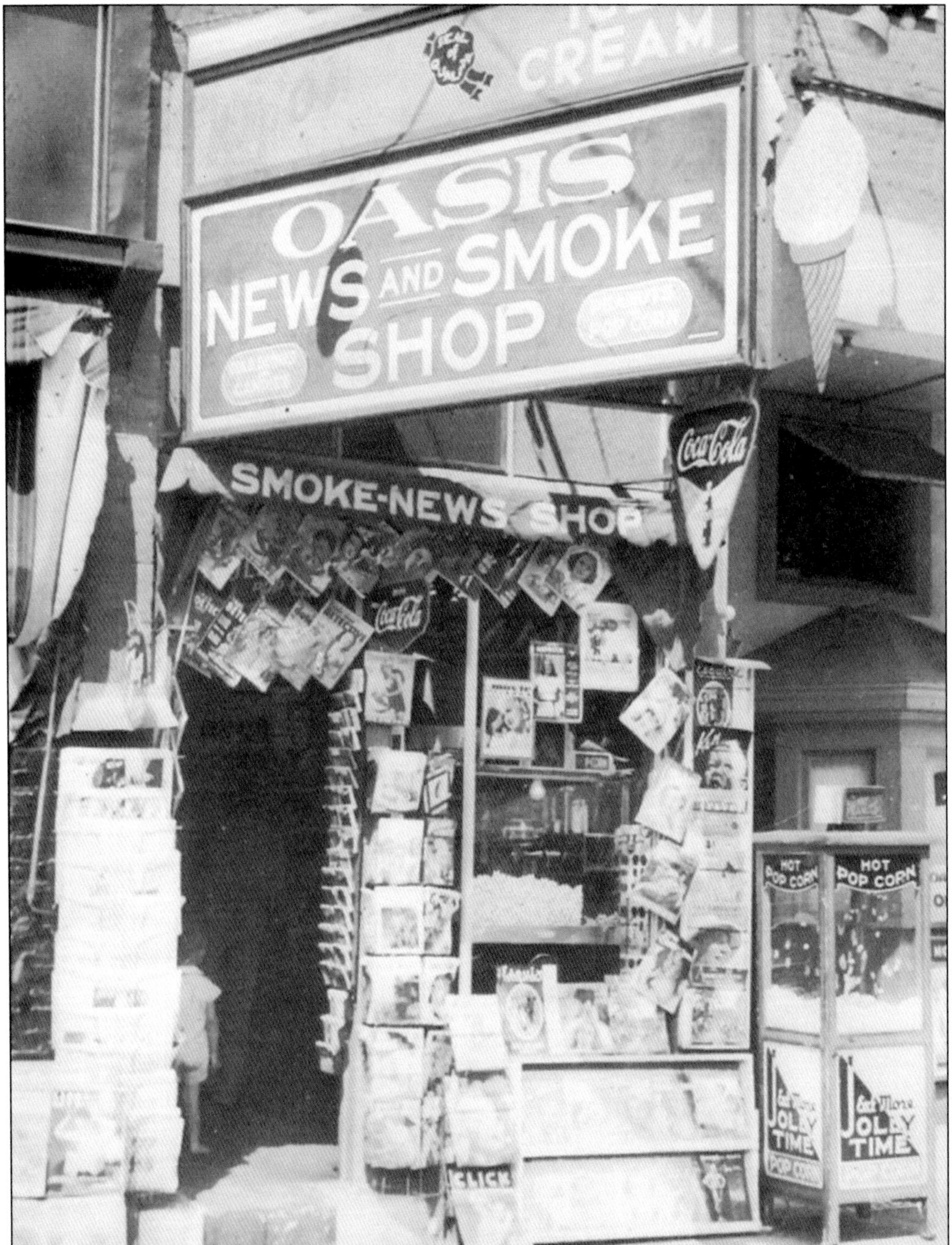

The Oasis News and Smoke Shop, pictured here in 1938, was a popular destination on the west side of Main Street for decades. Operated by Jim Lancaster, the Oasis stocked daily newspapers from Baltimore, Chicago, and Washington that were brought in by train. This photograph samples the variety of magazines that were offered: the men's monthly *Esquire*, detective magazines, several movie star titles, and *Ken*, a radical left-wing publication. Paperback books (especially Westerns) were stocked as well, but popcorn and cigarettes were the best-selling items. "Pop" Worley ran the business later. (Courtesy of Harvest Drive-In.)

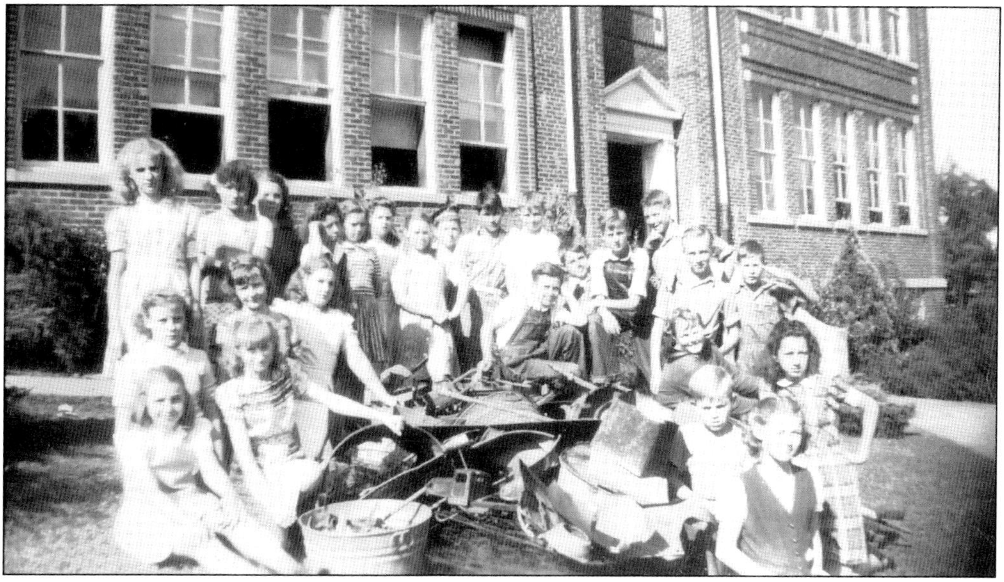

Clinchfield students contribute to the war effort by collecting scrap metal in 1942. Buckets, shovels, pieces of tin, and old toys would be melted down to make tanks, bombs, bullets, hand grenades, and other military supplies. Scrap metal drives were also important patriotism-boosters during the war, as evidenced by the young man saluting on the far right of the second row. (Courtesy of McDowell County Public Library.)

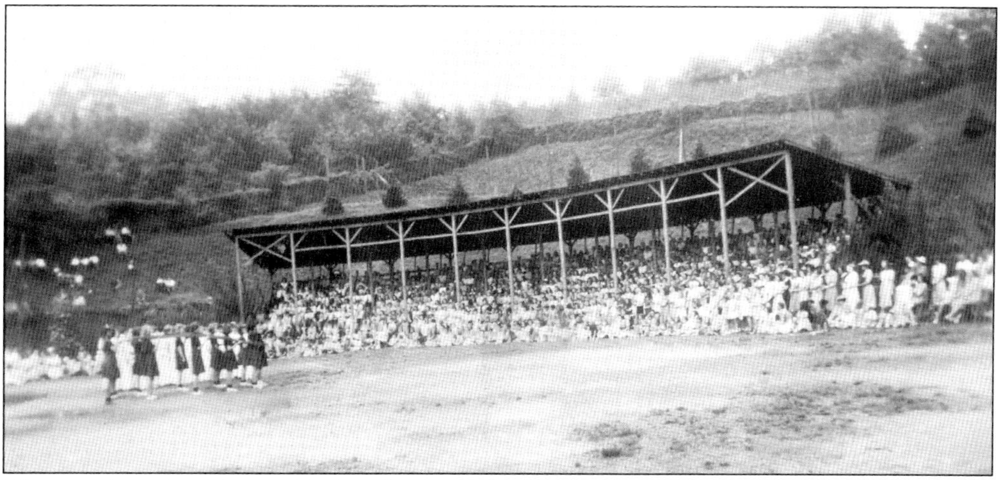

The grandstand at Marion High School on West Court Street is overflowing with spectators for the 1942 May Day festival. May 1 was once a major holiday, and this evening celebration attracted a crowd of nearly 1,000. Over 250 children from various schools in town participated in the program. Due to the war, this May Day celebration took on a decidedly patriotic theme. (Courtesy of Mountain Gateway Museum.)

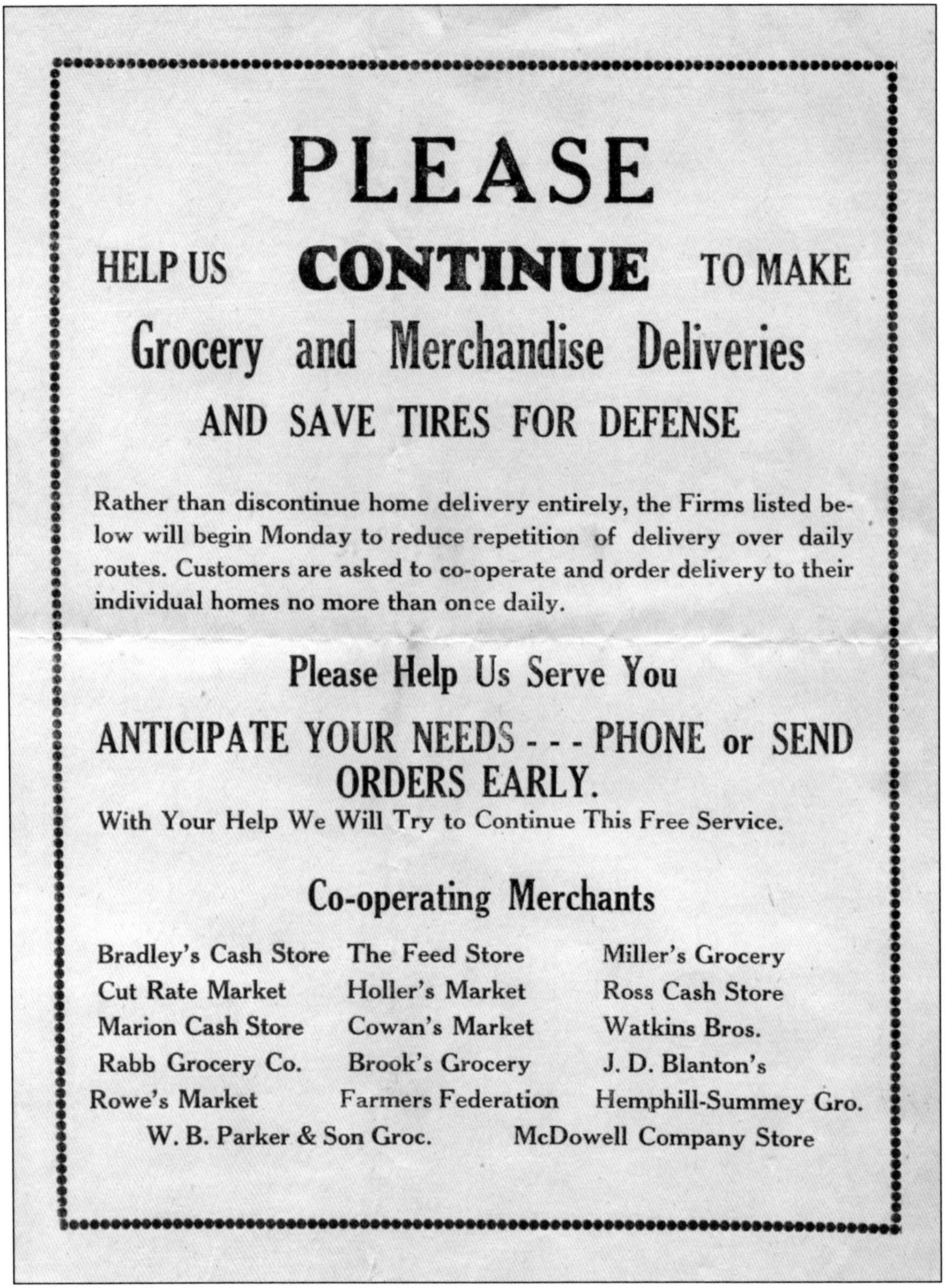

PLEASE

HELP US CONTINUE TO MAKE

Grocery and Merchandise Deliveries

AND SAVE TIRES FOR DEFENSE

Rather than discontinue home delivery entirely, the Firms listed below will begin Monday to reduce repetition of delivery over daily routes. Customers are asked to co-operate and order delivery to their individual homes no more than once daily.

Please Help Us Serve You

ANTICIPATE YOUR NEEDS - - - PHONE or SEND ORDERS EARLY.

With Your Help We Will Try to Continue This Free Service.

Co-operating Merchants

Bradley's Cash Store
The Feed Store
Miller's Grocery
Cut Rate Market
Holler's Market
Ross Cash Store
Marion Cash Store
Cowan's Market
Watkins Bros.
Rabb Grocery Co.
Brook's Grocery
J. D. Blanton's
Rowe's Market
Farmers Federation
Hemphill-Summey Gro.
W. B. Parker & Son Groc.
McDowell Company Store

Many items were rationed during World War II, including sugar, coffee, shoes, fuel, and tires. This flyer notifies patrons of many Marion stores that delivery routes will be curtailed until further notice in order to conserve tires. Pleasure driving was also discouraged during this period, and some estimates were that weekend traffic in the county dropped by 95 percent. Tires were rationed from January 1942 until December 1945. During that time, a local tire rationing board had to approve any new tire purchase or recapping. (Courtesy of Louis Wall.)

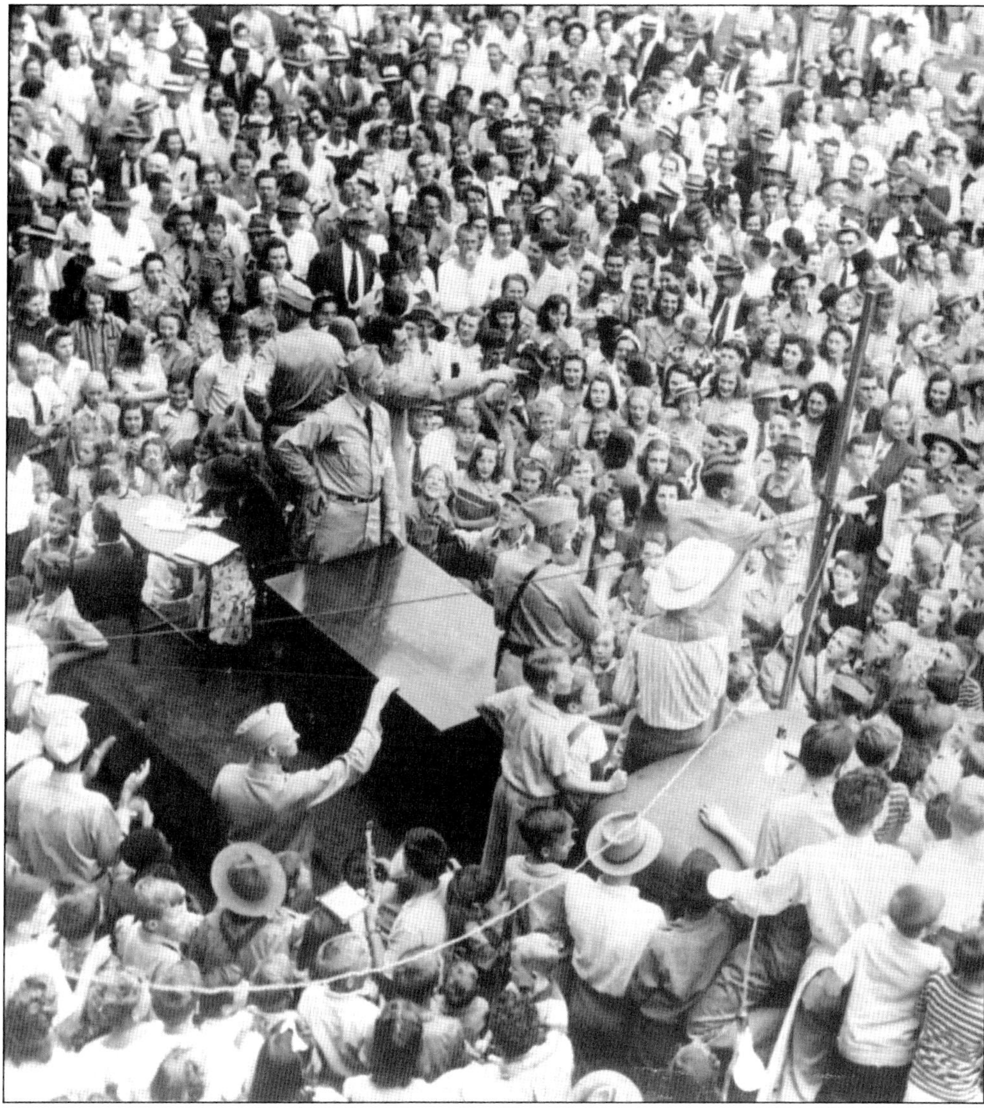

A Victory Bond Auction is held on Main Street during World War II. The prize for the most bonds purchased was a desk made for Gen. Douglas MacArthur by the Marion plant of Drexel Furniture. MacArthur's name was engraved on the top of the desk, with five stars over the word "General." When the War Department would not allow the finished desk to be shipped to MacArthur, it was given to Flemming Snipes, chairman of Victory Bond Drives for McDowell County. Main Street was roped off between Henderson and Court Streets for an auction, and hundreds of citizens attended. The winning bid was $4,800, and nearly $50,000 in total was raised. Also up for bid was nylon hosiery, which was a scarce item at the time due to the military's use of nylon to make parachutes, tents, and tires. (Courtesy of Mountain Gateway Museum, Warren Hobbs Collection.)

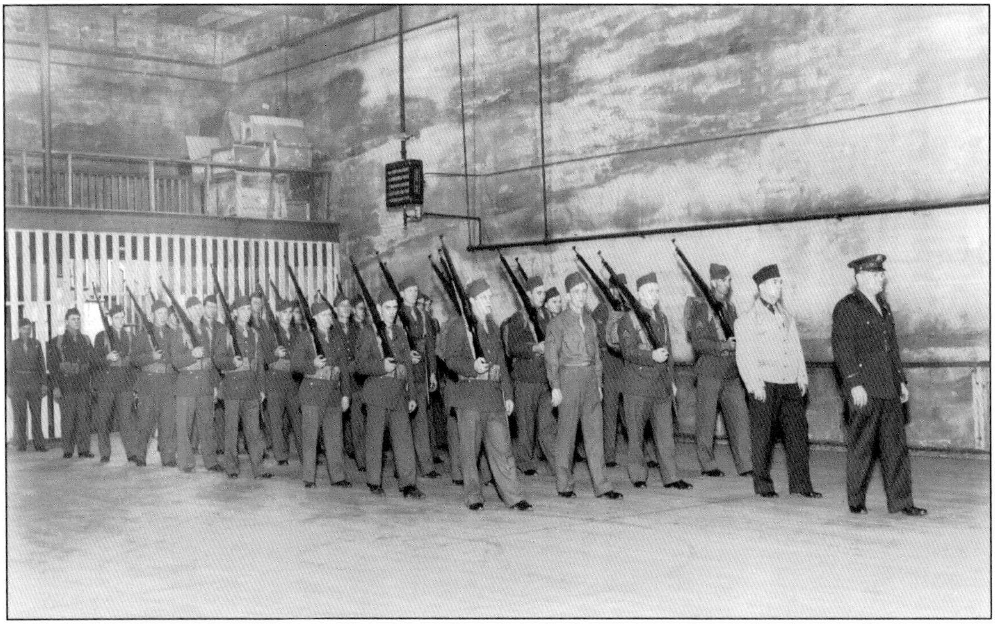

The McDowell County unit of the State Guard conducts drills in the basement of the Marion Community Building. Carl Bascom "C.B." Reynolds is second from the left, and the commander is Cecil Dobson. The State Guard was established in 1941 when the National Guard was mobilized into service to fight in World War II. The State Guard was disbanded in 1947 after National Guardsmen had returned home. (Courtesy of Gregg M. Hensley and Hensley Studio.)

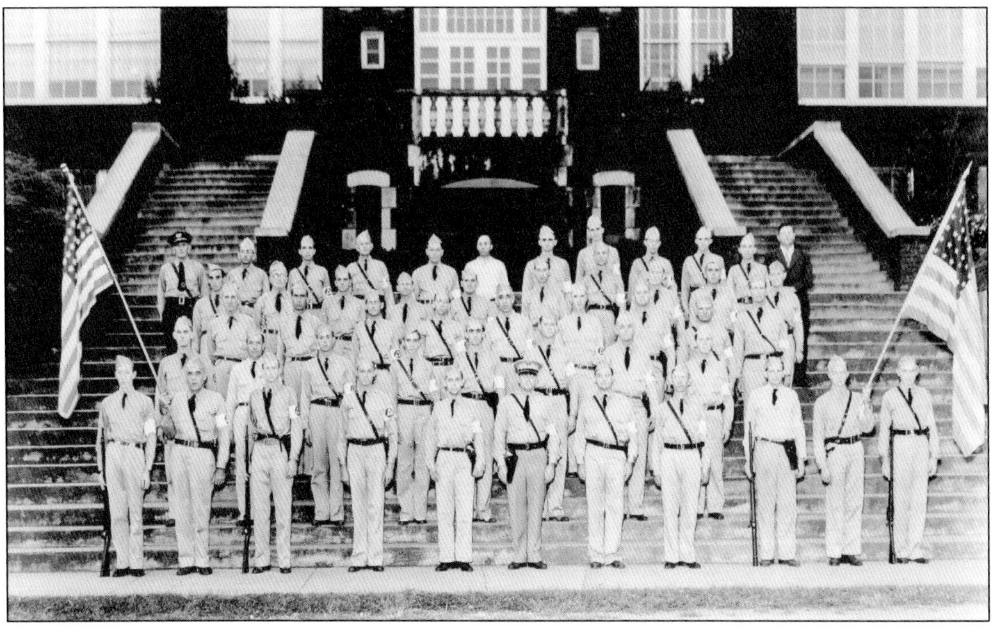

The Citizens Defense Corps of Marion stands at attention in front of Marion High School around 1943. The corps was run by the national Office of Civilian Defense and was trained to fight fires, provide first aid, perform chemical decontamination, and provide other services in the event of enemy attack. The armbands on the men indicate that this is an "auxiliary policeman" unit. (Courtesy of Gregg M. Hensley and Hensley Studio.)

Four

The Postwar Boom

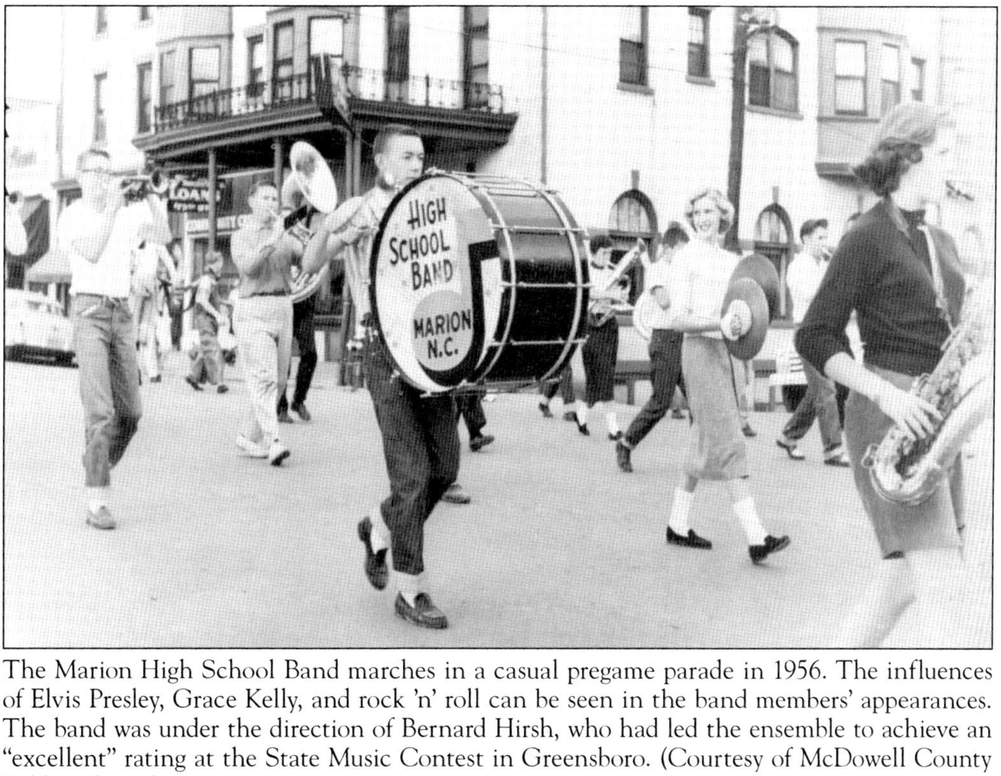

The Marion High School Band marches in a casual pregame parade in 1956. The influences of Elvis Presley, Grace Kelly, and rock 'n' roll can be seen in the band members' appearances. The band was under the direction of Bernard Hirsh, who had led the ensemble to achieve an "excellent" rating at the State Music Contest in Greensboro. (Courtesy of McDowell County Public Library.)

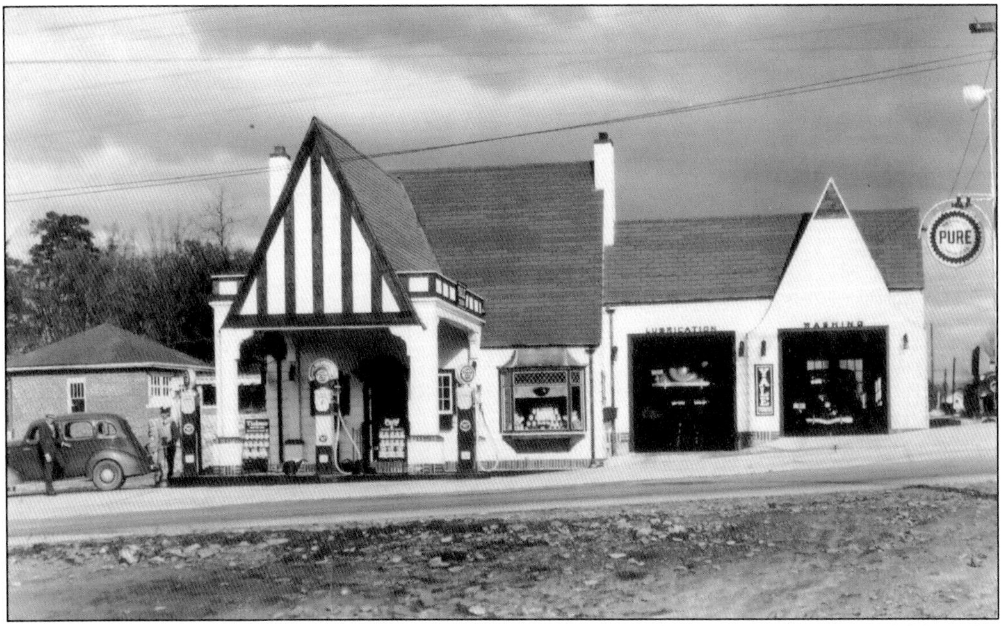

This 1940s-era full-service filling station was located on North Main Street. It would later be torn down to make way for new development, including an updated city hall building. The sight of an attendant pumping fuel, cleaning the windshield, and checking the oil while the driver relaxed was common at the time. Note the gravity-fed gasoline pumps. (Courtesy of Mountain Gateway Museum.)

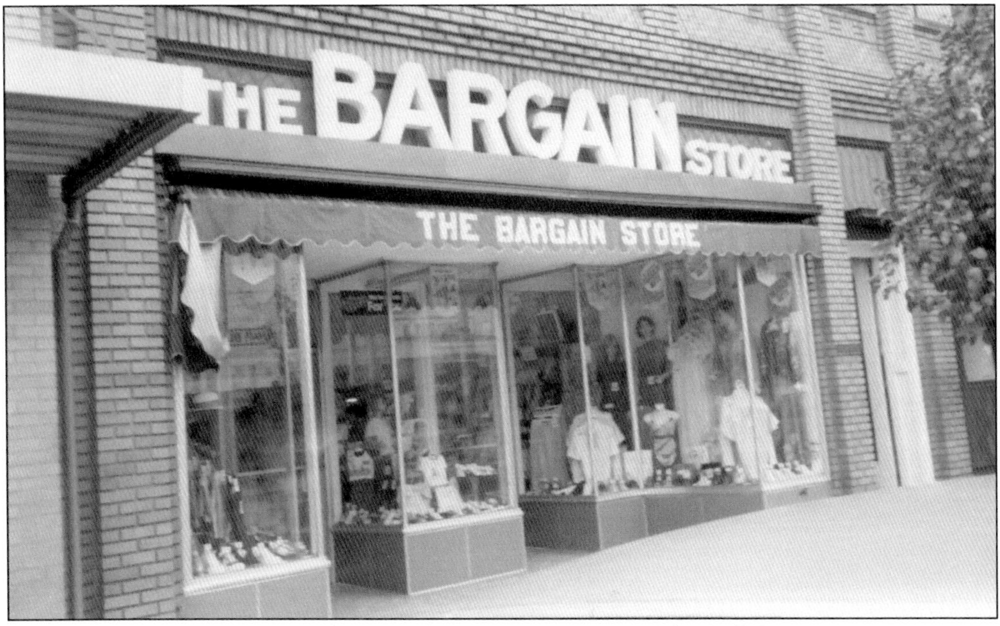

The Bargain Store was opened on South Main Street in 1945 by Belk-Broome store manager V.T. Eckerd. Pete and Ruby Eckerd bought it soon after and expanded into a larger neighboring building. The Bargain Store specialized in durable clothing and shoes at attractive prices. It remained in business into the 1990s. (Courtesy of McDowell County Public Library, Warren Hobbs Collection.)

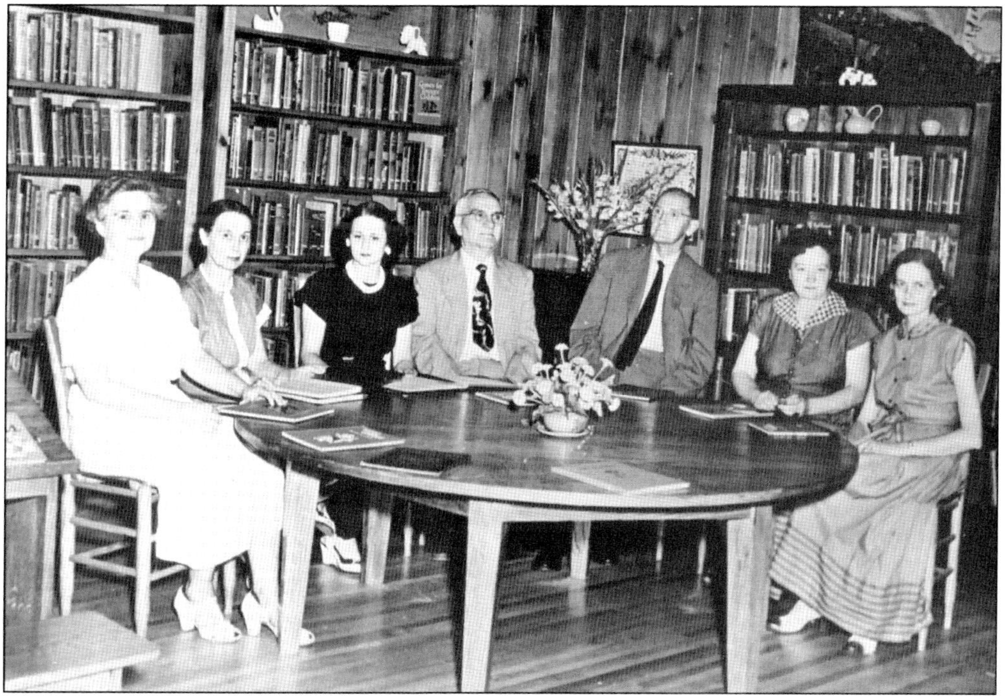

The Board of Trustees of the McDowell County Public Library meets in July 1949. From left to right are Mrs. J.F. Jonas, Mrs. Homer Beaman, Mrs. S.W. Blanton, T.L.Caplan, R.J. Noyes, Ruth Greenlee, and Alice Bryan. Bryan, hired in 1946, was the county's first full-time librarian. The McDowell library had evolved from the collection of Florence Irvin Thomas, who had begun lending from her private collection around 1920. (Courtesy of Mountain Gateway Museum.)

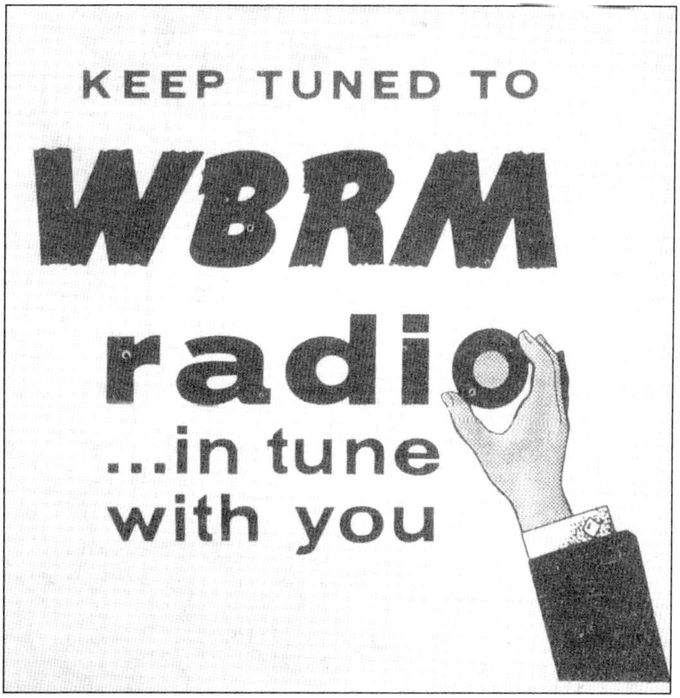

On May 9, 1949, Marion radio station WBRM began broadcasting 1,000 watts at 1250 on the dial. With minimal interference from other stations or communication devices, the station's programming could be heard in 18 states and in Canada. The first words to be broadcast after the initial station identification were those of a prayer by Rev. M.O. Owens. WBRM's studio and offices were located upstairs beside the Marion Theatre on West Court Street. (Courtesy of WBRM.)

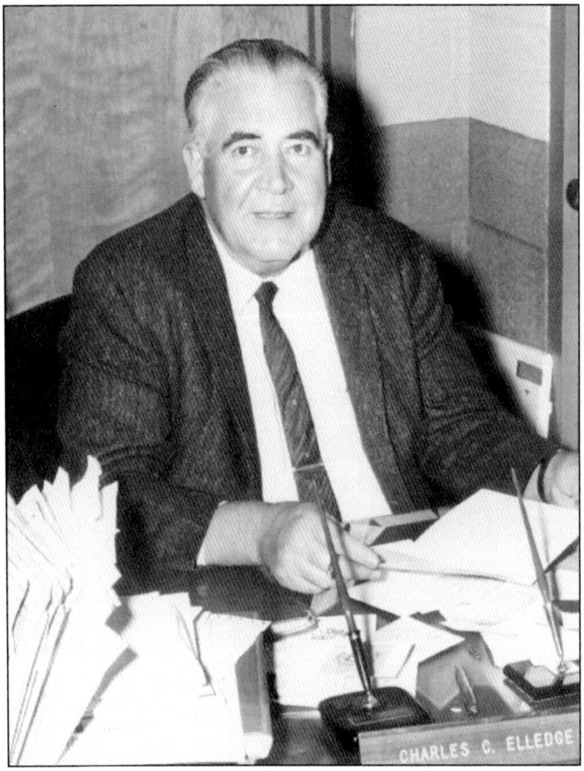

Charles Elledge was the principal at Marion High School from 1951–1966. He was also an accomplished actor. He appeared in eight feature films, in numerous television commercials, and for 33 seasons as Preacher Simms in the Boone outdoor drama *Horn in the West*. One month before his passing in 1986, a bronze bust of Elledge was unveiled at the Boone Theater. (Courtesy of McDowell County Public Library.)

This Sinclair service station was erected in the 1940s on the former site of the Flemming Hotel on North Main Street. The "HC" gasoline advertised on the sign is the high-octane "Houston Concentrate" by Sinclair. This location would later be occupied by a gazebo and city parking lot. (Courtesy of Gregg M. Hensley and Hensley Studio.)

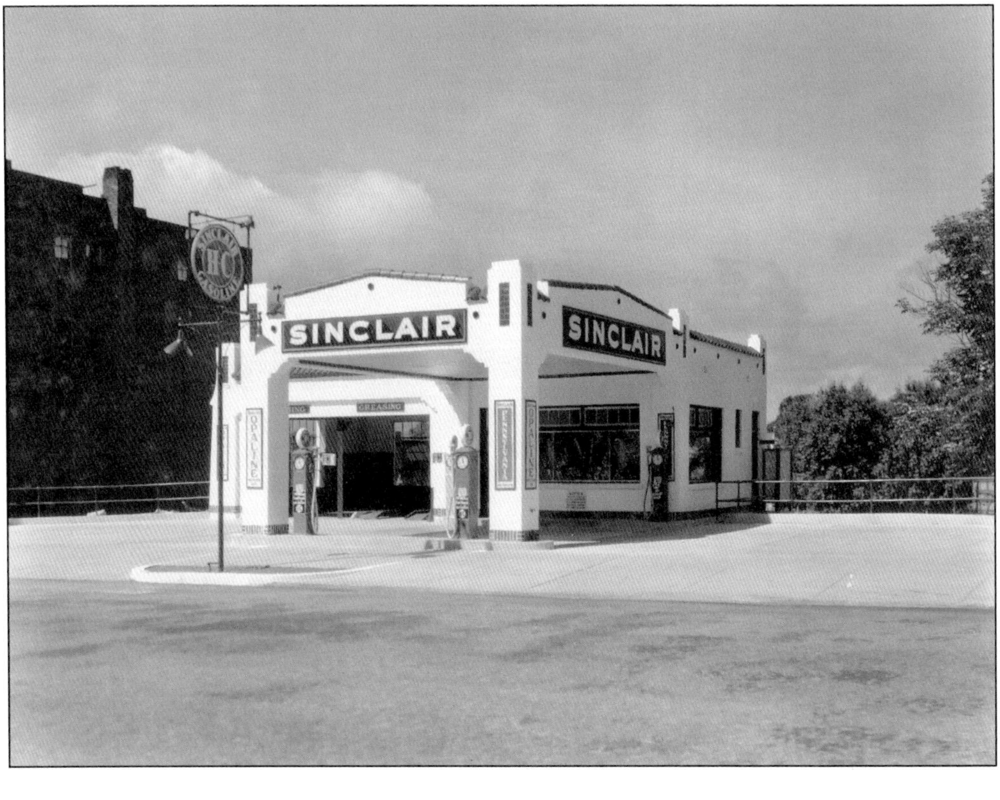

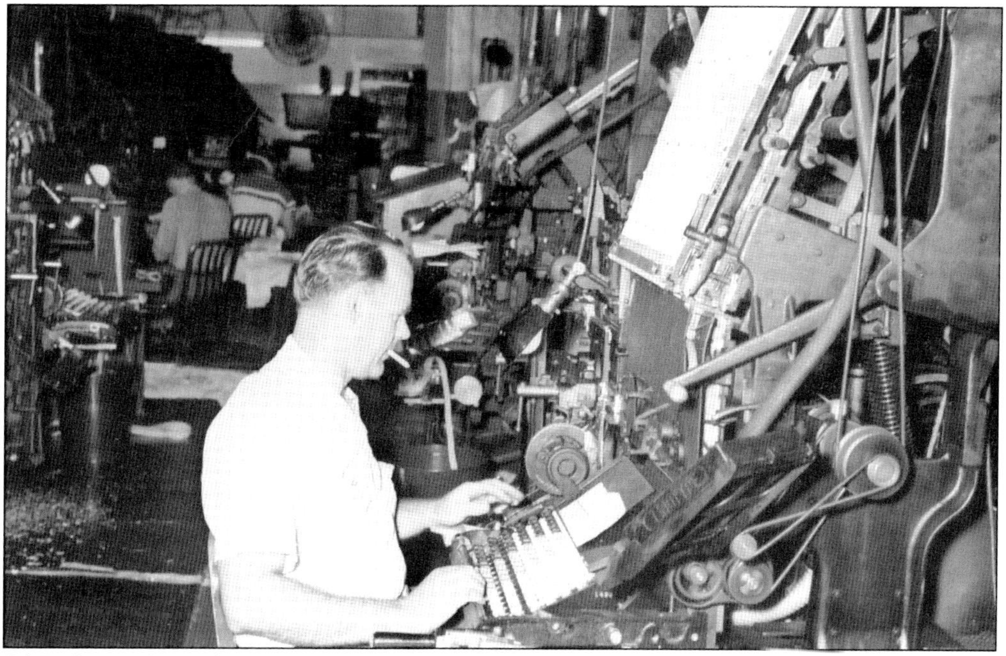

Ed Finley works at the Linotype machine at the *McDowell News* in the early 1950s. The notes for the story he is typing are on the paper above his keyboard. As he types, a mold of each letter drops down into a tray and a cast of each line is made in hot metal. The completed story mold will be taken to the printer. (Courtesy of DeEsta Baker.)

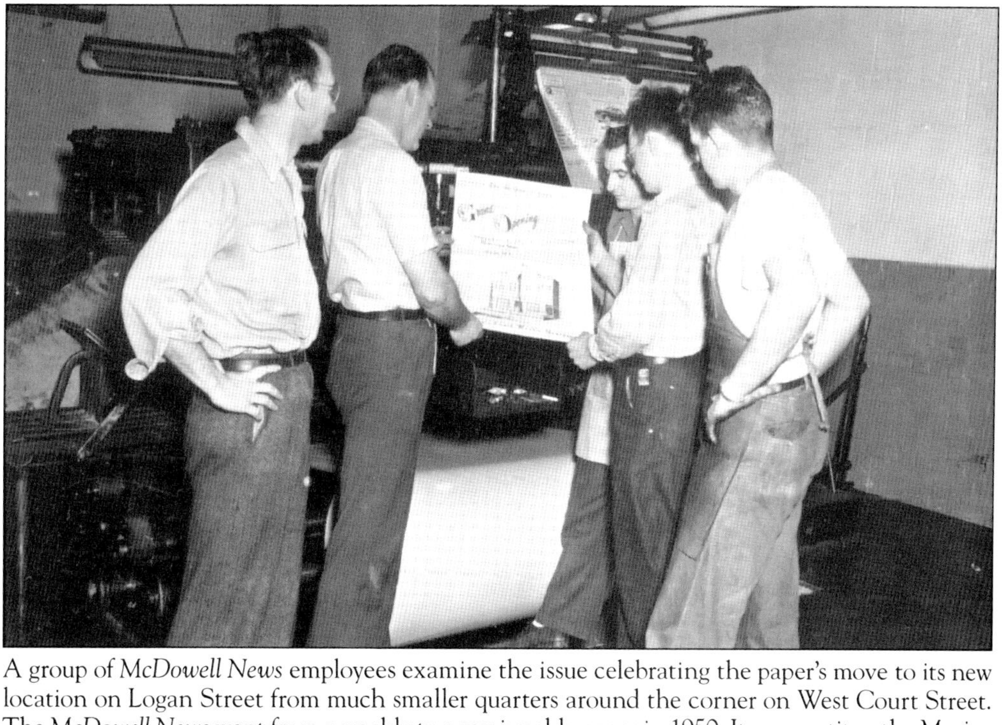

A group of *McDowell News* employees examine the issue celebrating the paper's move to its new location on Logan Street from much smaller quarters around the corner on West Court Street. The *McDowell News* went from a weekly to a semiweekly paper in 1950. Its competitor, the *Marion Progress*, ceased publication in 1956. (Courtesy of DeEsta Baker.)

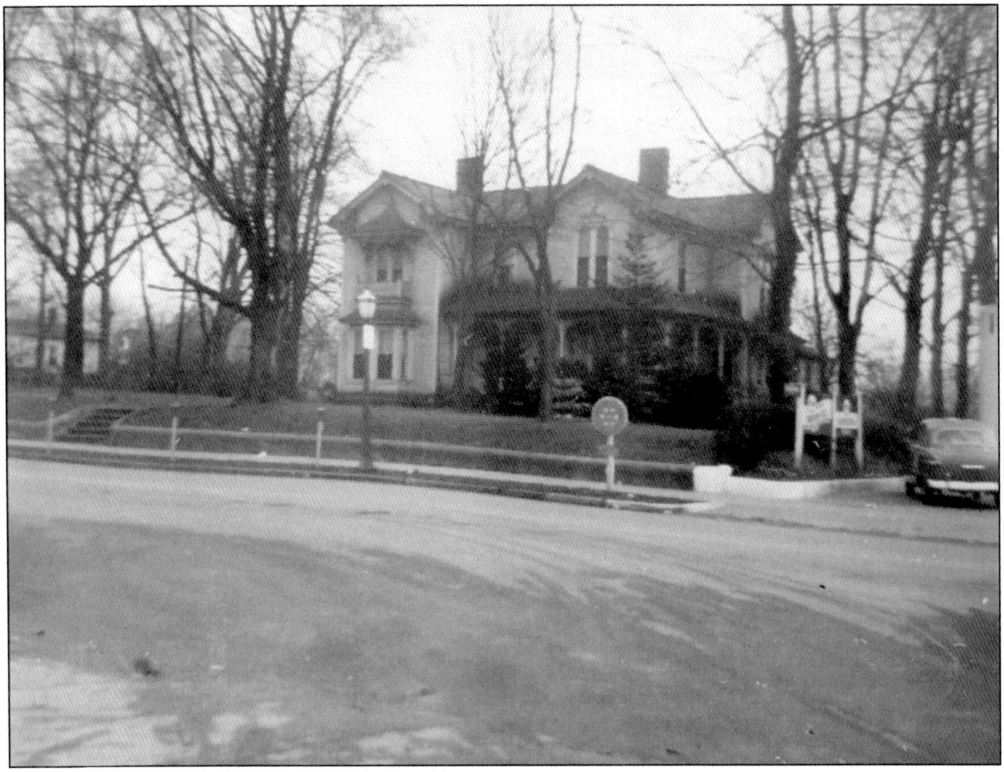

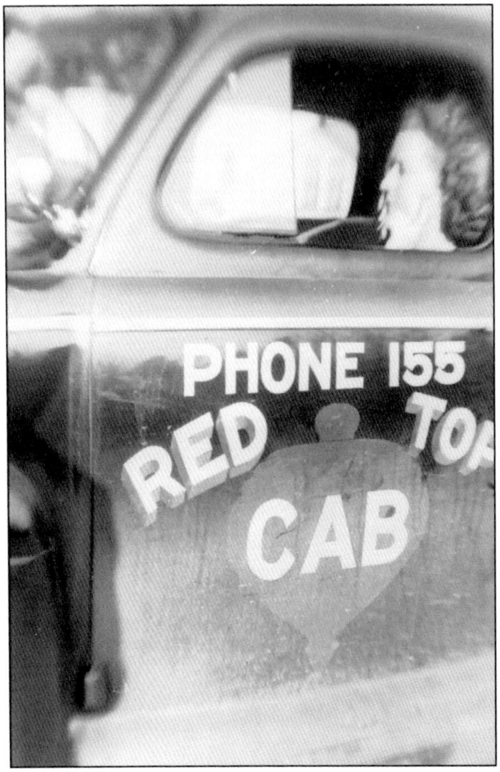

The D.L. Lonon home stood on the corner of Fort and North Main Streets. This photograph was taken shortly before it was torn down to make way for a Gulf service station. In the years following World War II, most of the Main Street homes were demolished to accommodate commercial development. (Courtesy of McDowell County Public Library, Robin Hood Collection.)

The Red Top Cab Company was one of several taxi services operating in Marion after the war. Other services in operation at the time were Eagle Cab, Black and White Cab, and Lake City Taxi. The identity of the Red Top female driver is not known. (Courtesy of David Vess.)

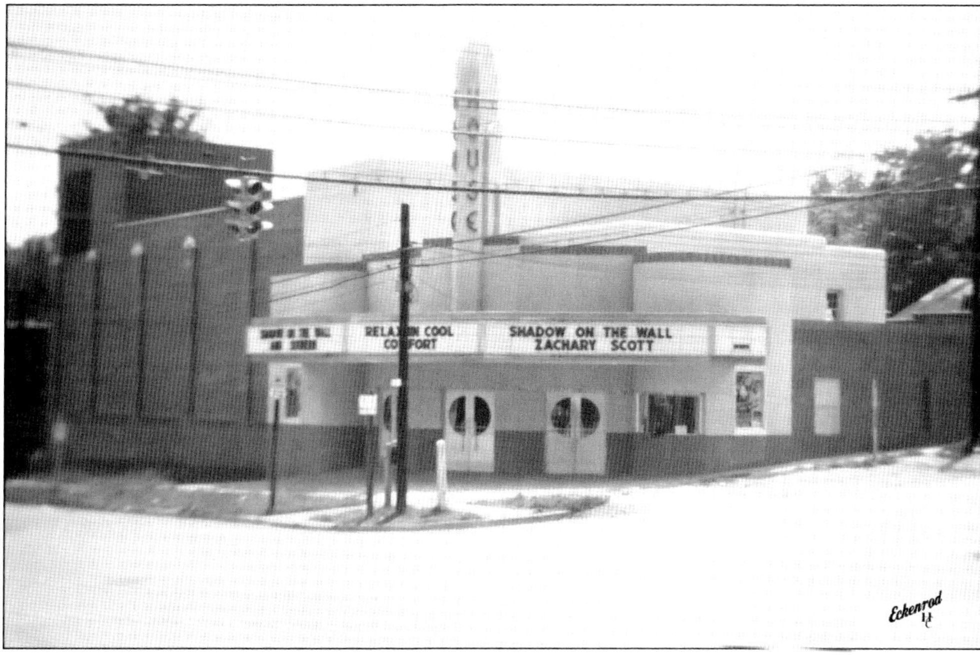

The House Theatre was opened on East Court Street in 1950 by Ernest House Jr.. Designed by C.C. Benton of South Carolina, the 550-seat venue hearkened back to the Art Deco architectural style of the late 1920s. The House Theatre closed in the 1980s shortly after the opening of the McDowell Twin Cinemas on North Main Street. (Photograph by Eckenrod Studio.)

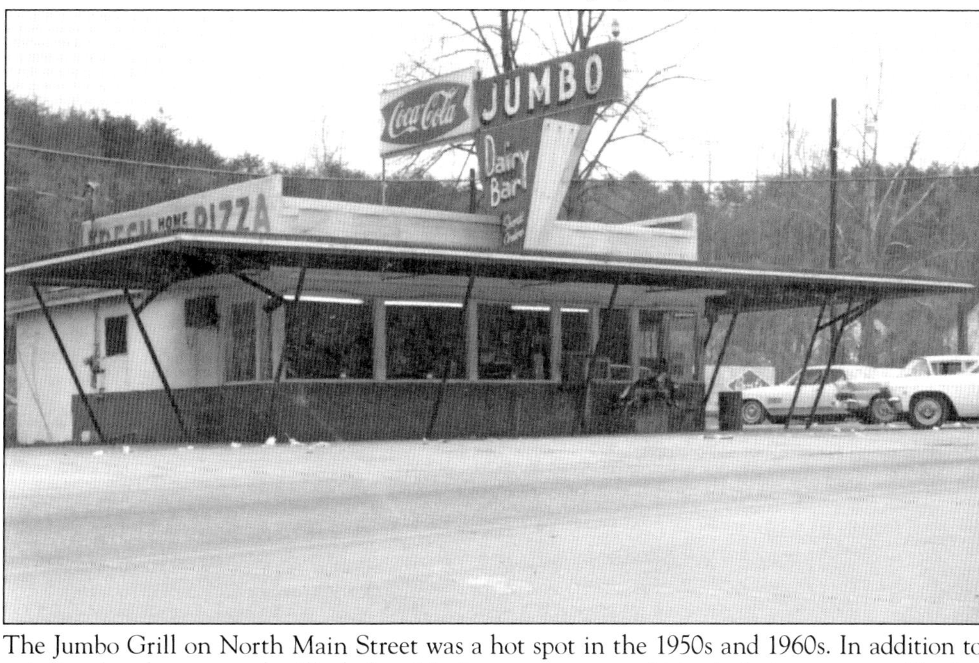

The Jumbo Grill on North Main Street was a hot spot in the 1950s and 1960s. In addition to enjoying hamburgers and milk shakes, Marion teenagers would back their cars up to Garden Creek behind the grill and hang out. Later, Garden Creek would be channeled through a pipe and paved over. The expanded site would be occupied by another Marion institution, The Steakhouse. (Photograph by Eckenrod Studio.)

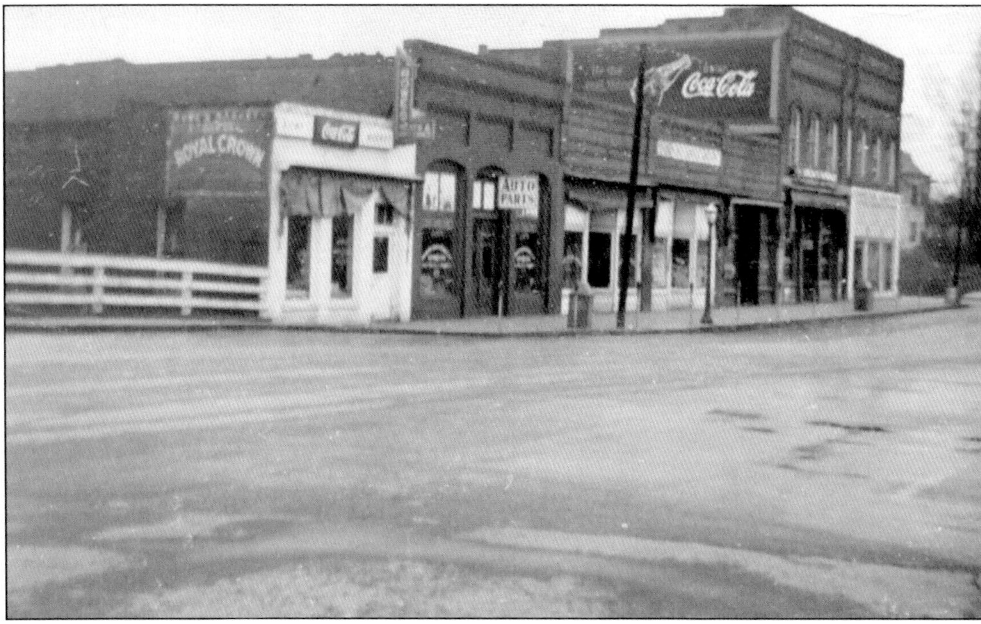

The following series of photographs was taken of various parts of downtown Marion in February 1950 by Robin Hood of the First National Bank. This view shows the stores on Main Street southeast of the railroad bridge. From left to right are Rowe's Market, Marion Auto Parts, Black Furniture Shop, Self Service Grocery, Jimeson's Hardware, and Rice & White Furniture. (Courtesy of McDowell County Public Library, Robin Hood Collection.)

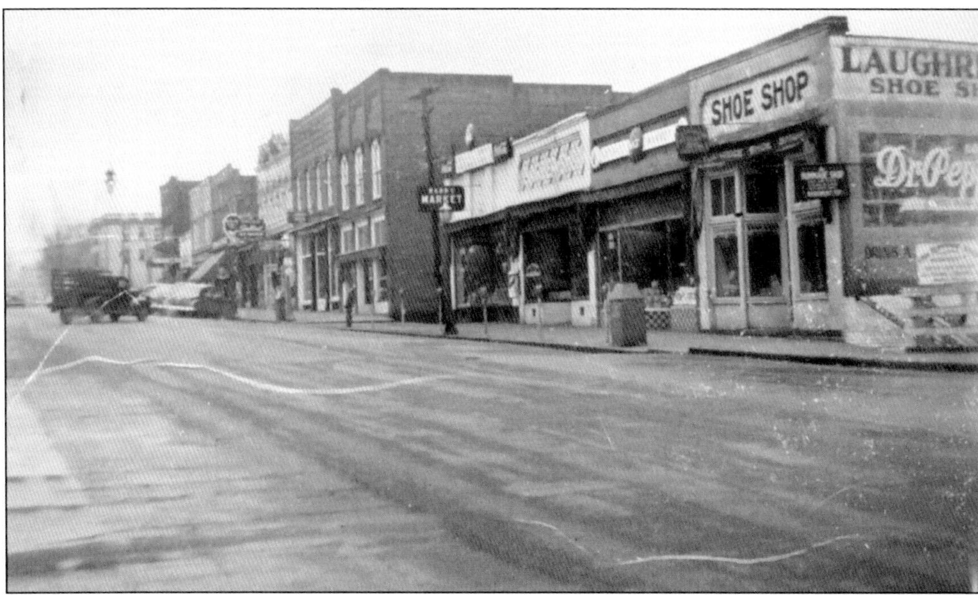

These are the stores northeast of the bridge. From right to left are Laughridge Shoe Shop, Cut Rate Market, Main Street Barbershop, Rabb's Market, J.D. Blanton's ready-to-wear, J.D. Blanton's hardware, Streetman's Drug, Western Auto, Holler's Market, Greene's Jewelry, and Workman's Department Store. Laughridge, Rabb, Blanton, Holler, Streetman, Greene, and Workman had been in business for decades. (Courtesy of McDowell County Public Library, Robin Hood Collection.)

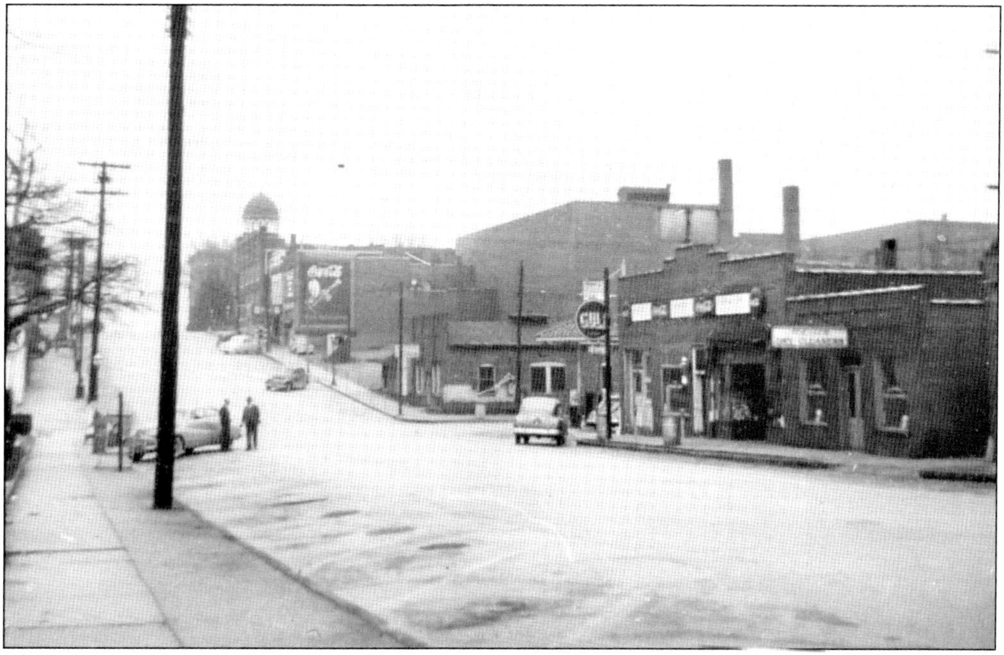

This photograph was taken in 1950 from West Court Street looking back up toward Main. From left to right are Marion Dry Cleaners, Mrs. John Steepe Store, Saunders Barbershop, Early Radio Shop, and Johnny Sullivan's Service Station. (Courtesy of McDowell County Public Library, Robin Hood Collection.)

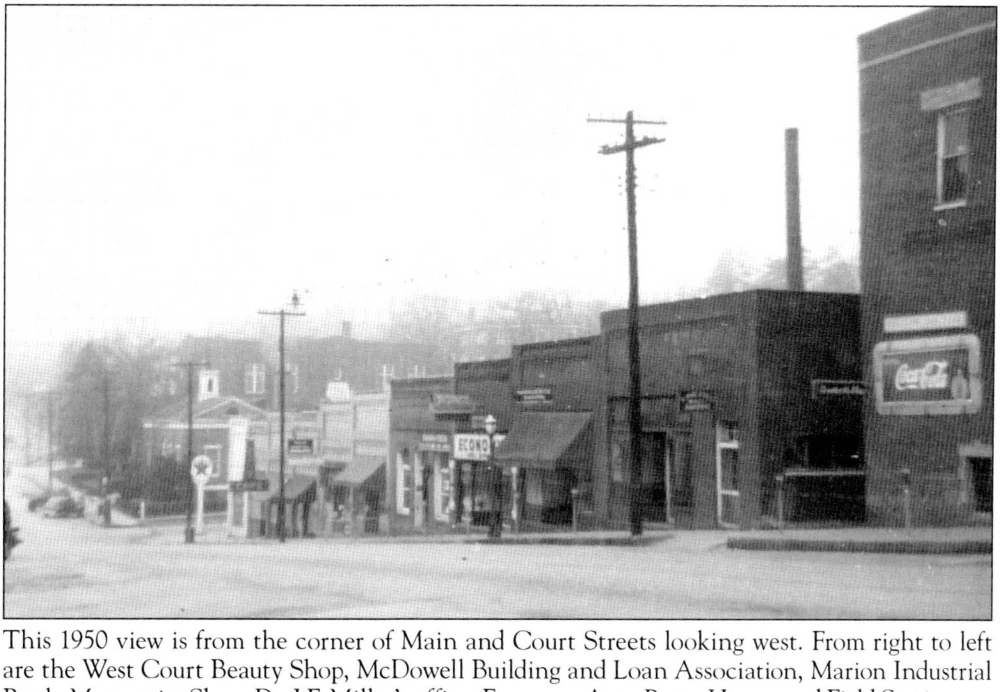

This 1950 view is from the corner of Main and Court Streets looking west. From right to left are the West Court Beauty Shop, McDowell Building and Loan Association, Marion Industrial Bank, Marguerite Shop, Dr. J.F. Miller's office, Economy Auto Parts, Hagna and Field Stationery, McDowell Insurance Agency, Silvers Grocery, Atkins Shoe Shop, and the Carolina Café. (Courtesy of McDowell County Public Library, Robin Hood Collection.)

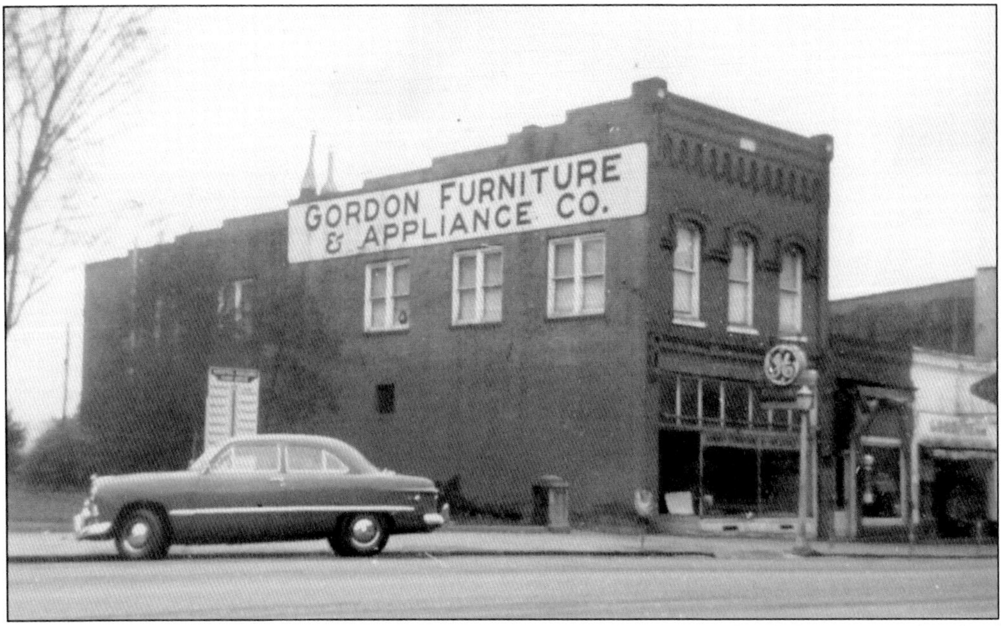

This building located beside the courthouse was the only one south of the square that had survived the 1894 fire. It would later be torn down for expansion of courthouse operations. On the courthouse lawn is a tally board for the hospital building fundraising-drive, showing the goal nearly achieved. This photograph was taken in 1950, and the new hospital opened in 1952. (Courtesy of McDowell County Public Library, Robin Hood Collection.)

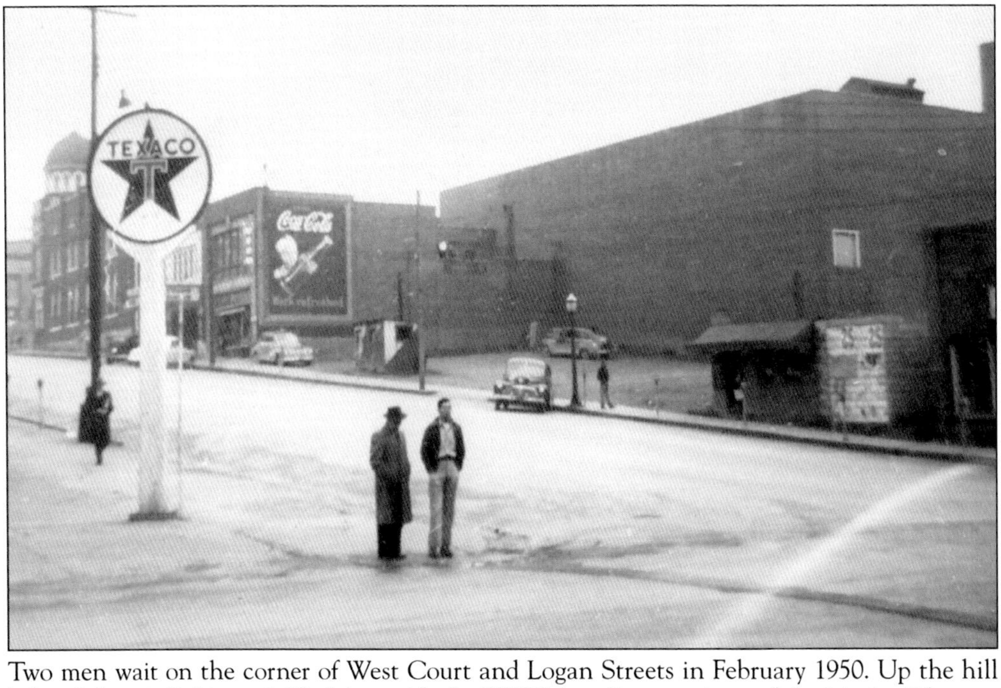

Two men wait on the corner of West Court and Logan Streets in February 1950. Up the hill behind them is Robinson's Clothing, with the WBRM studios upstairs, and the Marion Theatre. The site of the corner service station would later be occupied by the Marion Fire Department. (Courtesy of McDowell County Public Library, Robin Hood Collection.)

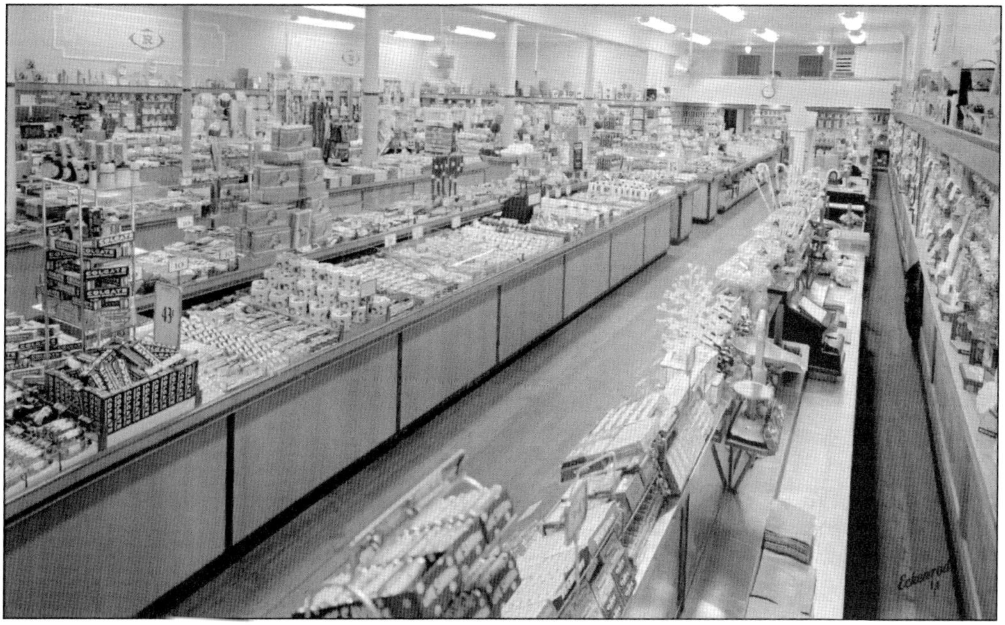

The beauty aids and gift departments of Rose's dime store are ready for business in this 1950s-era photograph. Rose's 5¢-10¢-15¢ Store opened on Main Street in Marion in the early 1930s. Note the scale for weighing candy and the wooden cash register to the right. Old-fashioned favorites Adams Clove chewing gum and Teaberry gum are featured just below the Life Savers. (Photograph by Eckenrod Studio.)

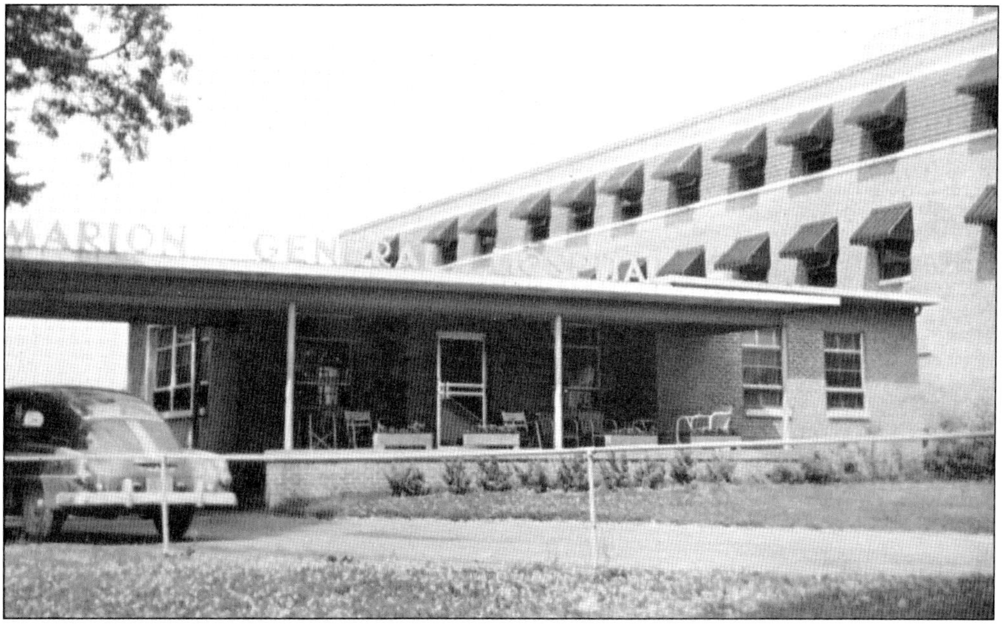

Marion General Hospital moved to Fleming Avenue in 1952. It boasted 62 beds and triple-X fireproof construction. This facility was preceded by Marion's first hospital located in a house on State Street, a West Henderson location built in 1914, the old Flemming Hotel beginning in 1924, and a building a few blocks away on James Drive built in 1930. (Courtesy of McDowell County Public Library, Warren Hobbs Collection.)

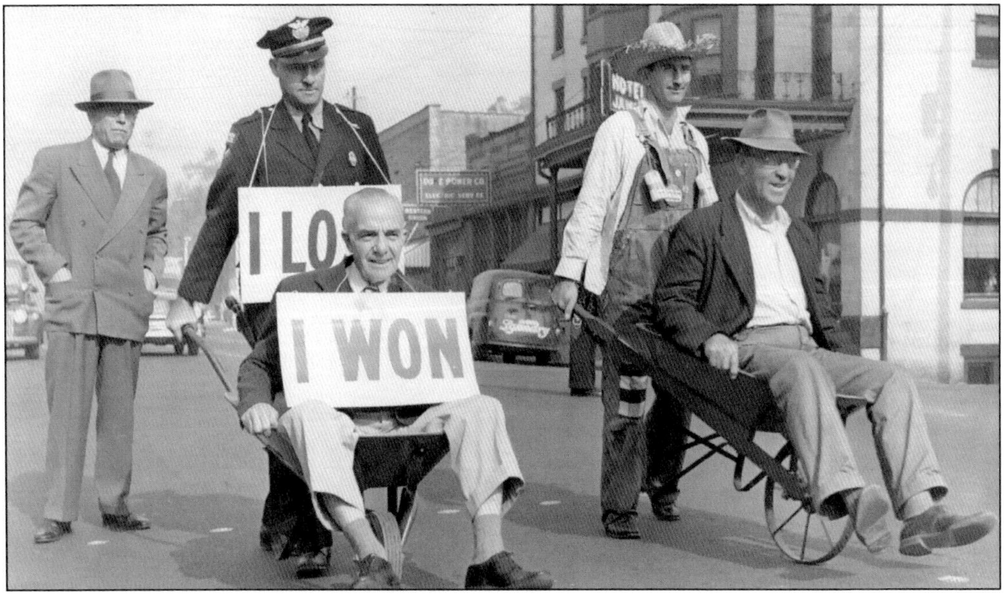

These men being pushed down Main Street in wheelbarrows won their bet on the 1952 presidential election. Victorious Eisenhower supporters J.E. Black (right) and Ralph Alexander enjoy the ride while disappointed Stevenson boosters Robert Jarrett (policeman) and Clyde Parker good-naturedly fulfill their end of the bargain. Stevenson was the candidate of the Democratic party, and McDowell Democratic chairman S.J. Westmoreland somberly observes the proceedings. (Courtesy of McDowell County Public Library, Robin Hood Collection.)

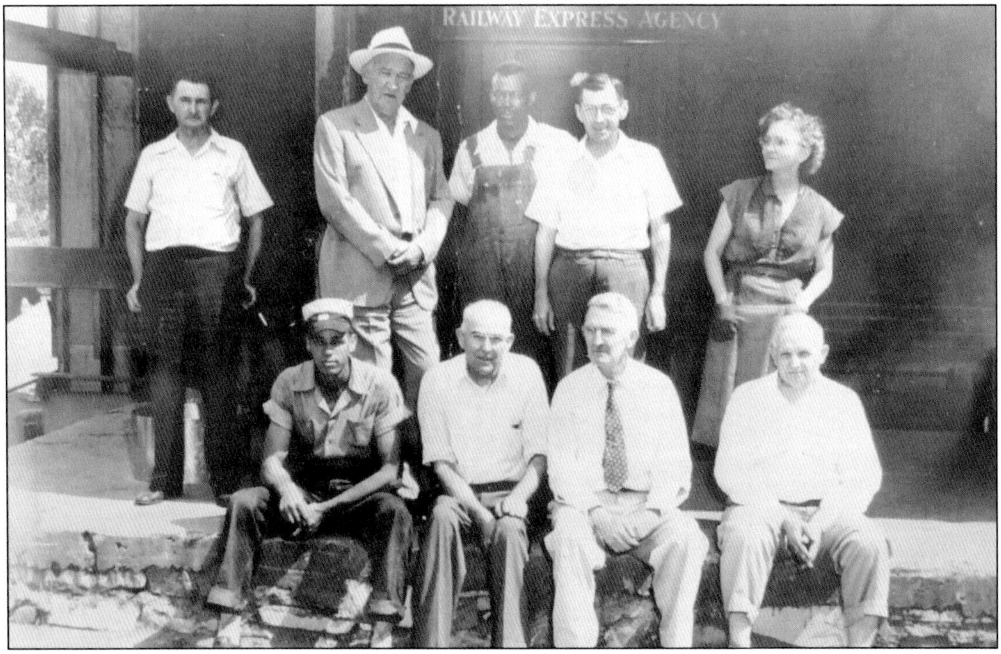

Personnel of the Southern Railway Office break for a photograph in 1952. From left to right are (sitting) Charles Presnell, Jake Raburn, J. Clay Conley, and John Wilson; (standing) Ernest Wair, George Sandlin, Tom Faucette, R.E. Patton, and Ruby Ledbetter. Wair and Patton were telegraphers, while the rest were clerks, agents, and laborers. (Courtesy of Mountain Gateway Museum.)

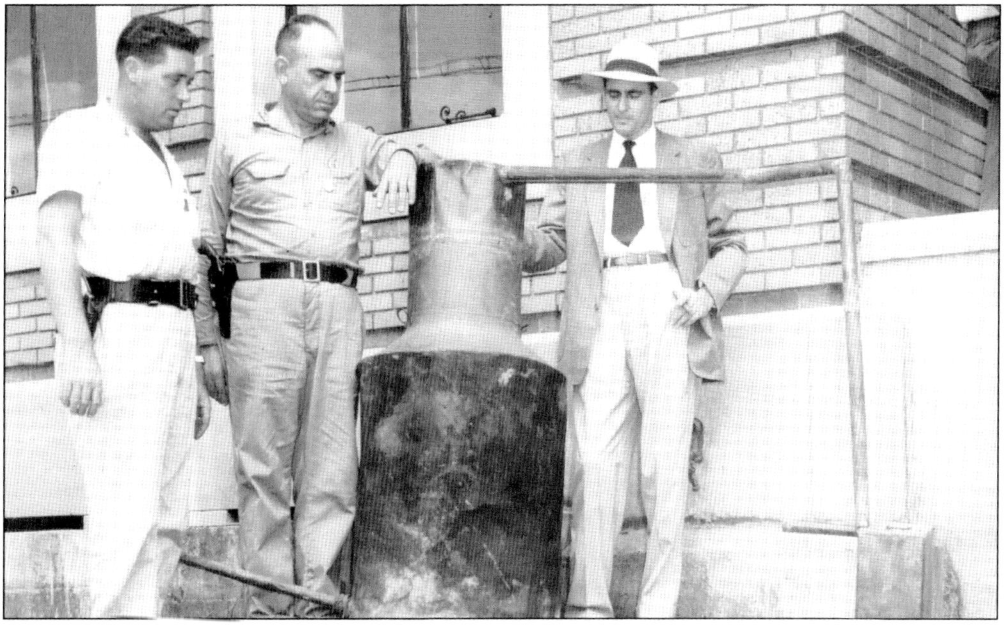

McDowell County sheriff Ashby Robinson (right) and Deputies Owens and Toney display moonshining evidence outside the courthouse in Marion. Breaking up illegal stills was a major focus of Robinson's tenure, and it was customary for a "trophy" to be brought to the courthouse after each successful operation. Robinson was sheriff from 1950 to 1958. (Courtesy of Mountain Gateway Museum.)

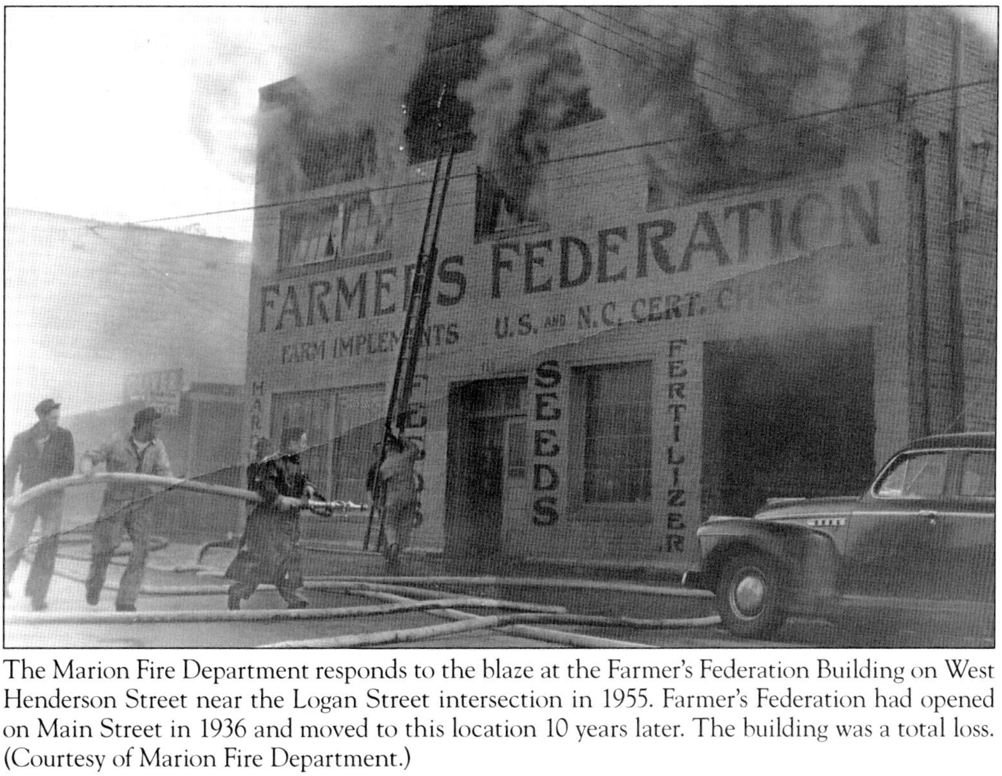

The Marion Fire Department responds to the blaze at the Farmer's Federation Building on West Henderson Street near the Logan Street intersection in 1955. Farmer's Federation had opened on Main Street in 1936 and moved to this location 10 years later. The building was a total loss. (Courtesy of Marion Fire Department.)

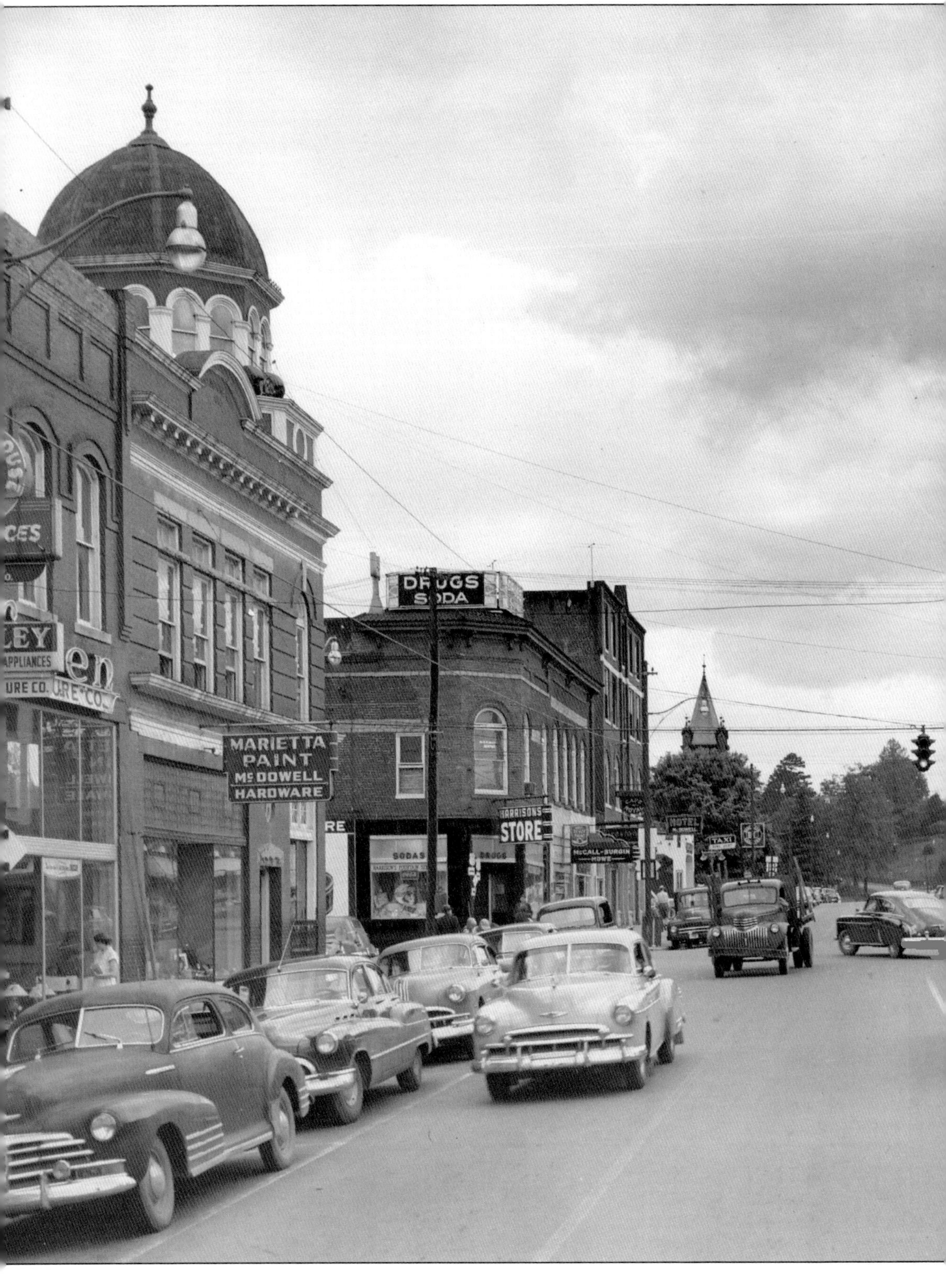
DRUGS
SODA
MARIETTA
PAINT
McDOWELL
HARDWARE
HARRISONS
STORE
SODAS
DRUGS
APPLIANCES
HOTEL
TAXI

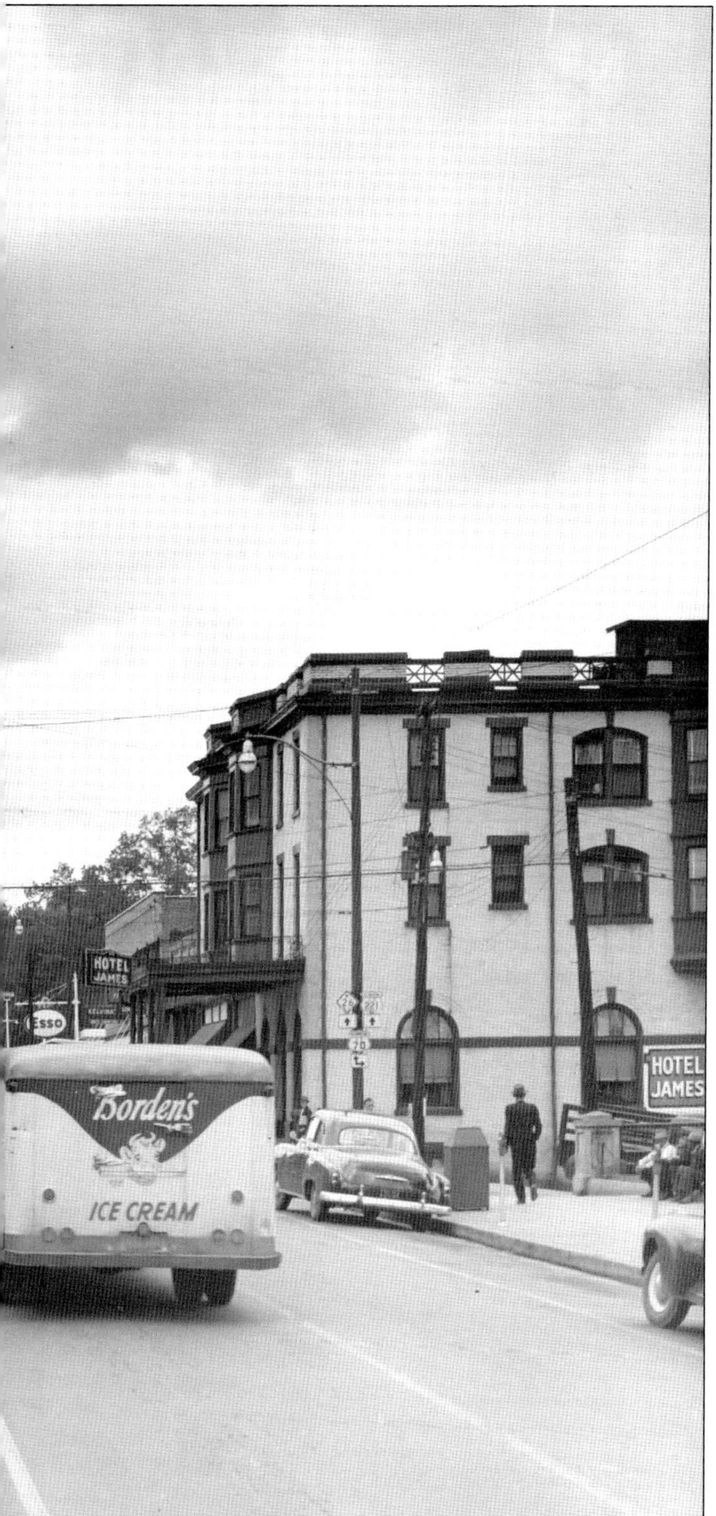

This view looking north on Main Street in May 1953 shows a bustling downtown. On the corner across from the bank is Harrison's Café, operated by "Doc" Harrison. With a soda fountain and jukebox, it was a popular gathering place for teenagers, especially on Saturdays. The Marion Theatre was located diagonally across West Court Street, making Harrison's a convenient stop for young people before and after a movie. Up the block from Harrison's was the Royal Café, one of the most popular dining establishments in Marion. It was operated by the Demetriou brothers, who would later relocate up the mountain to Fletcher and operate the Royal Steakhouse, which continued their reputation for excellent food. (Courtesy of McDowell County Public Library, Robin Hood Collection.)

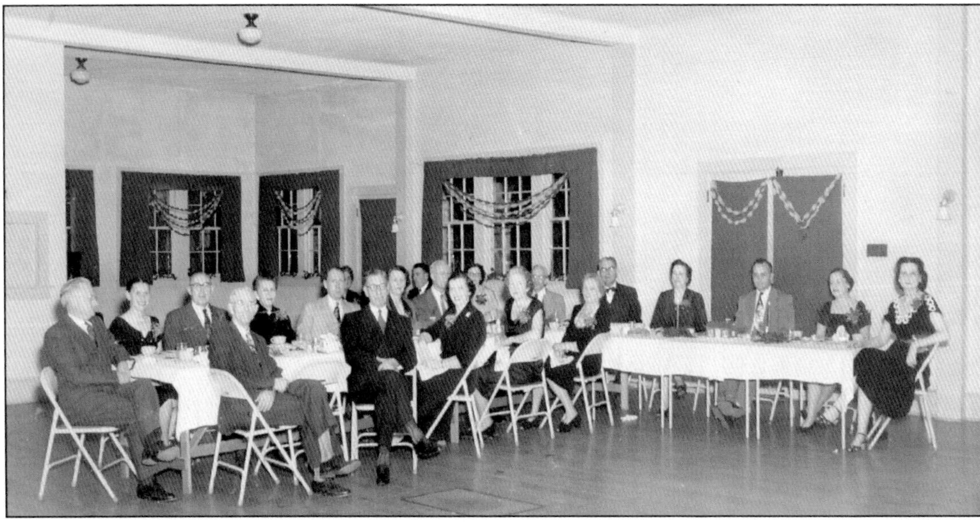

The McDowell Building and Loan Association holds its Christmas dinner in 1952. Starting at the far right and going counterclockwise around the table are the following: Doris Hill, Mrs. C.D. Blanton, Willis C. Truesdale, Mrs. C.A. Workman, W.R. Chambers, C.D. Blanton, Mrs. Willis C. Truesdale, Ben C. Epley, Mrs. J.F. Snipes, C.A. Workman, Mrs. W.S. Shiflet, Carter Hudgins, Mrs. Carter Hudgins, W.S. Shiflet, Mrs. Ben C. Epley, J.F. Snipes, J.H. Tate, A.S. Bradford, Kathryn Hunt, Mrs. A.S. Bradford, and Mrs. W.R. Chambers. (Courtesy of McDowell County Public Library.)

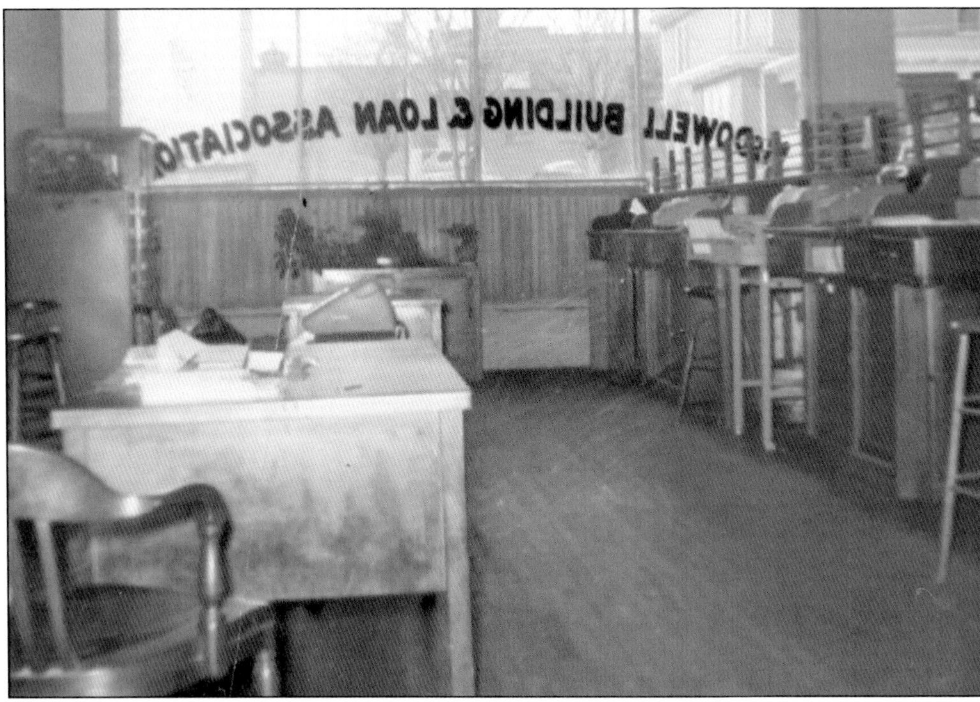

This is the interior of the office of McDowell County Building and Loan on West Henderson Street in 1957. The organization moved to this location in 1954, announcing that "the most modern bookkeeping equipment" was being installed to handle its $2 million in accounts. (Courtesy of McDowell County Public Library, Robin Hood Collection.)

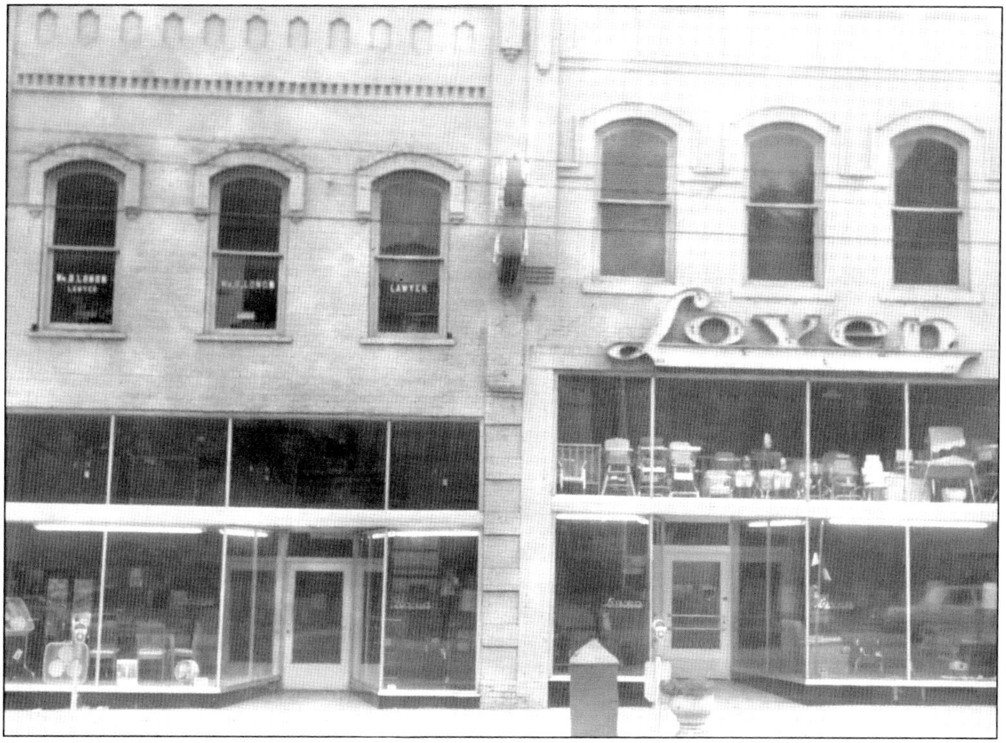

G. Carl Loven came to Marion from Spruce Pine in the early 1940s and operated Loven Furniture Company on the west side of Main Street for many years. Loven's emphasis was on fine furniture, but he also stocked Crosley appliances, Dexter washing machines, Siegler oil heaters, and more. Margaret Wall was a longtime Loven employee and a beloved figure in town. Loven passed away in 1969. (Courtesy of McDowell County Public Library, Robin Hood Collection.)

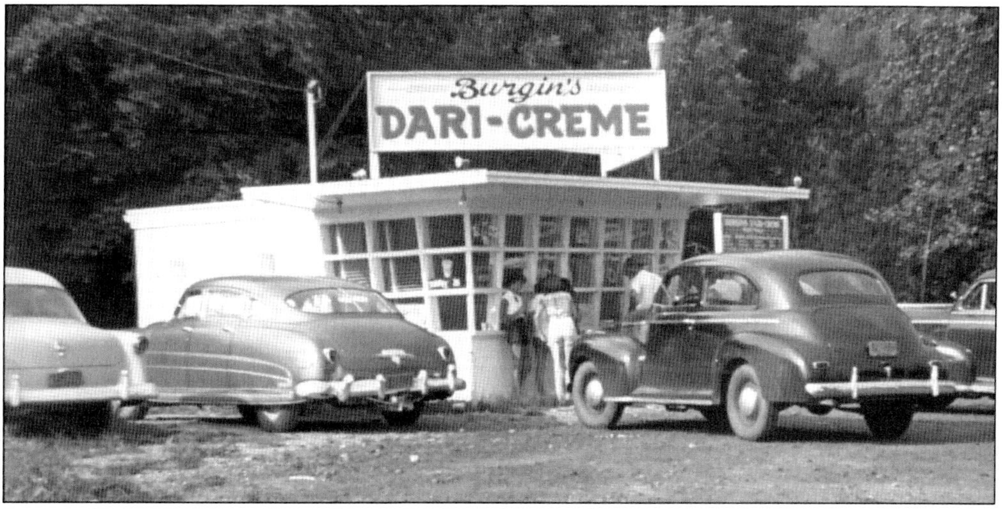

Burgin's Dari-Creme was opened in 1954 on Highway 70 by J.G. Burgin and his wife, Lena. Their son Jimmy and his wife, Mildred, extended the family business by establishing Jack Frost Dairy Bar on Sugar Hill Road in 1971, selling ice cream made using the same hand-stirred method. Jim Burgin Jr. continues to operate Jack Frost at the time of this writing, still offering "1950s-style" ice cream. (Courtesy of Jim Burgin.)

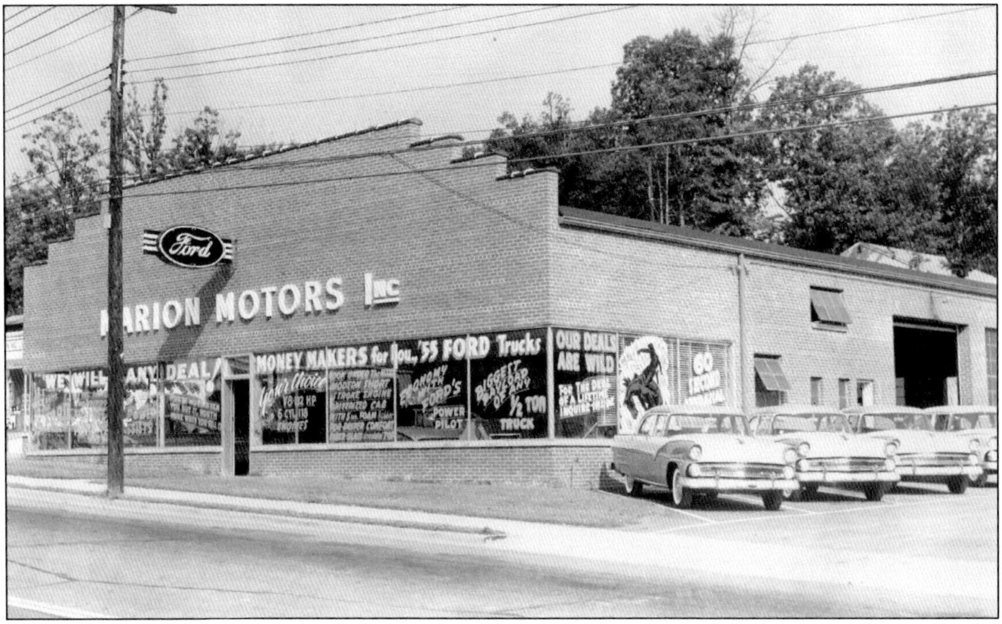

This Ford dealership was located on East Court Street. The 1955 Fords on display featured an "egg crate" grill, and a "panoramic" windshield was also being introduced. 1955 was the first year that seat belts were available as a dealer option. East Court Street was a popular place for car dealerships; a Pontiac lot was situated just across the street. (Courtesy of McDowell County Public Library.)

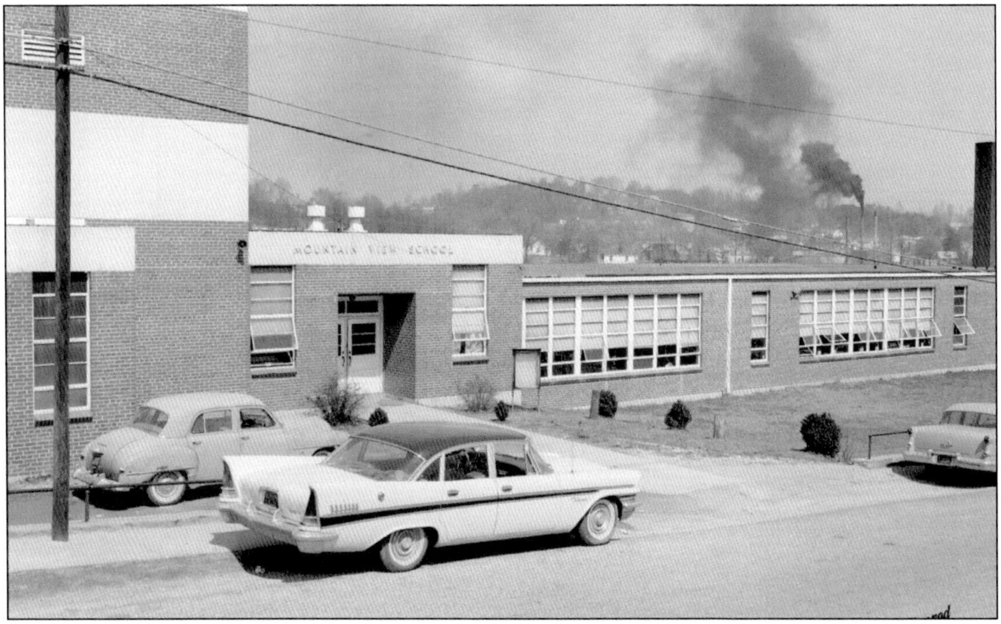

Mountain View School, seen here shortly after its opening in 1956 on Hudgins Street near West Henderson, replaced Hudgins School as Marion's educational facility for African American students. Hudgins had been a two-story wooden structure built in the late 1920s that was woefully outdated when it was finally replaced. Mountain View was closed when McDowell County schools were racially integrated in the 1960s. (Photograph by Eckenrod Studio.)

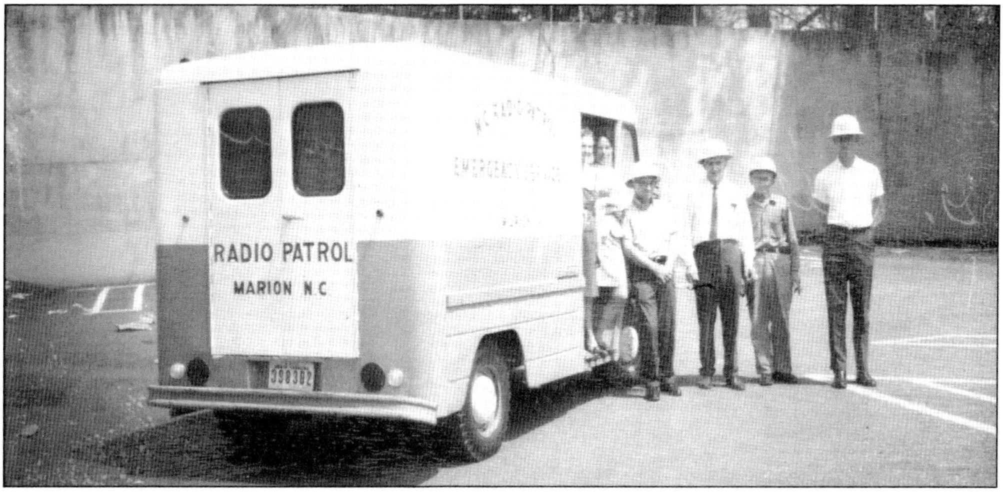

Members and officers of the Marion division of the North Carolina Radio Patrol pose by their truck around 1960. Pictured are, from left to right, Dollie Collins, Hollie Hollifield, Odell Hyatt, Nolan Lawing, L.G. Collins, and Clifford Epley. The Radio Patrol was a volunteer communications organization that assisted law enforcement. It later evolved into REACT. (Courtesy of McDowell County Public Library.)

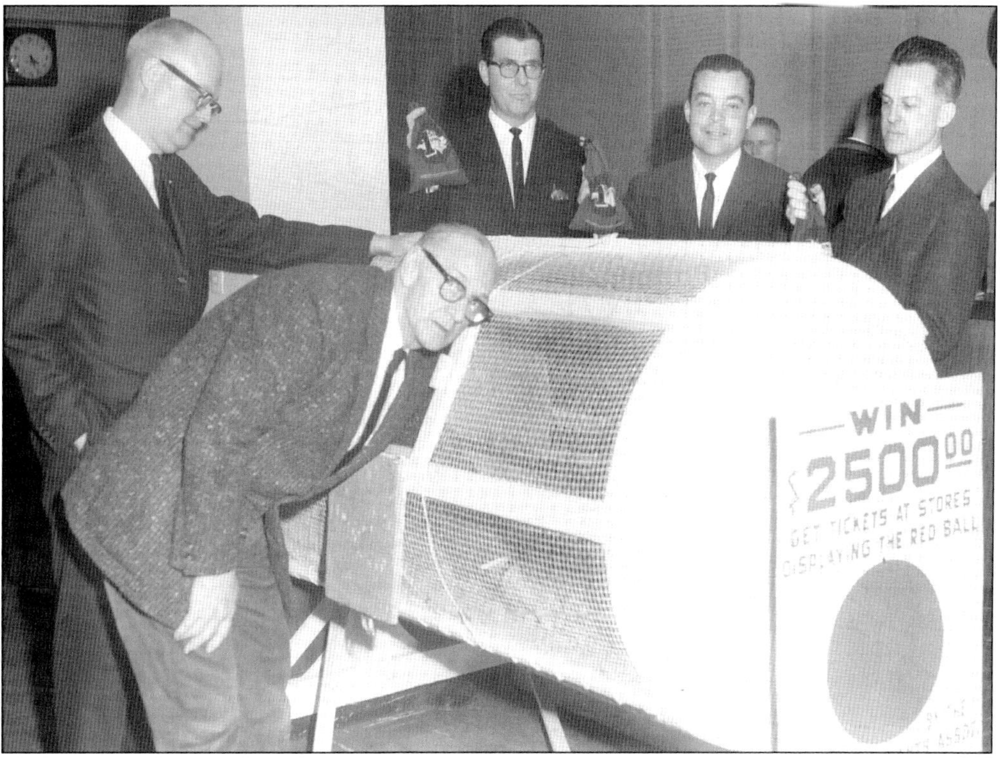

Representatives for the Marion Merchants Association pull the name of the winner of their 1963 Christmas drawing. Mayor J.W. Streetman draws the name while, from left to right, First National Bank vice president Robin Hood, jeweler William A. Griffith, Winslow G. Ballew of Ballew Motor Company, and Marshall Young of Young's Shoe Store look on. (Courtesy of McDowell County Public Library, Robin Hood Collection.)

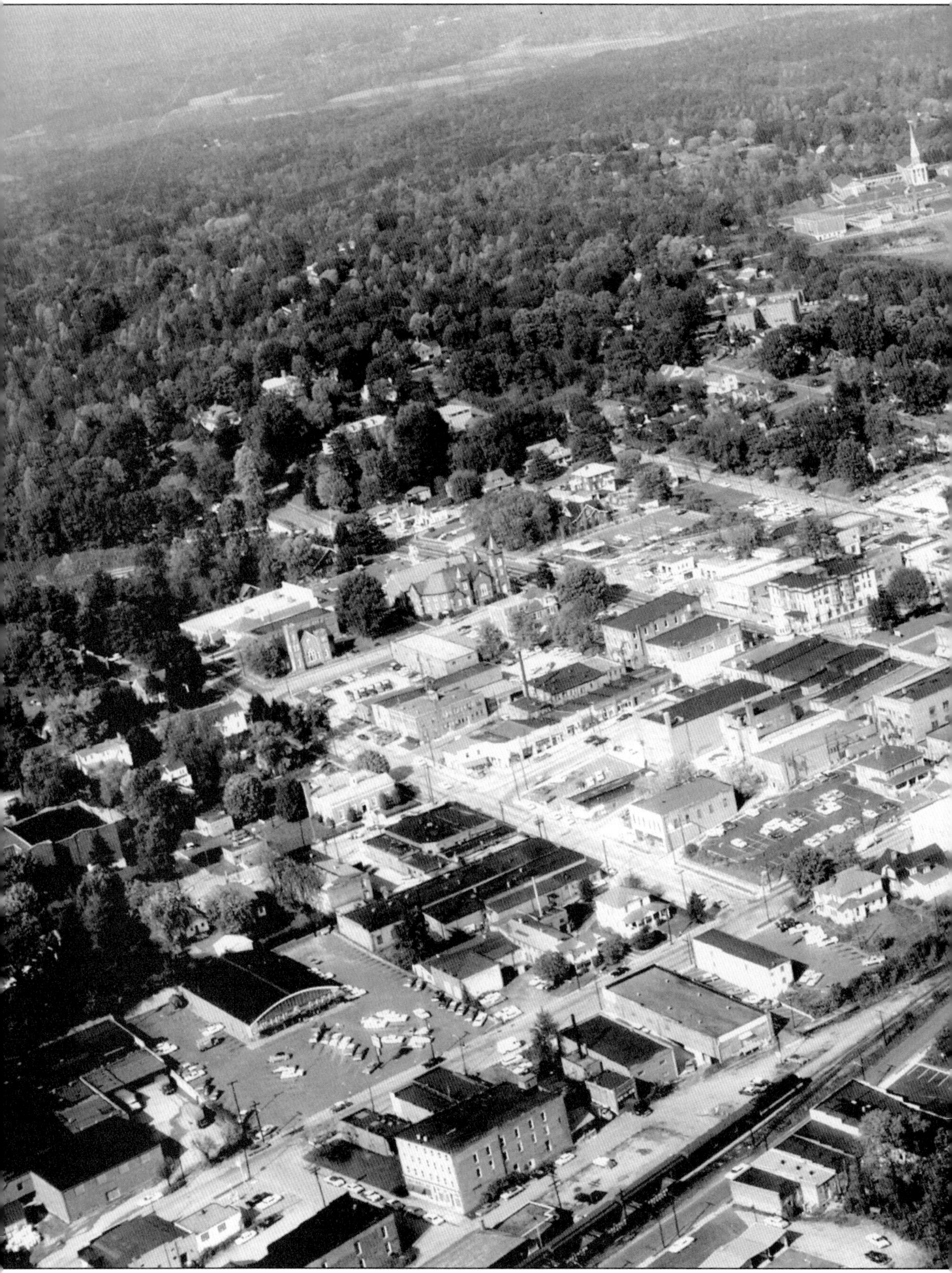

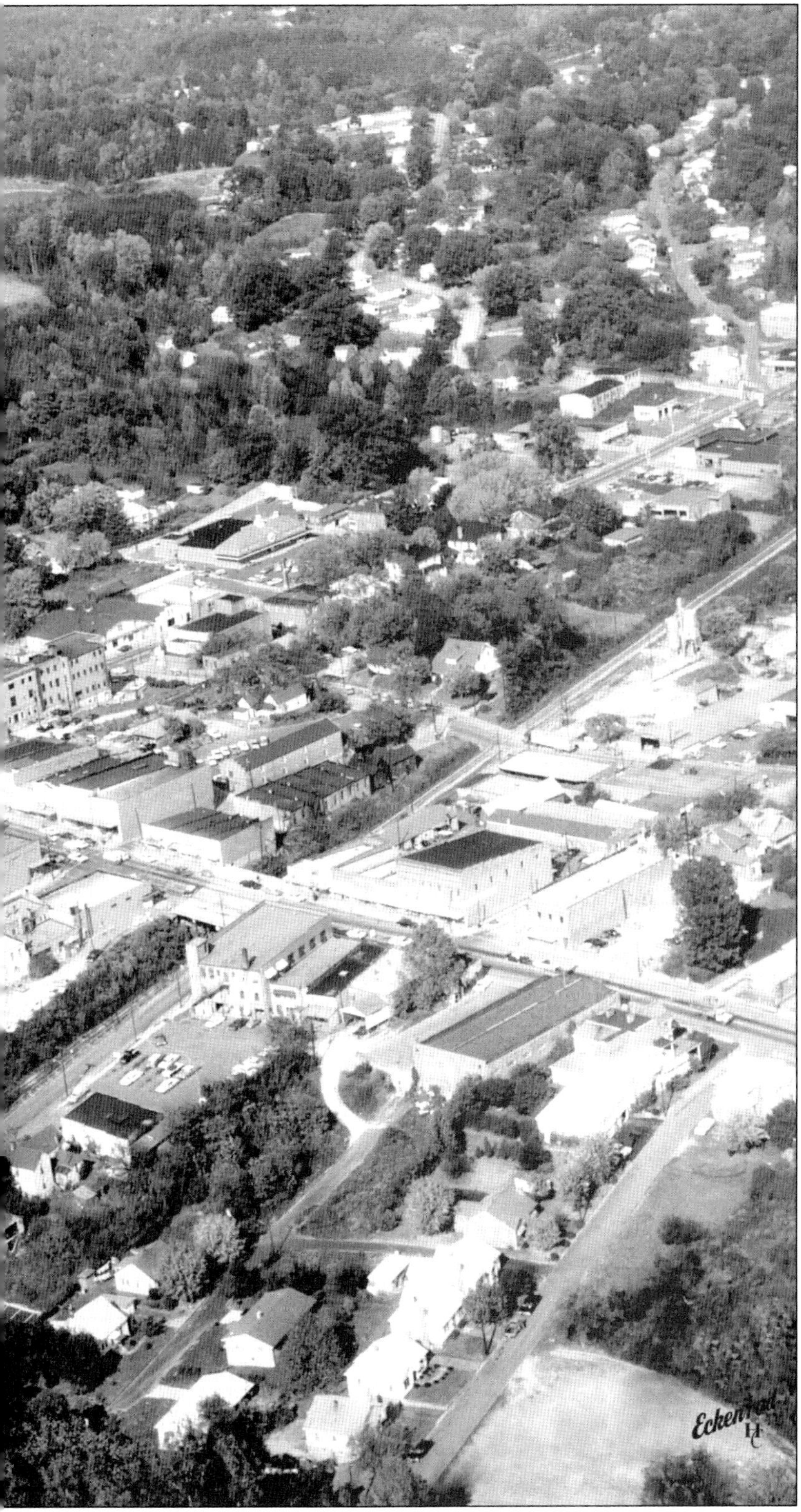

This aerial view of Marion was taken about 1960, with Main Street running horizontally across the middle of the image. Note the Winn-Dixie store on West Henderson near the lower-left corner. The new First Methodist Church on Robert Street can be seen near the upper middle, across the street from Marion Elementary School. The courthouse is at the approximate center of the picture, and the A&P store on East Court Street is visible two blocks behind it. Lake James is in the distance. (Photograph by Eckenrod Studio.)

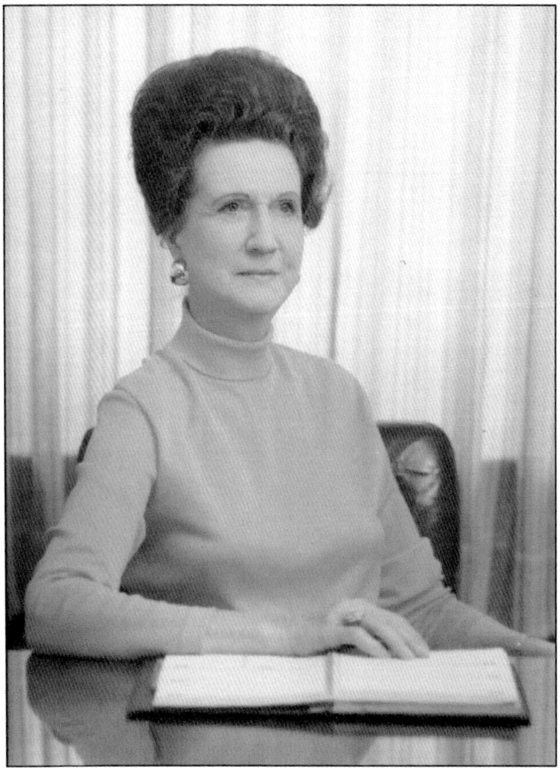

Doris Kraemer Hill (1910–2003) was one of Marion's most familiar faces due to her long banking career and civic involvement. Her father, William Homer Hill, came to Marion as a young man to work for the Southern Railway. He built a house near the railroad track on property purchased by his father-in-law Paul K. Kraemer, a native of Württemberg, Germany. Doris lived in the family home until her death. (Courtesy of McDowell County Public Library.)

This view from atop the Hotel James provides a good perspective of the central business district in the early 1960s. On the left side of the street are Shuford Furniture, Western Auto, and Moore's clothing store. On the right past the First Union National Bank are Loven Furniture Company, Evans Drug, Belk Department Store, Stelen's, Roses, Bill Griffith Jewelry, the Bargain Store, and Tainter's Drugs. (Courtesy of Harvest Drive-In.)

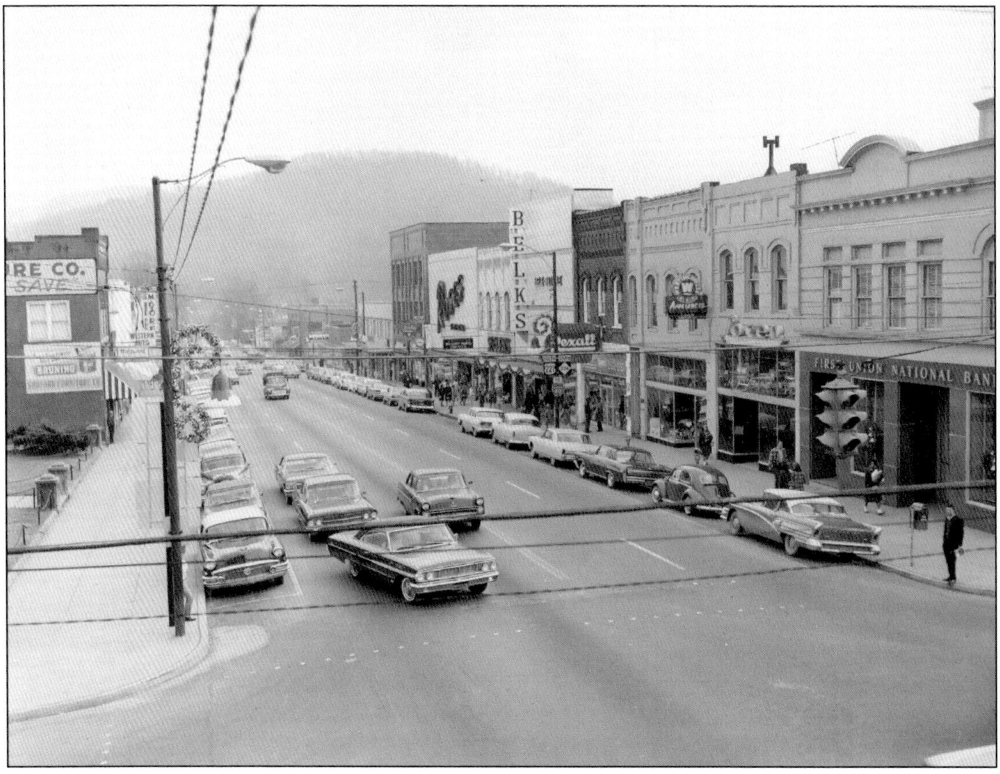

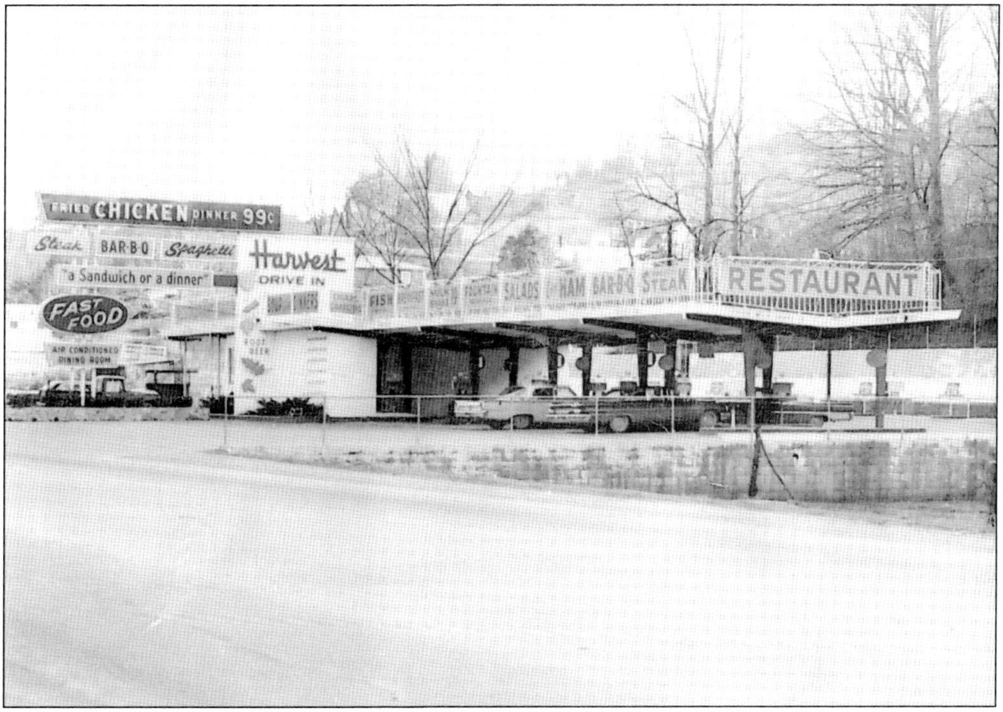

Jim and Helen Lancaster opened the Harvest Drive-In on North Main Street in 1962. Brothers Mack and Bob Gaddy purchased it in 1974 when their mother, a waitress there, told them it was for sale. A memorable feature has been the telephone at each dining room booth with which customers call in their orders to the kitchen. (Courtesy of Harvest Drive-In.)

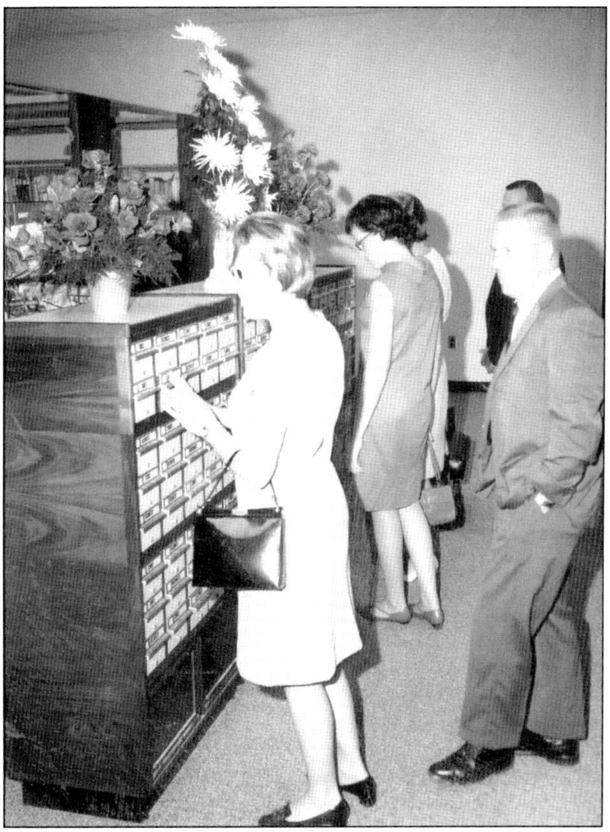

Patrons examine the card catalog in 1968 during an open house for the new McDowell County Public Library. A tax to build a permanent facility was defeated in a 1959 referendum, and the library closed following the vote. It reopened in 1961 on West Henderson Street when the measure passed on a second try. Finally, with the help of Congressman Roy Taylor, the old post office building was secured as a permanent location. (Courtesy of McDowell County Public Library.)

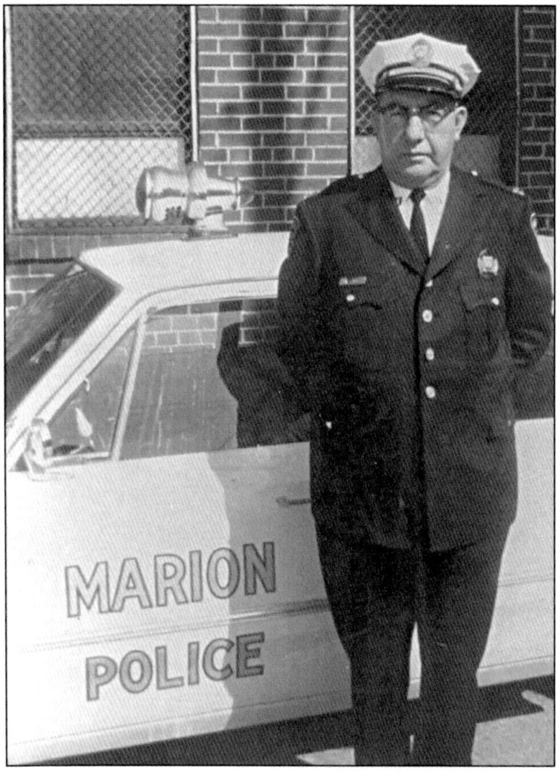

William "Bill" Wood was Marion chief of police from 1967 to 1973 and had been assistant chief for 16 years prior. He also helped start the McDowell County Rescue Squad. His father, D.L. Wood, was a Marion Manufacturing security officer for decades. Chief Wood's son Jack began working as second-shift dispatcher for the Marion Police Department during high school and also has had a long career in law enforcement. (Courtesy of Sarah Vess.)

Chief John Beck and Officer Silas Blankenship show off their new cruisers at the Brown Street entrance of the police department at the city hall building. Chief Beck had begun his career with the City of Marion in 1951 as a firefighter. In 1977, he was involved in the recovery of three priceless Audubon lithographs that had been stolen from a Key West museum and smuggled to Marion. (Courtesy of Sarah Vess.)

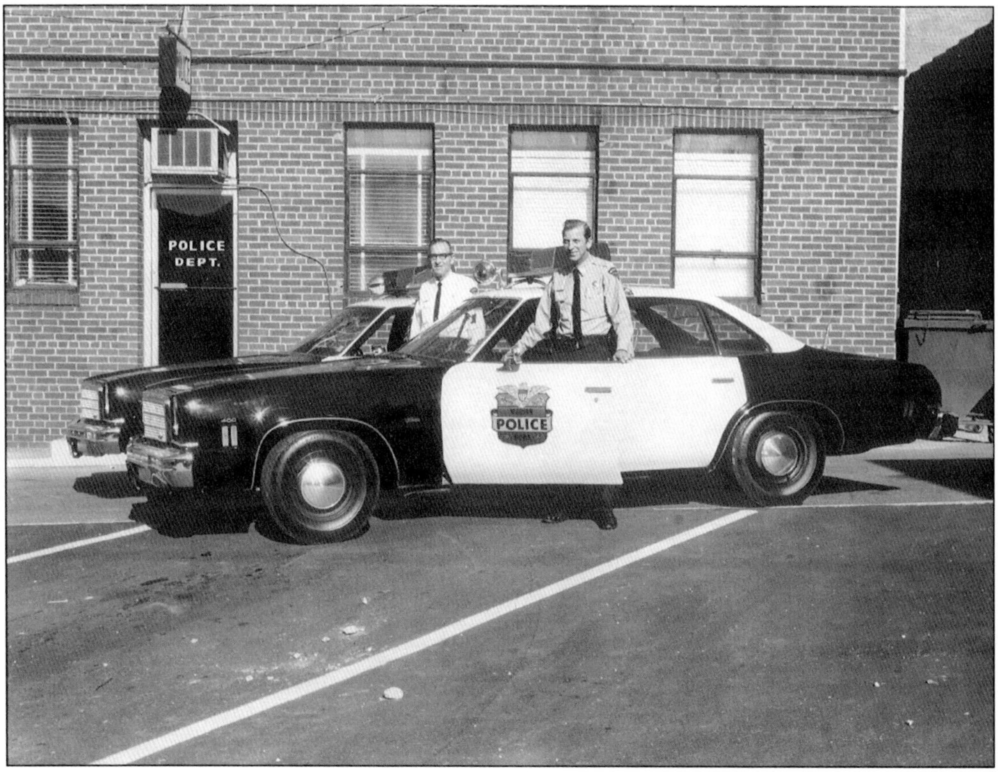

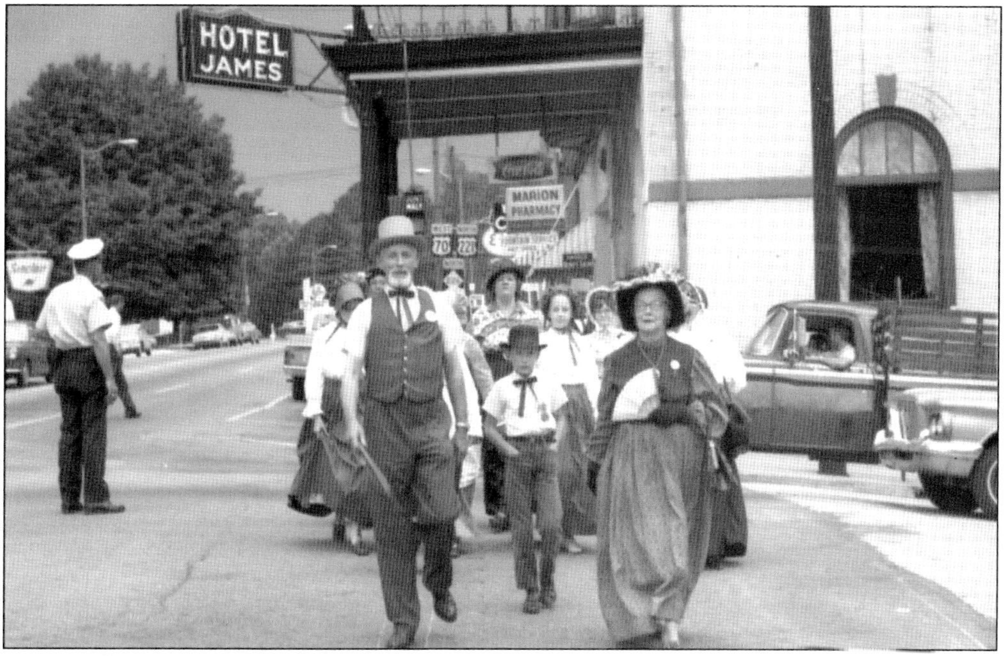

McDowell County observed its quasquicentennial (125th birthday) in 1968. The weeklong celebration included open houses, arts-and-crafts contests, tours of local industries, parades, dances, fireworks, and a nightly presentation of the historical pageant *So Rich Our Heritage*. Male residents were encouraged to grow full beards, and women donned long dresses and bonnets. (Courtesy of Gregg M. Hensley and Hensley Studio.)

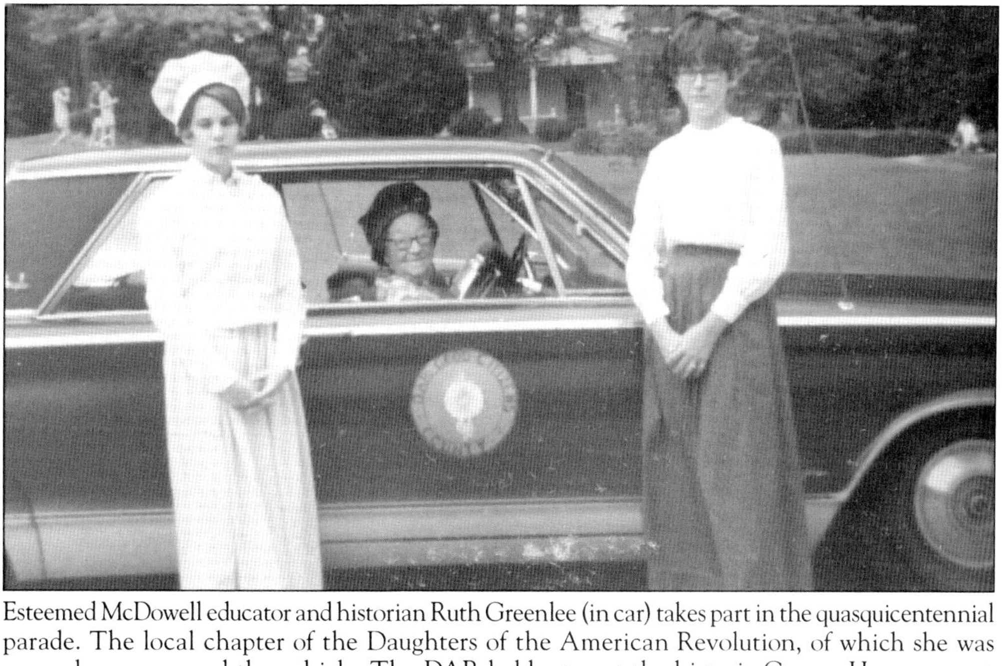

Esteemed McDowell educator and historian Ruth Greenlee (in car) takes part in the quasquicentennial parade. The local chapter of the Daughters of the American Revolution, of which she was a member, sponsored the vehicle. The DAR held a tea at the historic Carson House as part of the quasquicentennial festivities. (Courtesy of, McDowell County Public Library, Robin Hood Collection.)

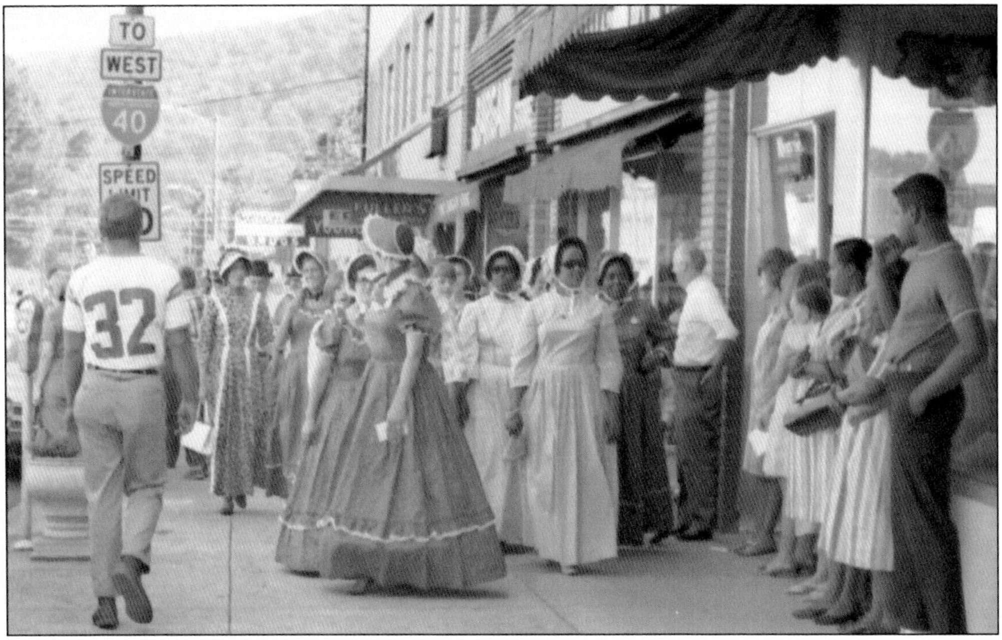

The clothing style of 1968 meets old-fashioned attire in this street scene from the quasquicentennial. The contrast between eras was also evident in some of the week's entertainment. The Friday night quasquicentennial ball featured a square dance band, followed by a "psychedelic rhythm band with go-go girls." (Courtesy of Gregg M. Hensley and Hensley Studio.)

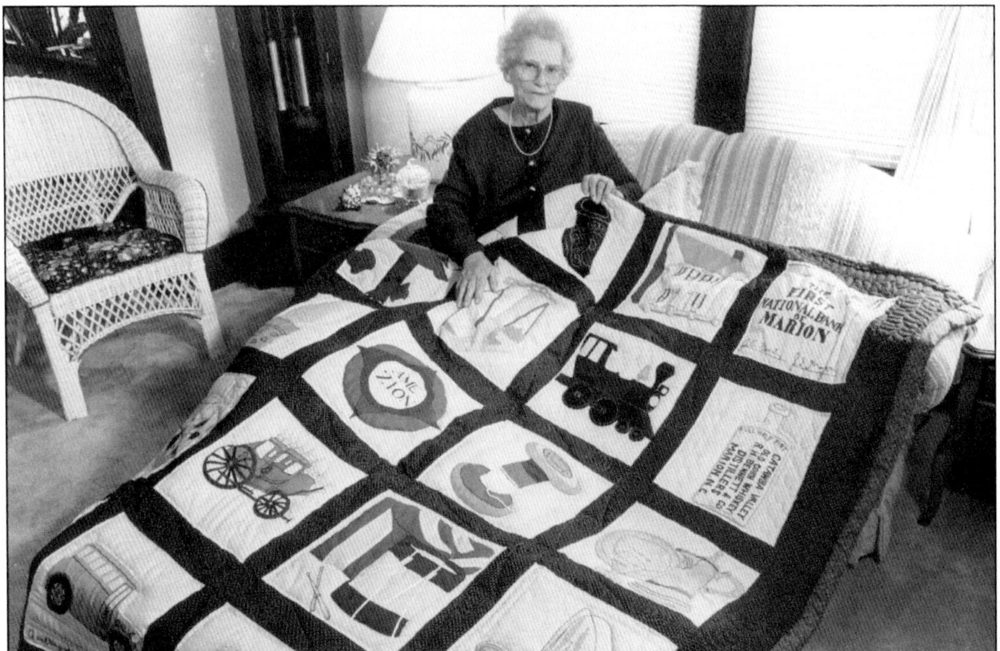

Vallie Martin hand-sewed each detail of this quilt, which was designed by quasquicentennial chairperson Warren Hobbs. Each square represents an important aspect of the history of McDowell County and Marion. After the 125th birthday celebrations had concluded, the quilt went on display at the McDowell County Public Library. (Courtesy of Mountain Gateway Museum.)

Five

The Mill Villages

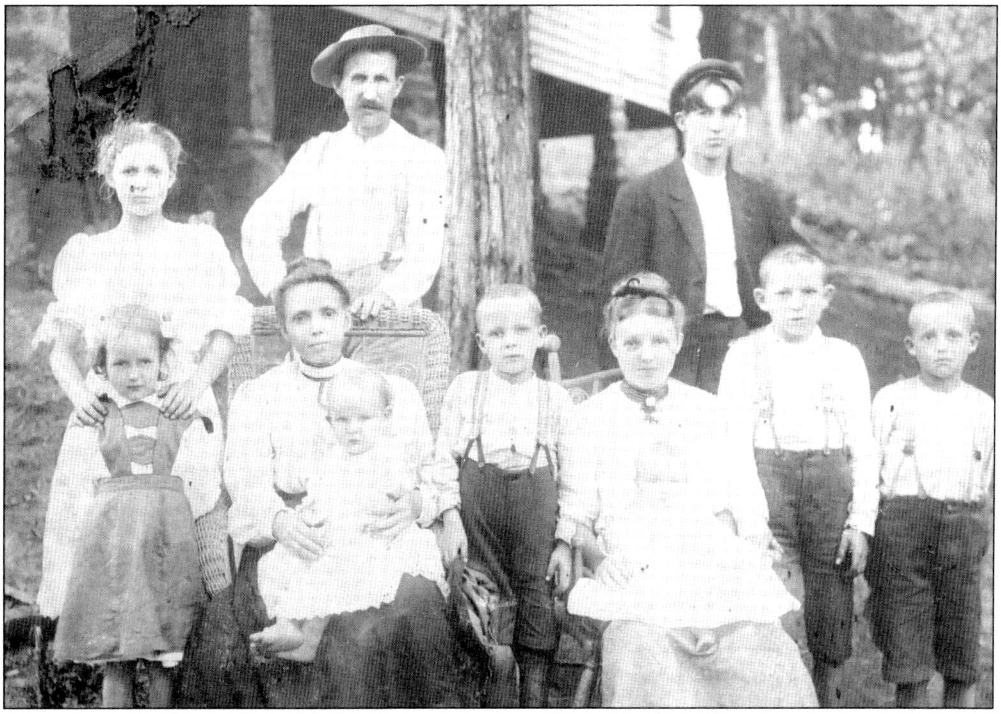

Isaac Leander Carrigan moved his family to Marion from Taylorsville to work at Cross Cotton Mill in 1917. Gathered at their mill village home are, from left to right, (first row) Daisy Morgan Carrigan, mother Sarah Ann Fox Carrigan holding Virginia Carolina, Fred Carrigan, Willie Carrigan holding her daughter Gwendolyn, Franklin Carrigan, and John D. Carrigan; (second row) Jessie Carrigan, father Isaac Leander Carrigan, and Glenn Carrigan. (Courtesy of David Vess.)

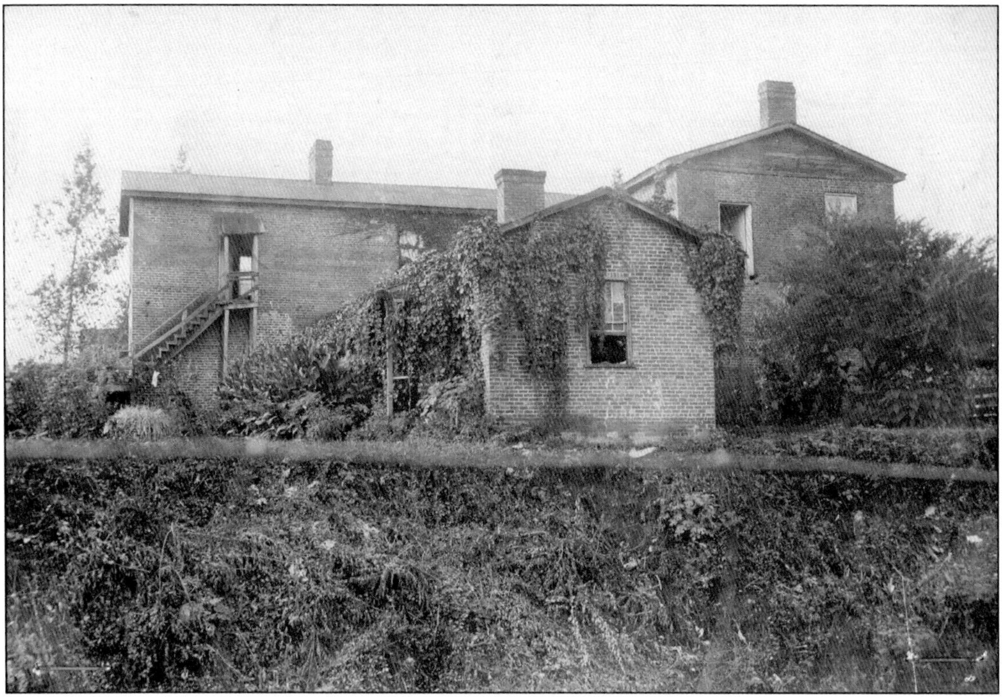

McDowell County's textile industry was born in the Craig Building, once located on the corner of West Henderson and Main Streets. In 1909, a group of businessmen evaluated locations in Western North Carolina for a cotton mill. They met with business leaders in the Marion Club Room of the Craig Building and agreed to build Marion Manufacturing Company. (Courtesy of McDowell County Public Library, Robin Hood Collection.)

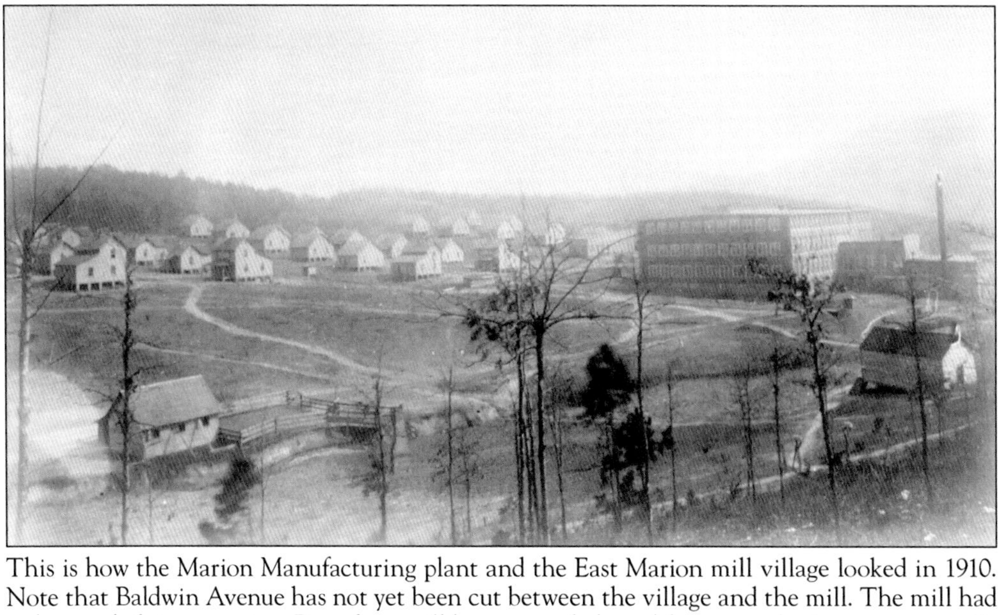

This is how the Marion Manufacturing plant and the East Marion mill village looked in 1910. Note that Baldwin Avenue has not yet been cut between the village and the mill. The mill had only one shift in operation. Rent for a mill house was deducted from a worker's wages, generally at the rate of 10¢ per room per week. (Courtesy of McDowell County Public Library, Robin Hood Collection.)

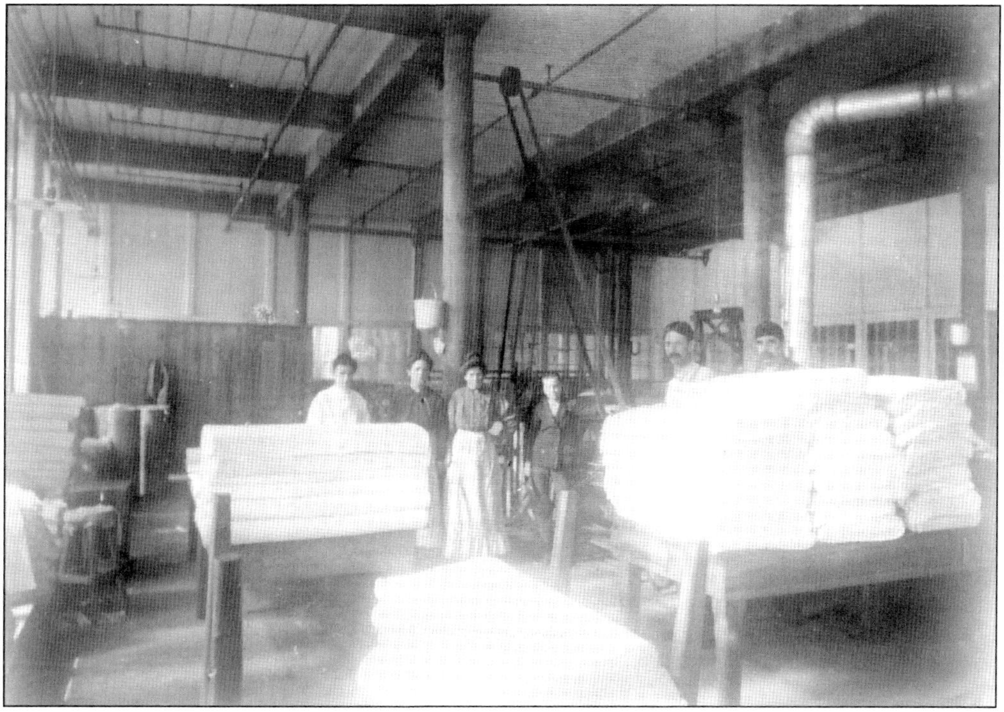

Overseer Tom Davis and five employees are gathered in 1911 in Marion Manufacturing's first cloth room. The company produced cotton cloth exclusively until 1938, when rayon was introduced. For decades, the sole selling agent for Marion Manufacturing's goods was J.P. Stevens and Company of New York, one of the biggest firms in the American textile industry. (Courtesy of McDowell County Public Library, Robin Hood Collection.)

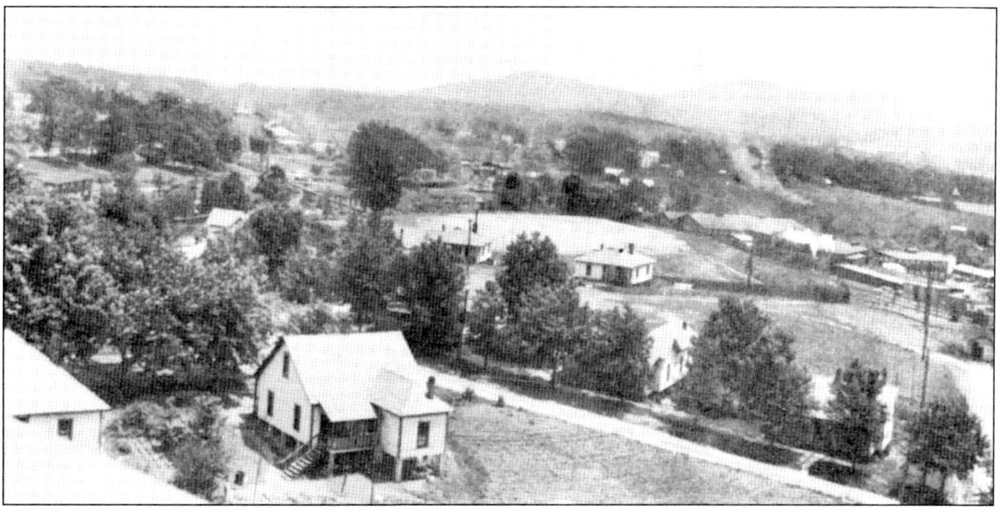

This is view of the Cross Mill village in 1937. At that time, there were 75 houses in the village and 175 mill employees. Unlike Marion Manufacturing and Clinchfield Mills, which made cotton cloth, Cross Cotton Mill specialized in double-corded and combed yarns. In the 1930s, it was producing 50,000 pounds of yarn per week. (Courtesy of McDowell County Public Library, Warren Hobbs Collection.)

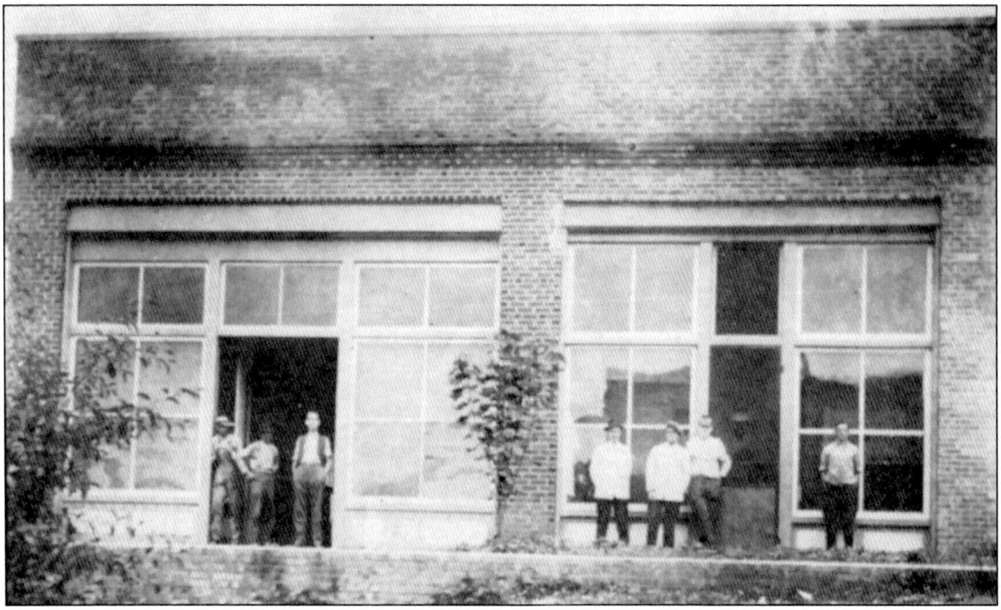

The Marion Manufacturing company store was located across from the main gate and also housed a barbershop. Note that the man second from the right still has lather on his face. The store also served as the village post office. It closed in 1948, and the building was remodeled for company offices. This is the earliest known photograph of the structure. (Courtesy of McDowell County Public Library.)

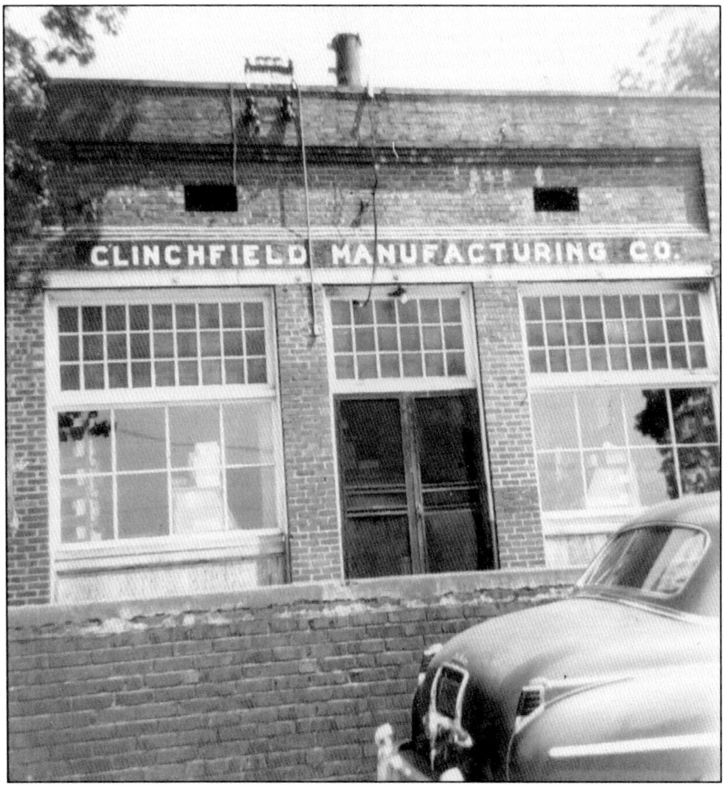

This photograph of the Clinchfield company store dates to the 1940s. The store opened shortly after the mill was established in 1914 and sold groceries, meat, dry goods, basic clothing, and household staples. When an employee bought goods, he signed a chit (voucher). The amount of the purchase would be deducted from the week's wages. (Courtesy of City of Marion.)

An unidentified woman holds baby Dorothy Duncan in front of the Cross Mill Methodist Church around 1927. Dorothy was the firstborn of Elmer and Leona Duncan. In addition to hosting worship services, Cross Mill Methodist had also served as a school for the children of mill employees until a permanent schoolhouse was built. (Courtesy of Carolyn Andrews.)

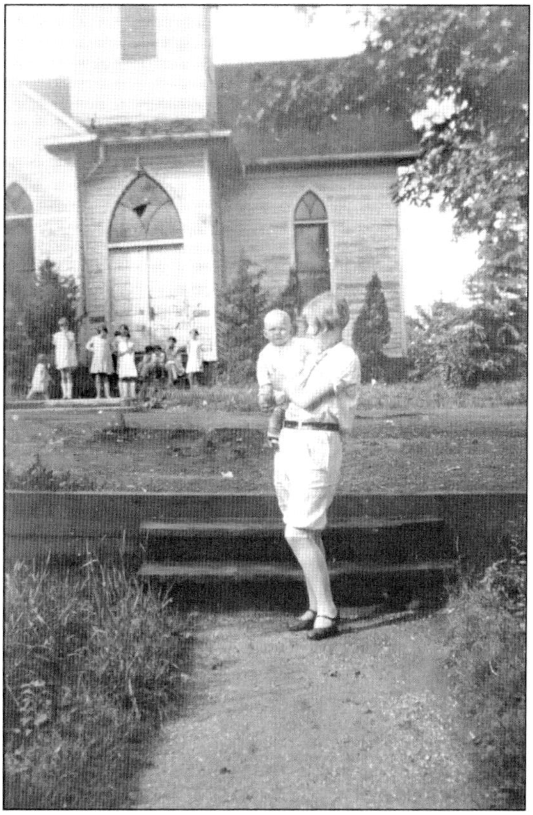

Card room operatives at Marion Manufacturing take a break in 1913. The man in the center wearing the tie is overseer Jim Frye. To his left is D.L. Wood, who came to Marion from Jackson County in 1911 and would remain a mill employee into the 1960s. In the second row are, from far left to right, Dolph Duncan, Jasper Duncan, and Walter Hyatt. (Courtesy of McDowell County Public Library.)

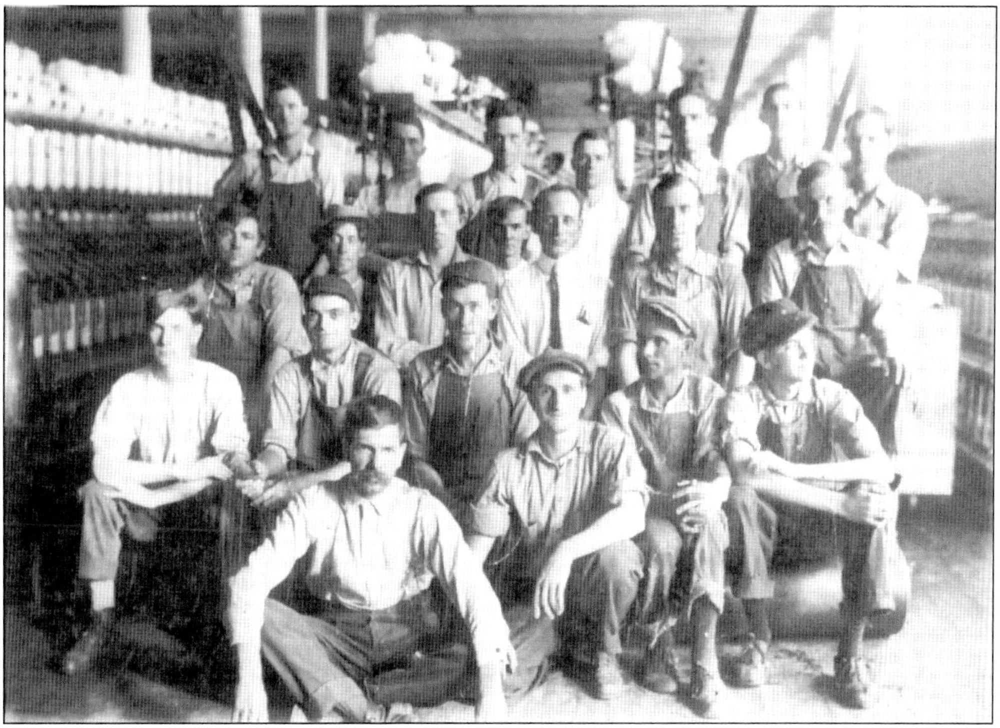

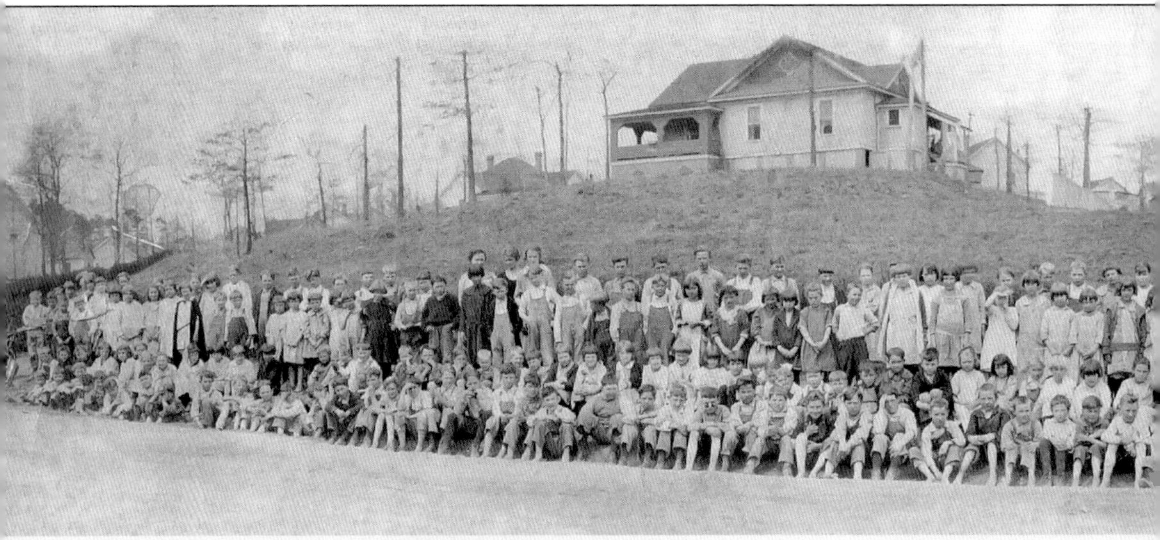

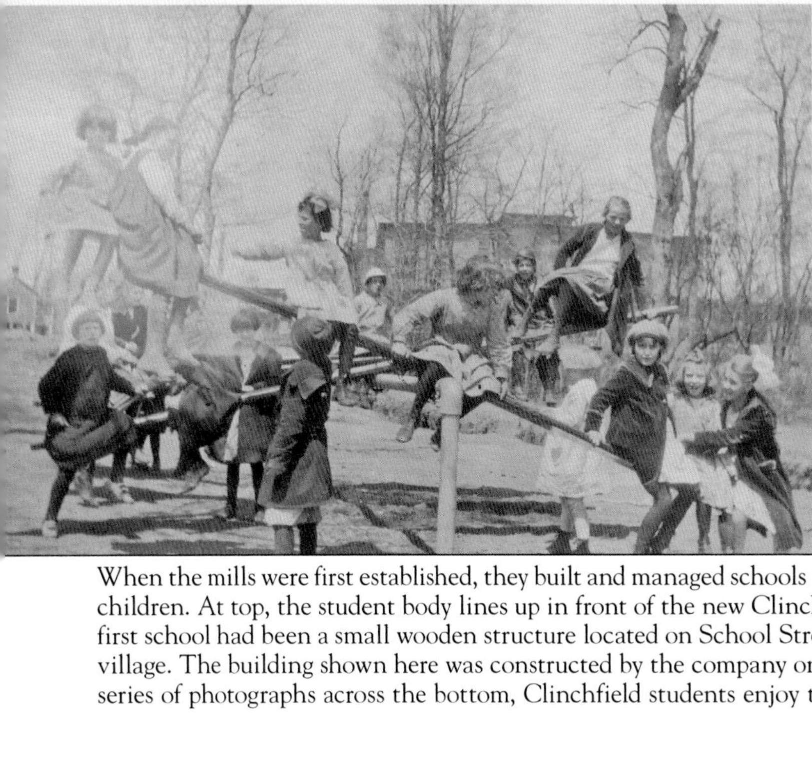

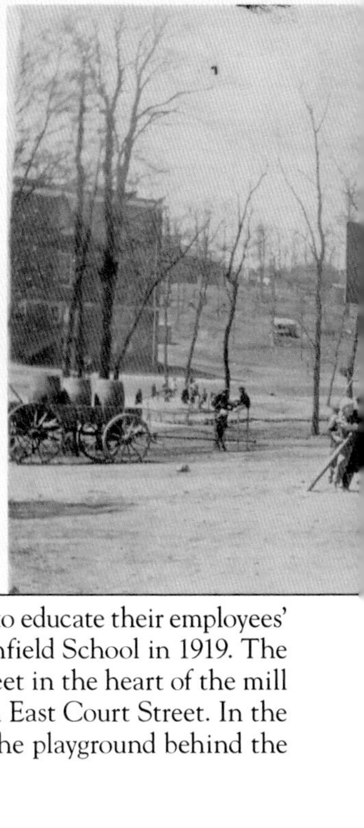

When the mills were first established, they built and managed schools to educate their employees' children. At top, the student body lines up in front of the new Clinchfield School in 1919. The first school had been a small wooden structure located on School Street in the heart of the mill village. The building shown here was constructed by the company on East Court Street. In the series of photographs across the bottom, Clinchfield students enjoy the playground behind the

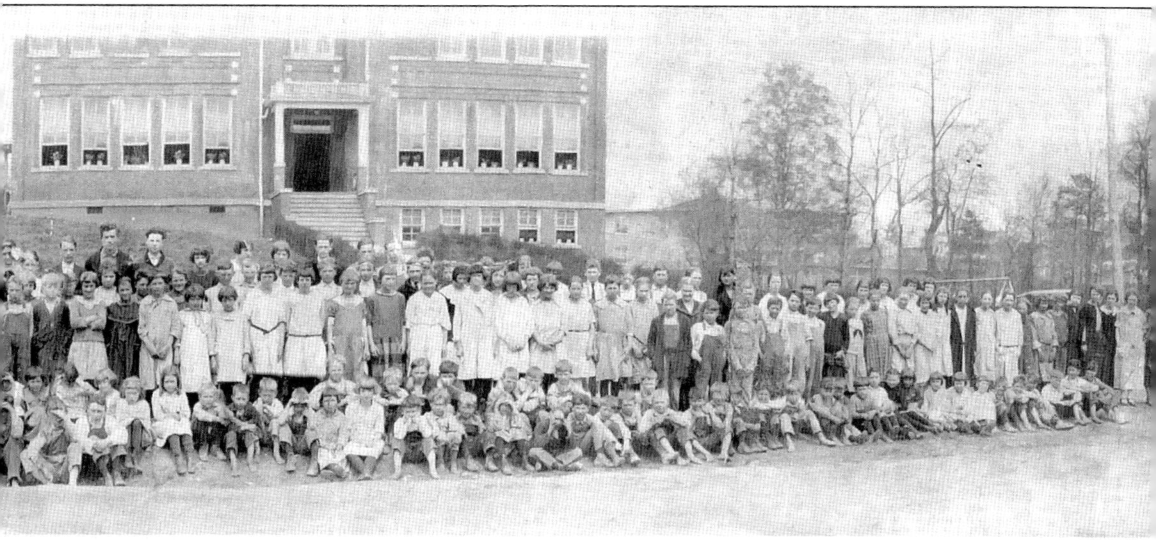

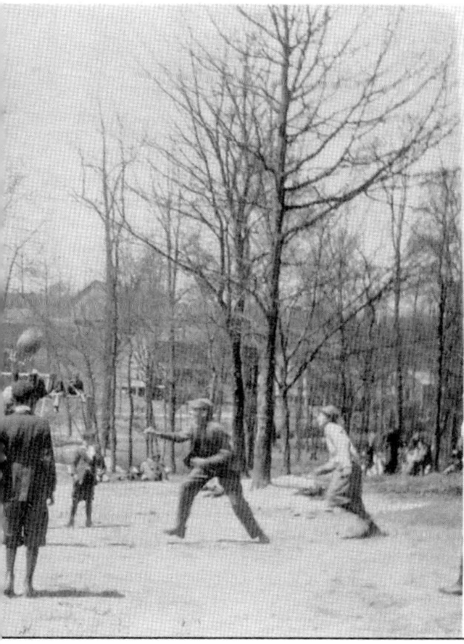

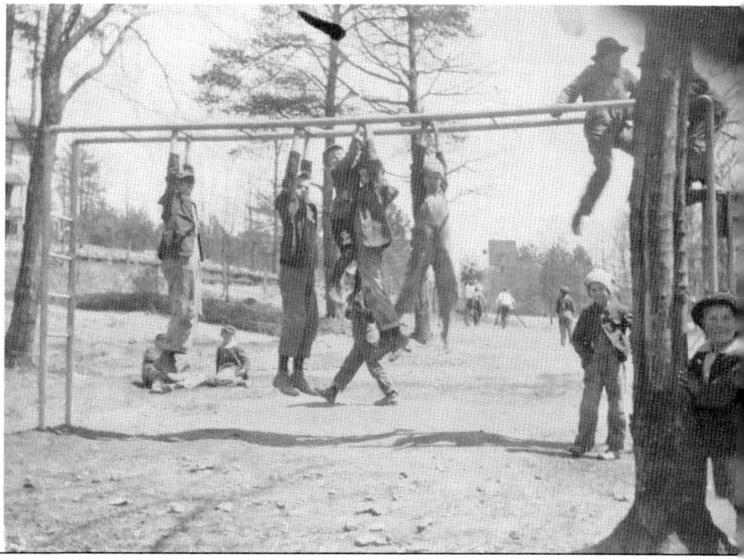

school in the winter of 1922. Glimpses of the mill and village are visible in the background. Standards were high at Clinchfield, leading it to be one of the first schools in the county to be state-accredited. By the early 1930s, oversight of all of the mill village schools had been taken over by the county. (Top image, courtesy of Scotty Elmore; three images at bottom, courtesy of McDowell County Public Library, Greenlee Collection.)

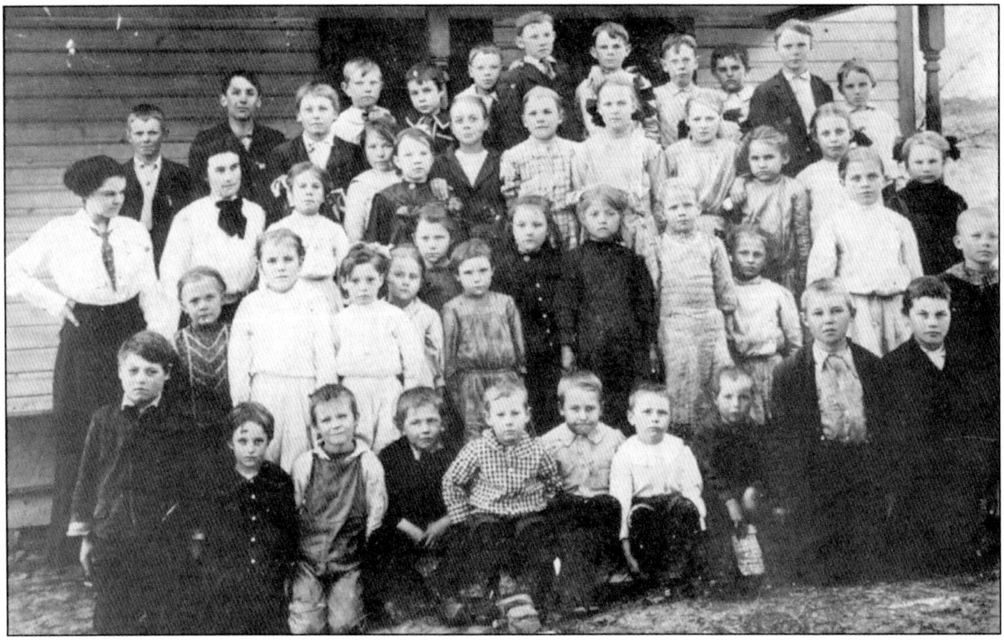

East Marion students pose with their teachers in 1911 in front of the first school built by Marion Manufacturing for the children of its employees. It was a two-room house on Sixth Street in the village. Another room was added later, and then a newer school was built on Baldwin Avenue, the main thoroughfare through the community. (Courtesy of McDowell County Public Library.)

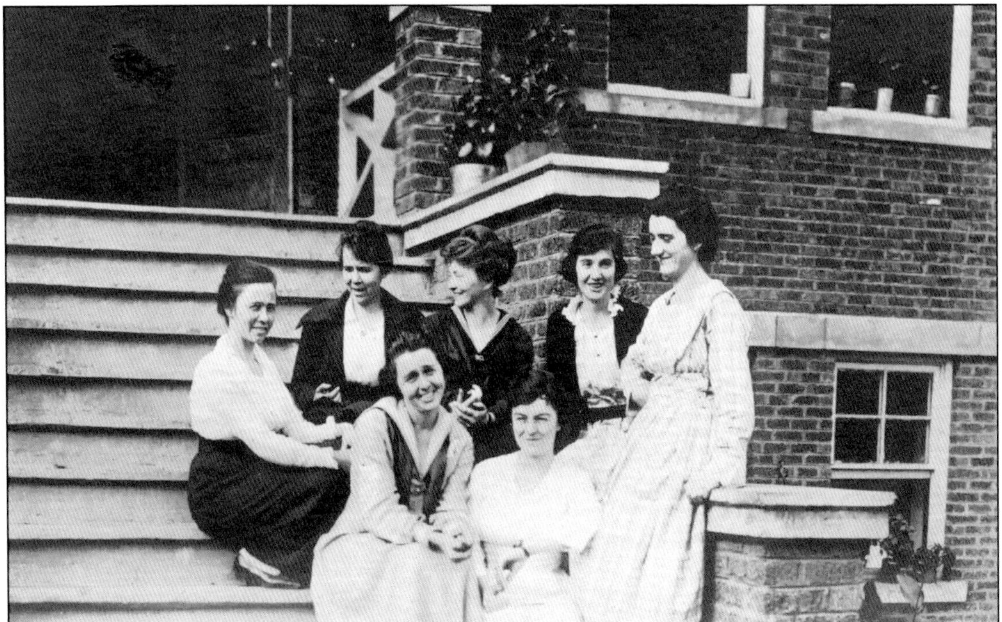

The Clinchfield School faculty of 1918–1919 shares a lighthearted moment. Pictured are, from left to right, Lona Goforth, Mamie Goforth, Abby Runion, principal Mary Greenlee, unidentified, Charlotte Mckoy, and Ola Wall. Like her sisters Ruth and Nina, Greenlee was a tireless educator and McDowell County historian for her entire life. The genealogical research library at the Historic Carson House bears her name. (Courtesy of McDowell County Public Library.)

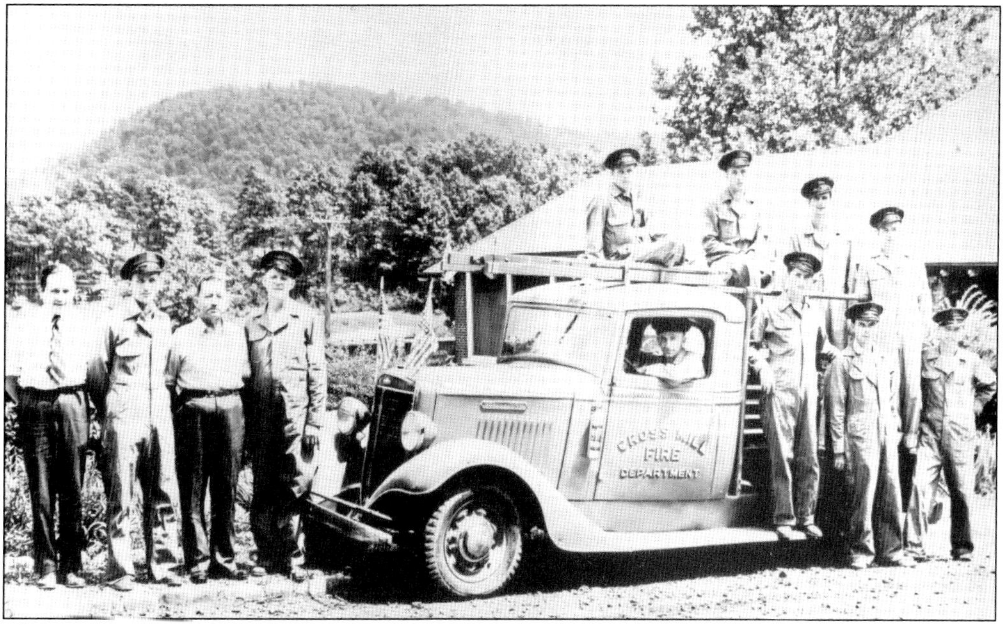

The Cross Mill Fire Department poses with its truck. Semeon Cross is on the far left. Also pictured are Virgil Bradford (second from the left), Fred Williams (third from the left), Mac Hester (driver), and W.F. Morris (second from the right). The others are unidentified. The Cross Mill Fire Department headquarters was located just above Webb Street in the mill village. (Courtesy of Blue Ridge Terrace.)

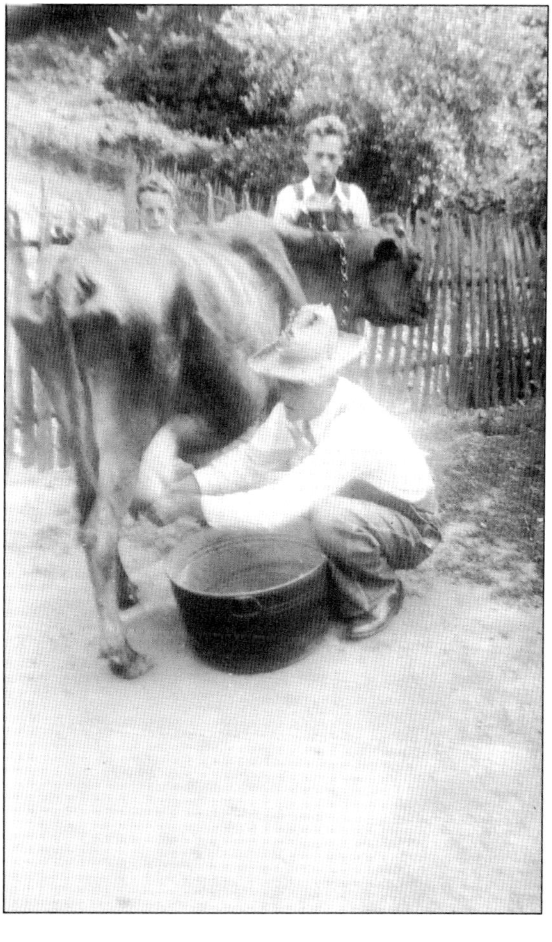

Even though they were no longer living off the land, many in the Marion mill villages continued to exercise some degree of self-reliance by keeping livestock. Here, Clyde Davis milks his cow in Cross Mill. Marion Manufacturing and Clinchfield Mills offered communal pastures to allow their employees to keep cows, pigs, and goats. Many mill village families also kept chickens. (Courtesy of David Vess.)

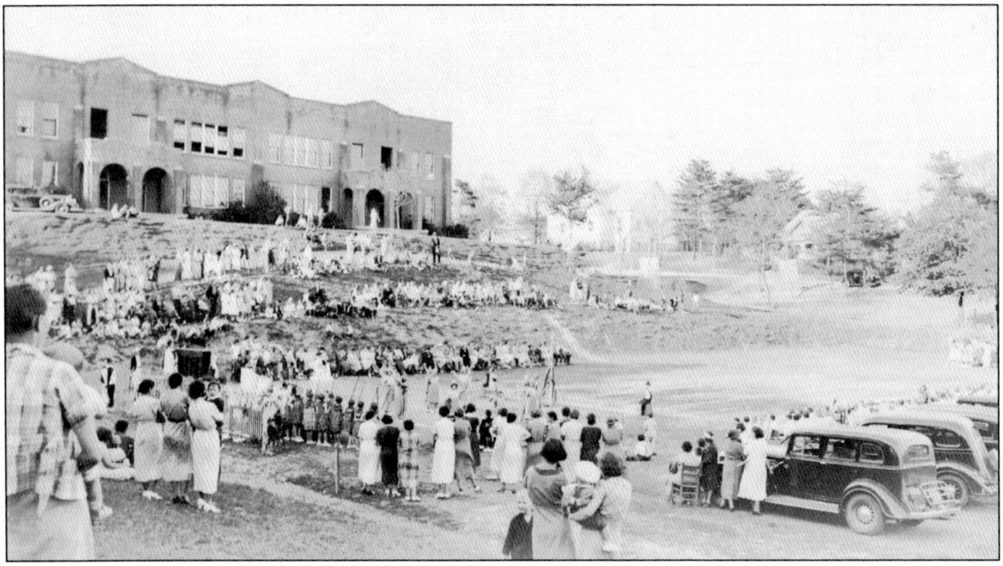

An audience at East Marion School enjoys a May Day program in the 1930s. The original East Marion Baptist Church can be seen across Baldwin Avenue at upper right. This impressive school was built in 1923 during Marion's post–World War I movement to construct larger and more modern educational facilities. It would later be torn down to make way for East Marion Elementary School. (Courtesy of Gregg M. Hensley and Hensley Studio.)

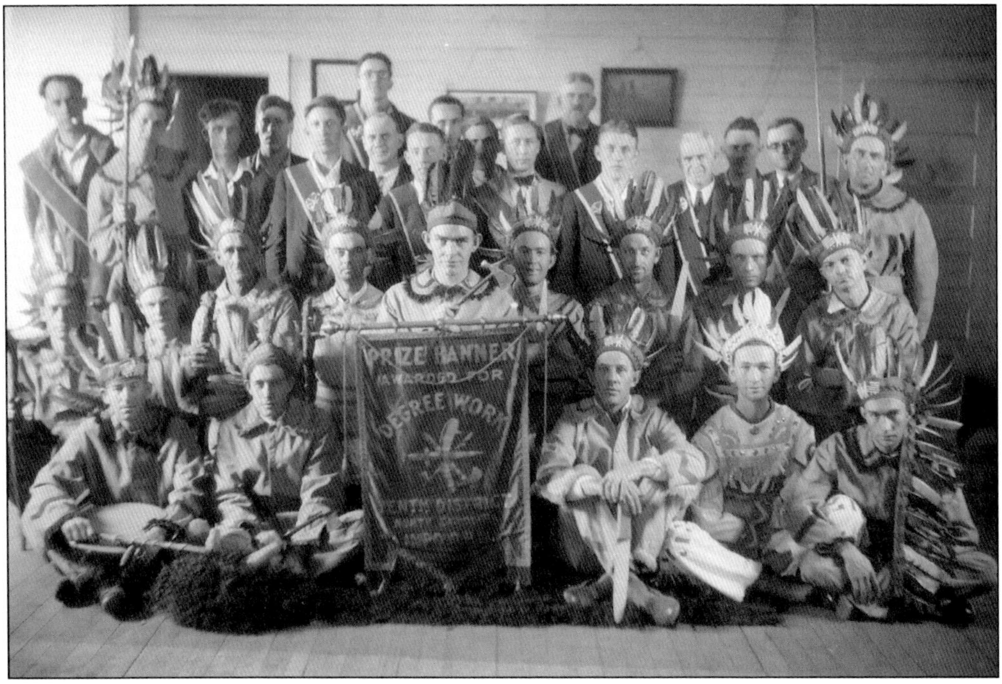

The Clinchfield chapter of the Improved Order of Red Men proudly displays a prize banner. The Red Men were a nationwide patriotic and service fraternity descended from the Sons of Liberty, which had taken part in the Boston Tea Party dressed as Native Americans. On V-J Day in 1945, the Clinchfield Red Men dressed in full regalia and danced around a bonfire on the courthouse lawn. (Courtesy of Louis Wall.)

Cross Cotton Mill and Marion Manufacturing both produced monthly newsletters for their employees. The *Cross Spinner* was a relatively simple publication, while Marion Manufacturing's *Picks and Hanks* was a slick magazine-style affair. *Picks and Hanks* editor and photographer Wilton E. Carter won several regional and national awards for his work. Each month, Carter would pay East Marion boys to stand outside the Marion Manufacturing gate at shift change to hand out copies of the latest issue. Company information, employee milestones, industry news, and community activities were covered. (Right, courtesy of Jim Long; below, courtesy of McDowell County Public Library.)

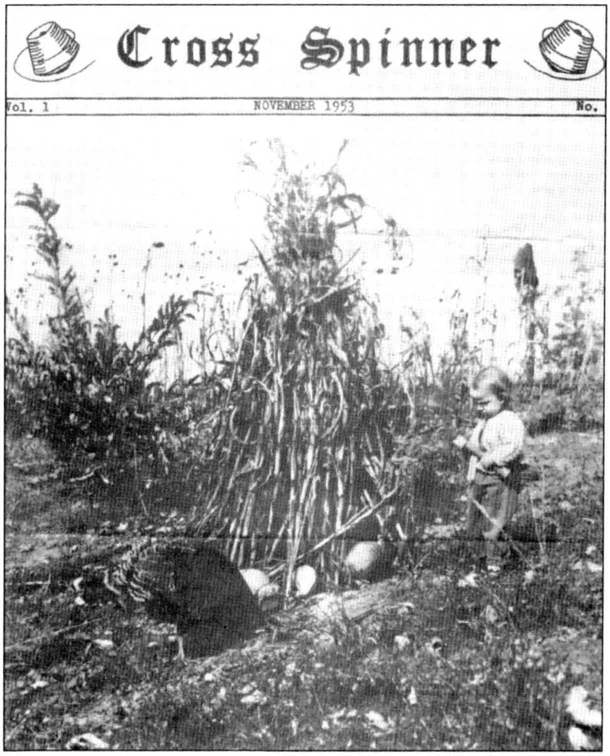

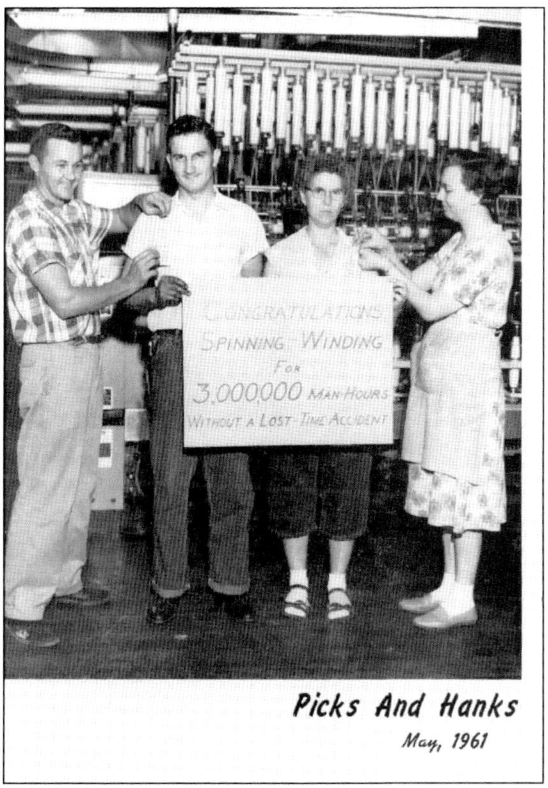

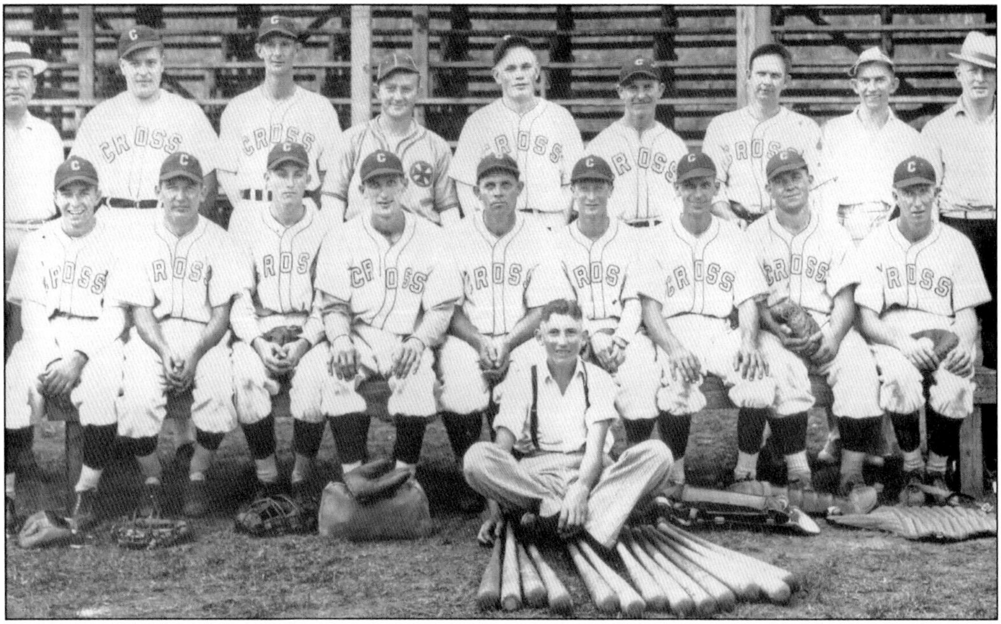

The mills organized baseball teams for local and regional play. This Cross Mill team includes Fred Williams, Eugene Cross, and Bandy Williams from far left to right in the back row and Bill Lonon at the far right. In the front row, third and fourth from left are "Fat" Murray and Virgil Bradford. Red Arrowood is at the far right, and Ralph Webb is sitting on the ground. The other players are unidentified. (Courtesy of Blue Ridge Terrace.)

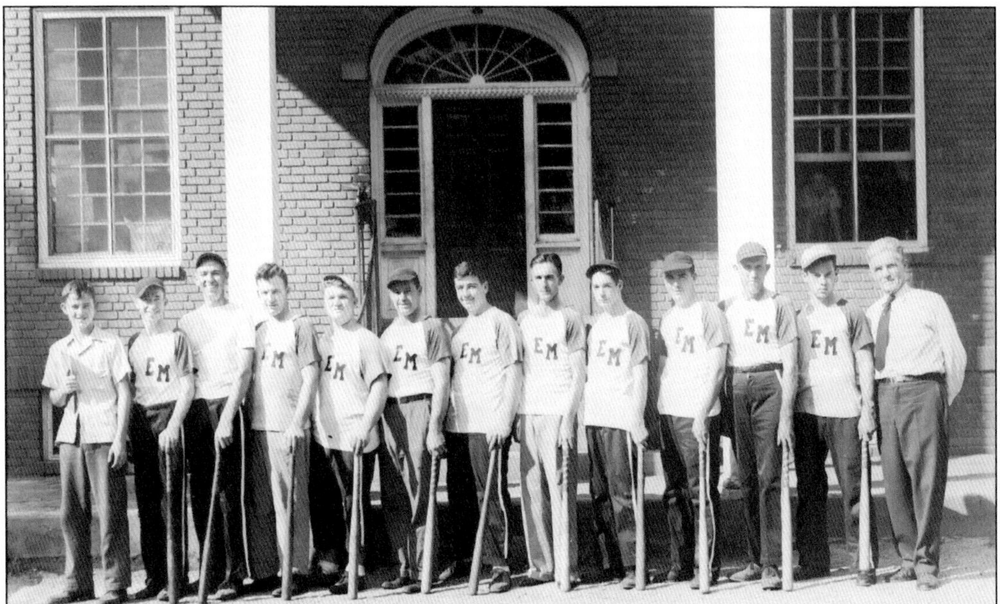

An East Marion baseball team lines up in front of Carroll Baldwin Hall in the 1940s. At right is its coach Jim Gourley. The fifth player from the left is "Goat" Fender. East Marion boys had a penchant for assigning each other amusing nicknames. In the village, there were young men known as "Dill," "Frog," "Little Creed," "Tater," "Bounce," "Frosty," and many other monikers. (Courtesy of Gregg M. Hensley and Hensley Studio.)

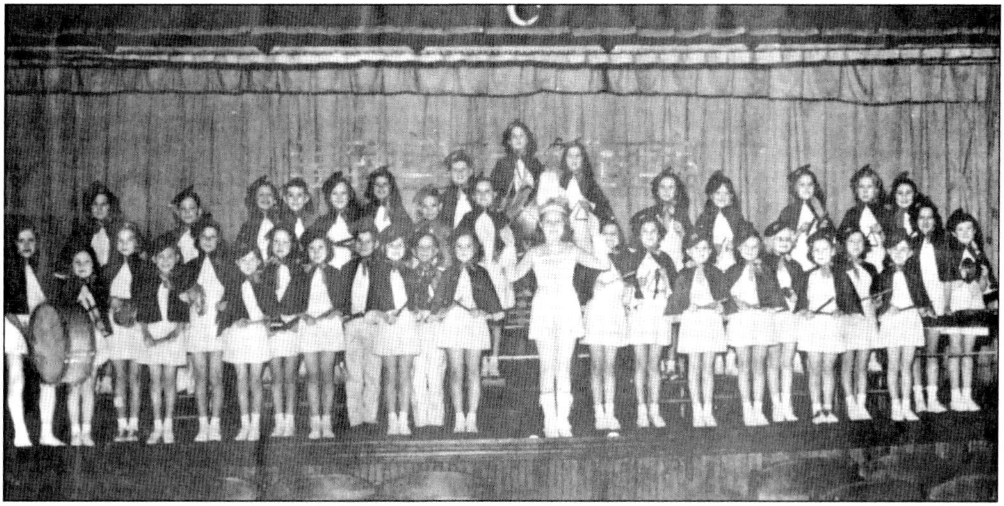

The Clinchfield Rhythm Band was started by teacher Rebecca Lowe in 1936. The ensemble performed on bells, sticks, tambourines, castanets, triangles, marimba, drums, and xylophones with Lowe accompanying on piano and was in high demand for parties and public gatherings. When it performed for the Clinchfield Mills Board of Directors in 1940, attendees were so impressed that they donated $200 for new uniforms and more instruments. (Courtesy of McDowell County Public Library, Greenlee Collection.)

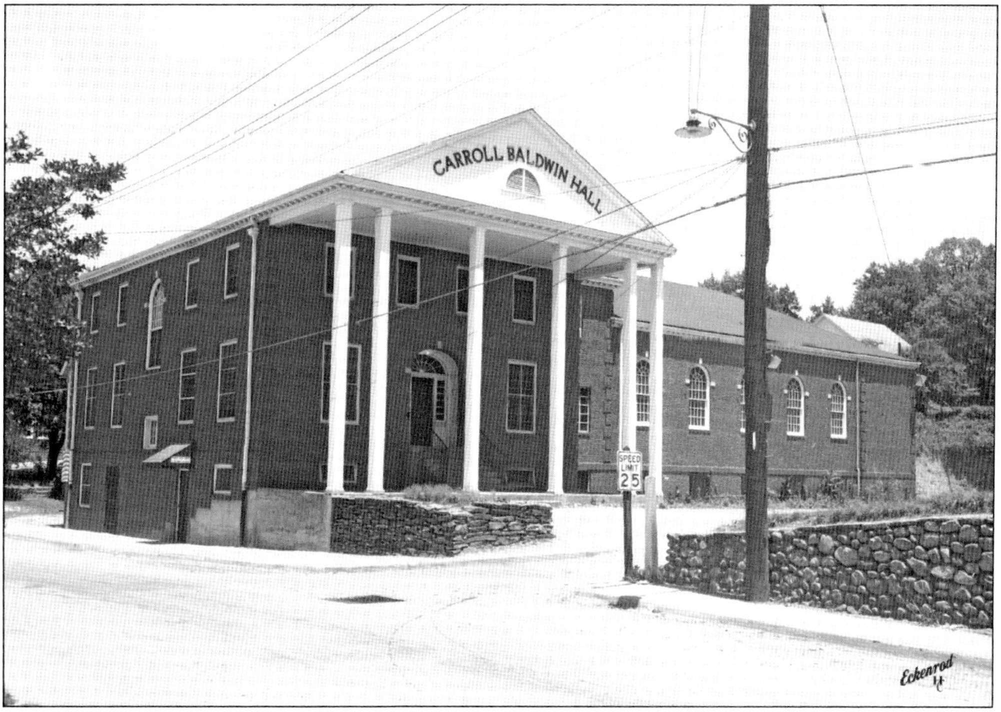

Carroll Baldwin Hall was built by Marion Manufacturing in 1928 across the street from the mill. The facility included a bowling alley, gymnasium, swimming pool, and meeting rooms. The project was conceived by company president Rignal Baldwin and named after his father, who had founded the mill. The "Y," as it was commonly called, was open to all employees and their families. It is seen here in 1959. (Photograph by Eckenrod Studio.)

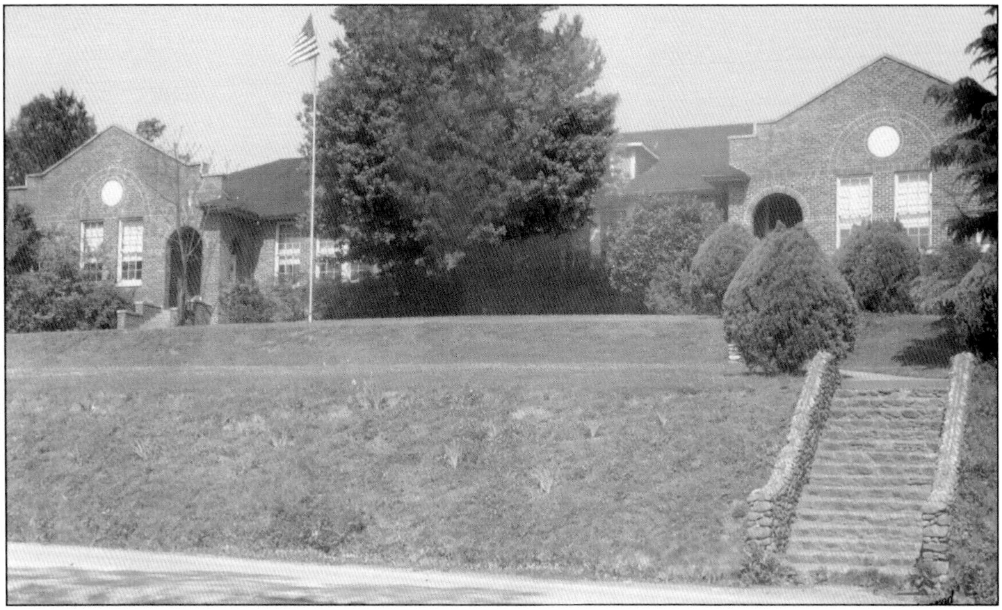

Cross Mill's first school was a one-room building, with students taught by Rev. R.G. Shoup. Cross Cotton Mill founder Eugene Cross established this larger school in the 1930s, supervised its construction, and kept in close touch with its operation through the years. The State Employees Credit Union stands on this site today. (Photograph by Eckenrod Studio.)

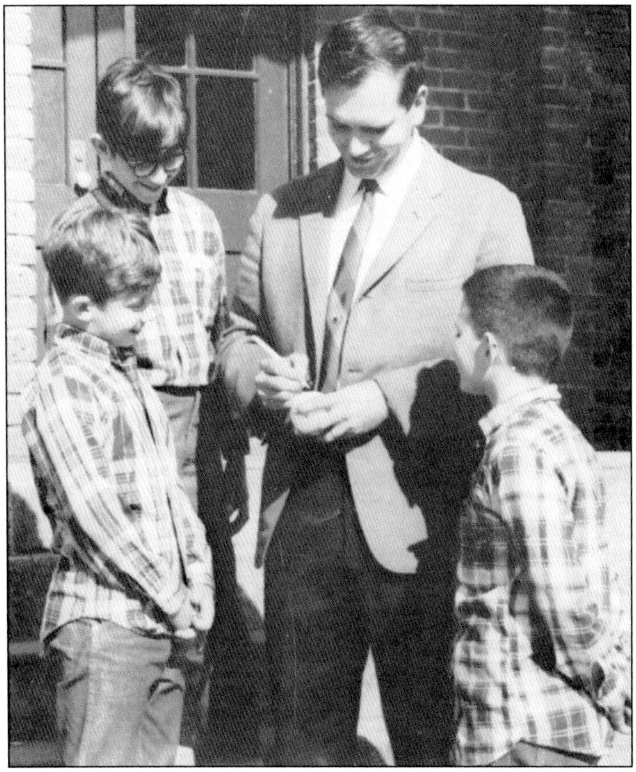

Former New York Yankee star second baseman Bobby Richardson signs a baseball for East Marion students Robert Lingerfelt, Dennis Blake, and Buddy Mills. Marion Manufacturing president R.W. Twitty arranged the 1966 visit through a former college classmate. Richardson spoke to a group at Carroll Baldwin Hall, toured the mill to greet employees, and visited the school. Richardson had been a teammate of Mickey Mantle and Yogi Berra. (Courtesy of McDowell County Public Library.)

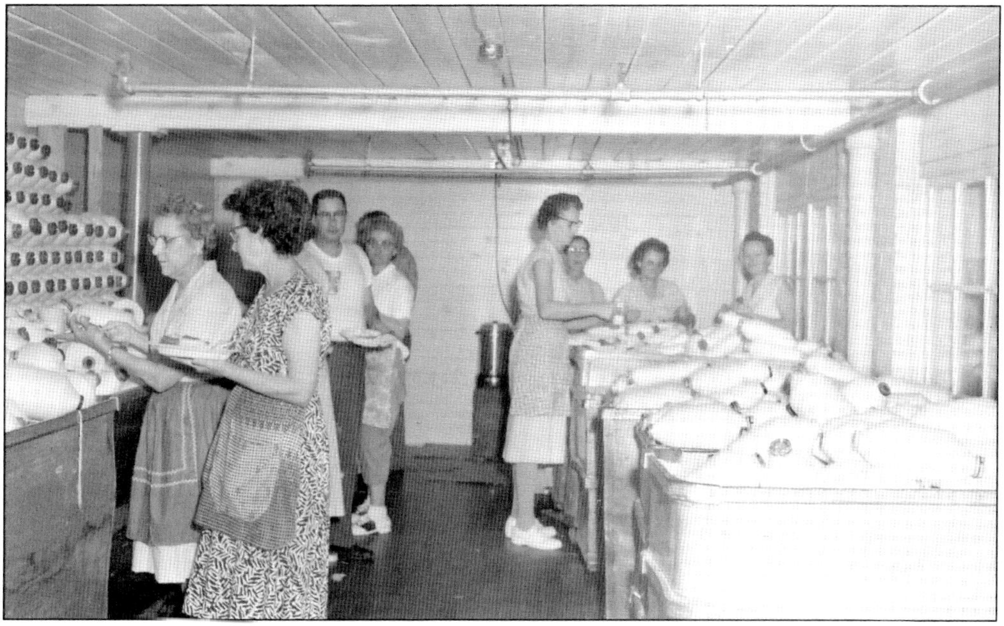

Cross Mill workers take a break in the spool room to enjoy a meal celebrating a coworker's retirement. Note the ladies' long aprons, the pockets of which were used to hold lint and strings—and usually a tin of snuff. Cross Mill employees and village residents were an exceptionally close-knit community. The operation was small compared to the other mills, it was family owned, and most workers were natives of McDowell County. (Courtesy of Carolyn Andrews.)

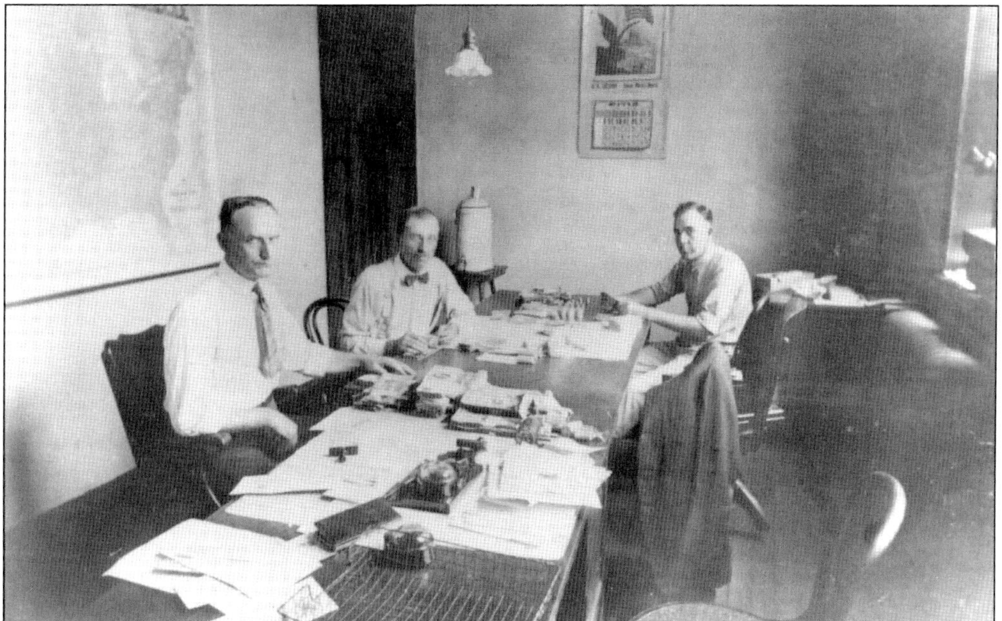

Paymasters for the Clinchfield and Marion Manufacturing mills are seated around a worktable in the First National Bank in 1920. Assembling pay packets are, from left to right, A. Elisha Neal and Boyd Farrow of Clinchfield and Ray Kanipe of Marion Manufacturing. (Courtesy of McDowell County Public Library, Robin Hood Collection.)

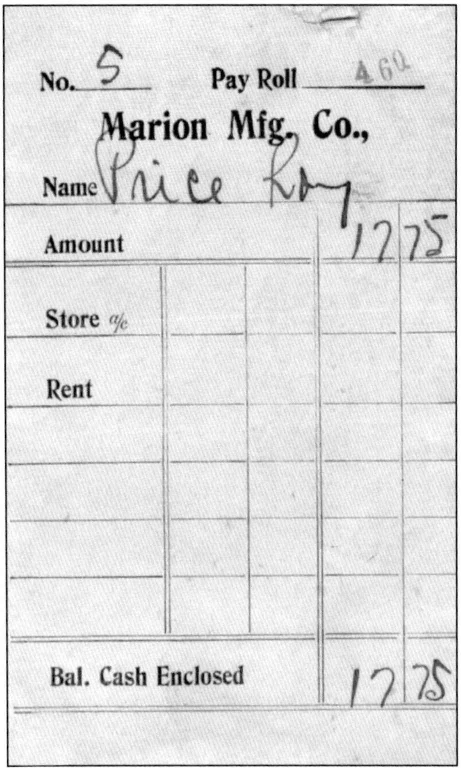

No. 5 Pay Roll 460

Marion Mfg. Co.,

Name Price Roy

Amount	17 75
Store a/c	
Rent	
Bal. Cash Enclosed	17 75

Mill employees received their wages in cash, with deductions made for house rent and charges at the company store. This pay envelope was issued to Roy Price in 1929 for a regular workweek of 65 hours. Price was instrumental in bringing the United Textile Workers Union to Marion in the spring of 1929 to address grievances with the management of Marion Manufacturing and Clinchfield mills. He served as the local chapter's first president. (Courtesy of Don and Janette Price.)

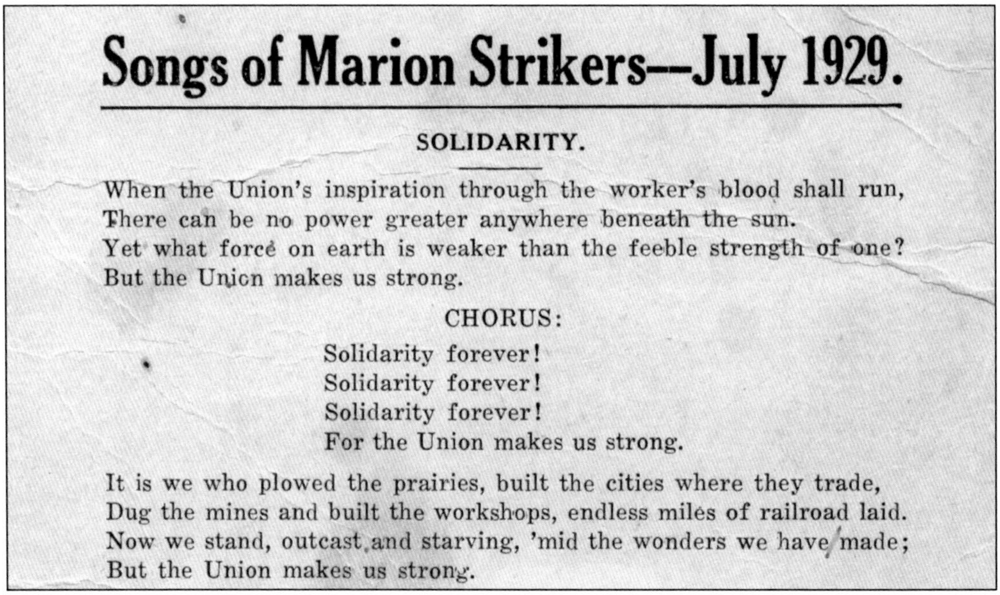

Songs of Marion Strikers—July 1929.

SOLIDARITY.

When the Union's inspiration through the worker's blood shall run,
There can be no power greater anywhere beneath the sun.
Yet what force on earth is weaker than the feeble strength of one?
But the Union makes us strong.

CHORUS:

Solidarity forever!
Solidarity forever!
Solidarity forever!
For the Union makes us strong.

It is we who plowed the prairies, built the cities where they trade,
Dug the mines and built the workshops, endless miles of railroad laid.
Now we stand, outcast and starving, 'mid the wonders we have made;
But the Union makes us strong.

This song card was distributed to Marion union members by the United Textile Workers of America. A key complaint against Marion Manufacturing and Clinchfield management was the use of the stretch-out, where mill hands were required to work longer hours with no increase in pay. In July 1929, when Marion Manufacturing began firing union members, a walkout took place. A temporary settlement was reached in September but quickly collapsed. (Courtesy of David Vess.)

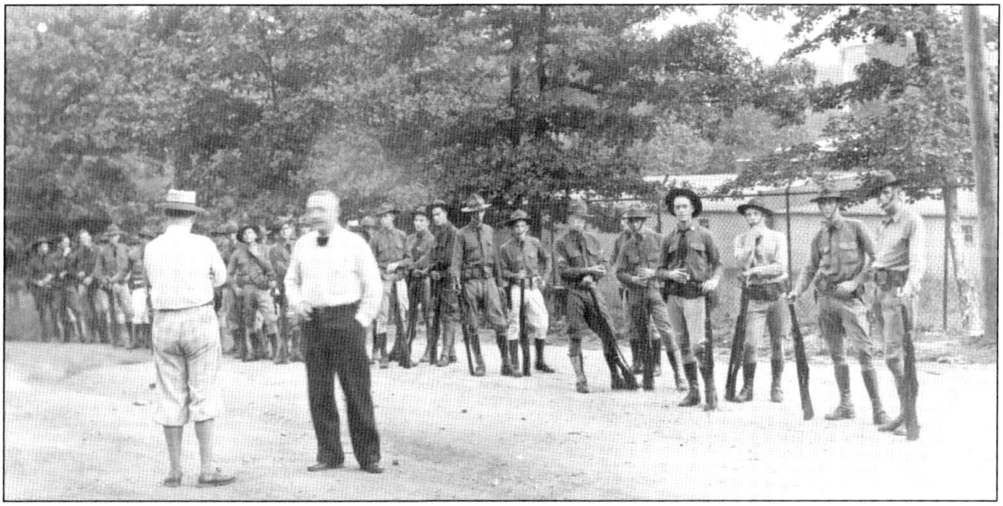

As tensions escalated during the strike at Marion Manufacturing and Clinchfield, National Guard troops at Clinchfield await orders from Major Patterson of Statesville, seen here consulting with Judge N.A. Townsend (in hat and golf clothes). This photograph was taken on September 1, 1929, two days after a dynamite explosion had started a fire in the Clinchfield opening room and strikers had physically forced the sheriff and deputies from the village. (Courtesy of Bill Wornall Textile Postcard Collection.)

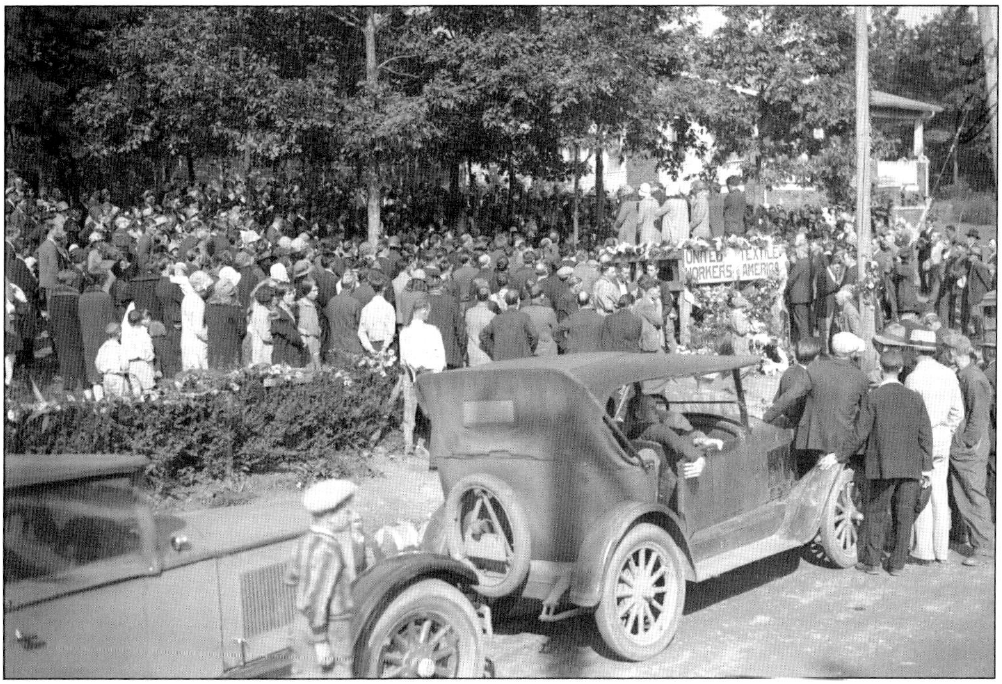

The 1929 strike reached a tragic climax on October 2 when a barrage of shots was fired during a confrontation between sheriff's deputies and strikers at the Marion Manufacturing gate. Six strikers were killed and dozens wounded. No East Marion church would hold services, so this funeral for three of the strikers was held in a clearing across from the mill. The coffins rested on sawhorses. (Courtesy of Wilson Library, University of North Carolina Library at Chapel Hill, North Carolina Collection.)

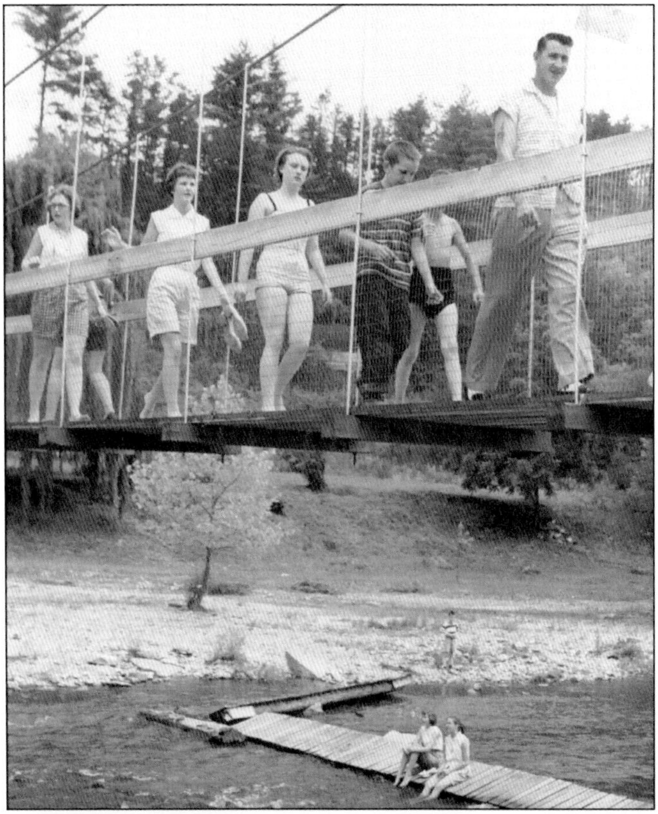

Company picnics were much-anticipated and well-attended annual events. The most popular site for the outings was Optimist Park in Morganton, where these photographs were made. At left, a group from Clinchfield crosses the river at a 1958 gathering. Below, East Marion families are entertained by a very clever dog at the 1960 Marion Manufacturing picnic. Over 1,250 people attended that year. A highlight was the train ride offered to the children on Biltmore Dairy Farms' "Winky Special." (Left, courtesy of City of Marion; below, courtesy of McDowell County Public Library.)

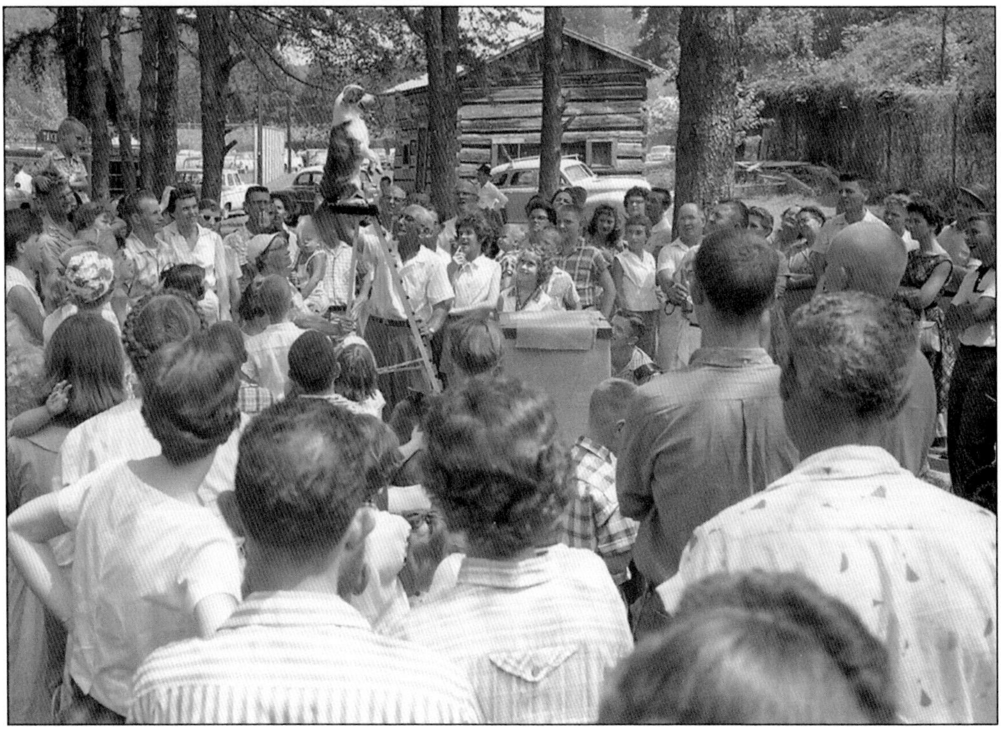

A humorous tradition at Cross Mill to celebrate a birthday was for a coworker to surprise the unsuspecting employee with a dusting of soot to the face. The deed was generally done by a doffer since they had more freedom of movement within the mill. Other workers who were in on the plot would erupt in laughter. In this picture, the birthday girl manages to hide the results from the camera. (Courtesy of Carolyn Andrews.)

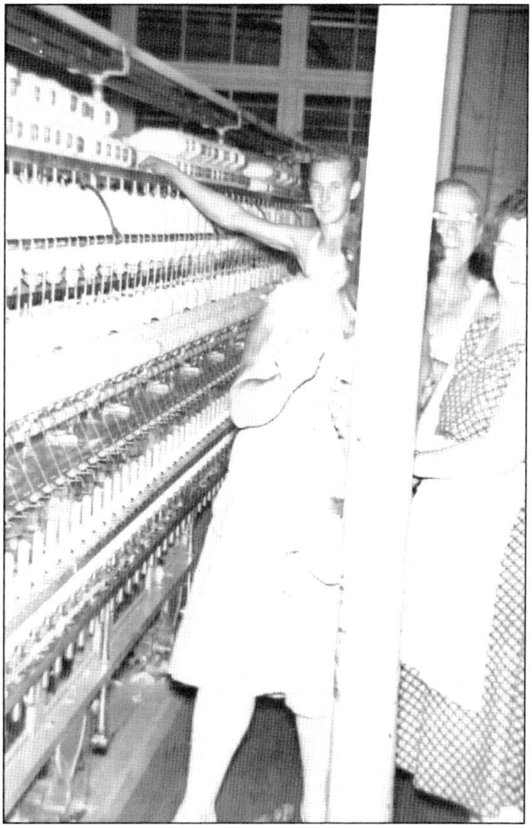

Clinchfield was the largest of the Marion textile mills and consisted of two buildings, the 325-foot-long Clinchfield No. 1 and the 550-foot-long Clinchfield No. 2. The sound of the machines in No. 2 was near deafening. In a 1940 feature in the *McDowell News*, writer Paul O. Nafe notes the noise level is "more than a thousand batteries of machine guns." Latter-day additions to both buildings are evident in this 1953 photograph. (Courtesy of McDowell County Public Library, Robin Hood Collection.)

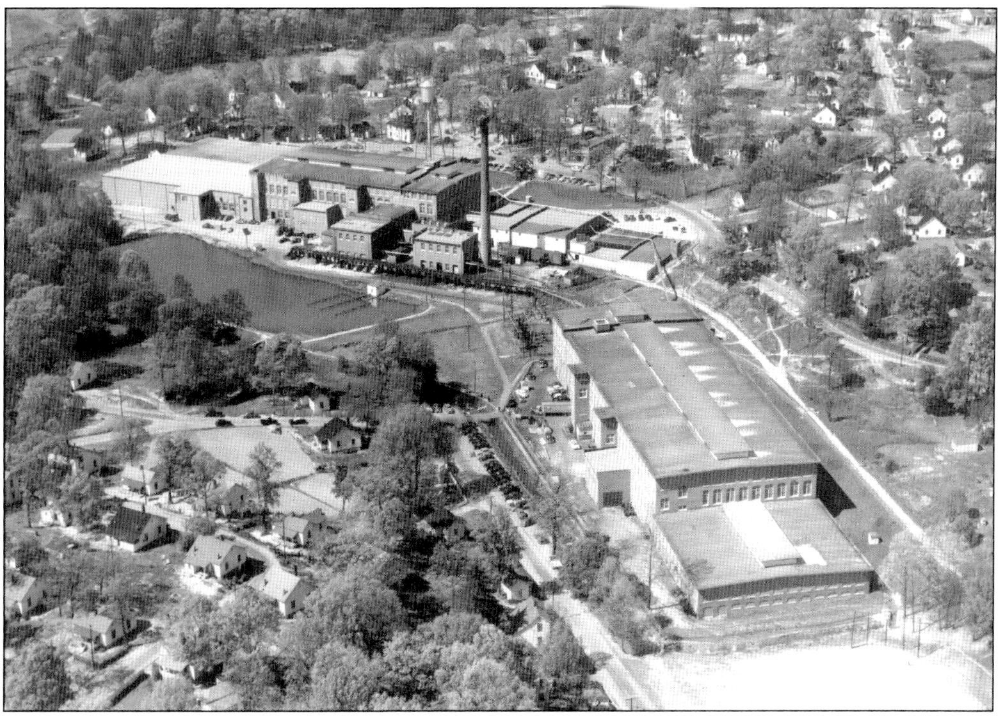

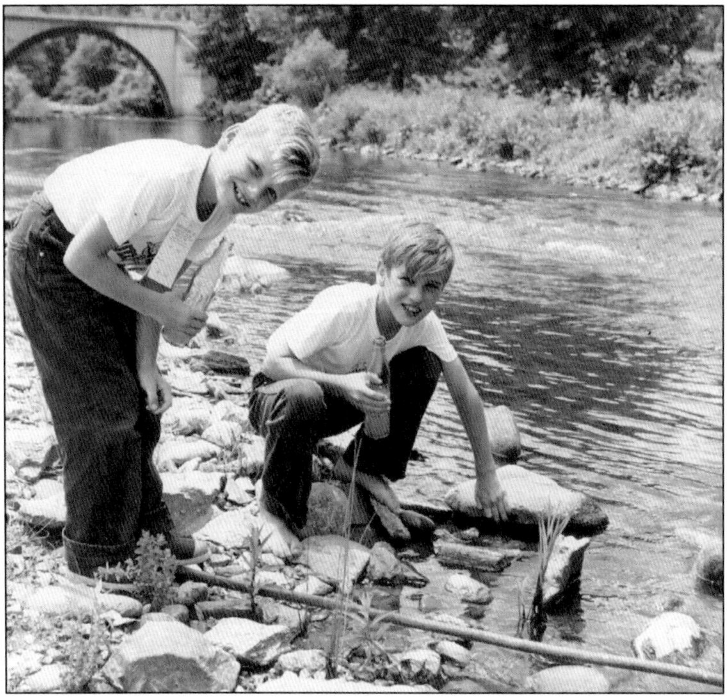

Life in Marion's mill villages in the 1950s and 1960s is remembered fondly. Children played and roamed safely throughout the communities. The companies sponsored ball teams, tournaments, classes, contests, and more. The work in the mills was still demanding, but the villages of that era are recalled as very "Mayberry-like." In this photograph, Ted and Dean Woodby enjoy an outing sponsored by Clinchfield Mills in 1958. (Courtesy of City of Marion.)

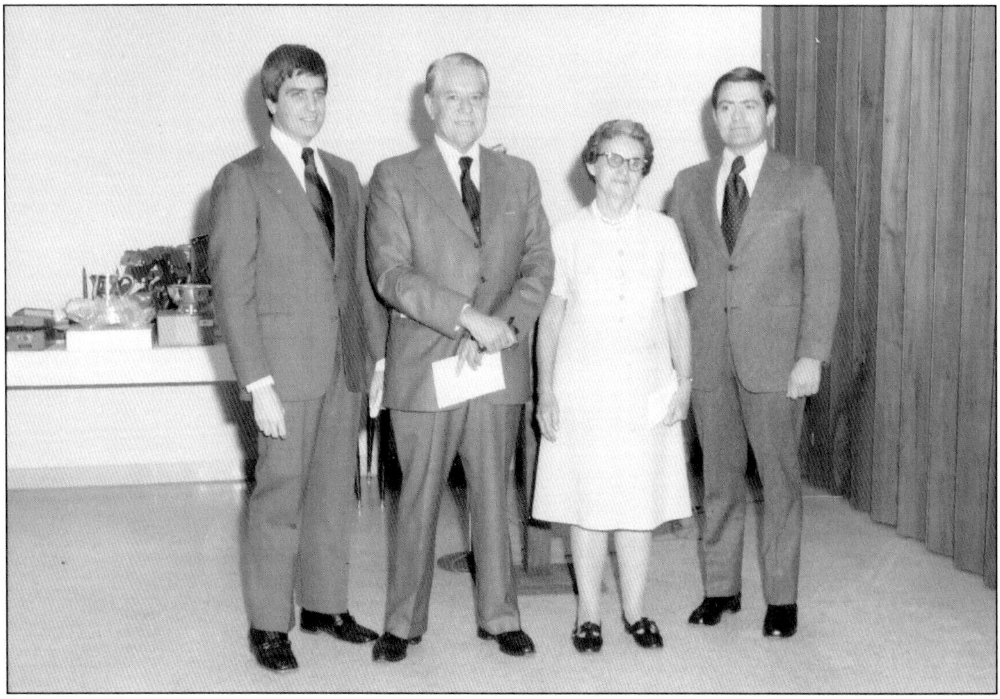

Leona Duncan receives recognition from the Cross family for 50 years of service in their mill. With Duncan are, from left to right, John Cross, Eugene Cross II, and Eugene Cross III. She was given a pin, a gold watch, and a dollar for every year worked. Such ceremonies were common, and it was not unusual for one family to have multiple members who had worked 30 or more years in the same cotton mill. (Courtesy of Carolyn Andrews.)

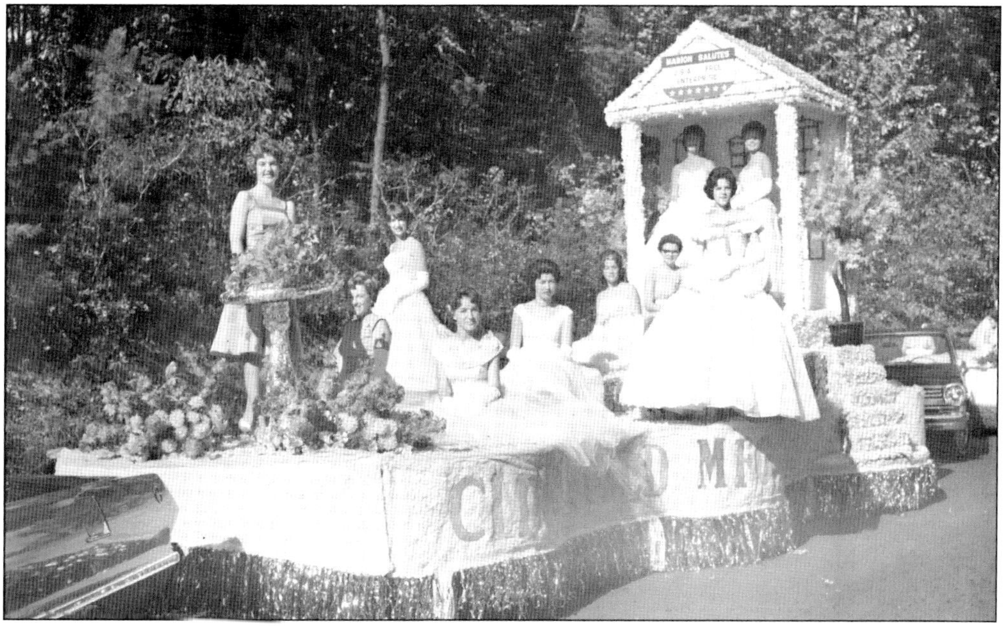

The ladies aboard Clinchfield Manufacturing's "Free Enterprise Day" float prepare for the parade to begin in October 1963. Inspired by Cold War competition between communism and capitalism, the chamber of commerce planned the day to highlight American ingenuity, efficiency, and innovation. Most McDowell manufacturing companies participated in the parade and in a product showcase that took place downtown. (Courtesy of City of Marion.)

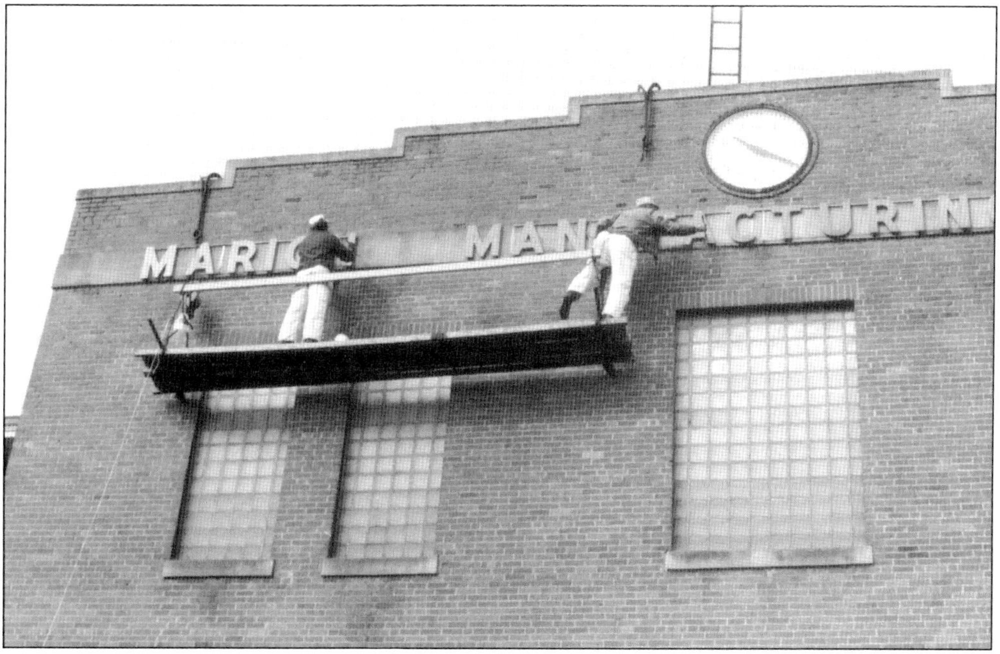

The Marion Manufacturing front tower and clock were familiar sights to drivers on Baldwin Avenue for decades. They were added to the building during a 1945–1947 remodel, along with glass-block windows. The lettering of the company name was added in 1958 and is seen here later being repainted. (Courtesy of McDowell County Public Library.)

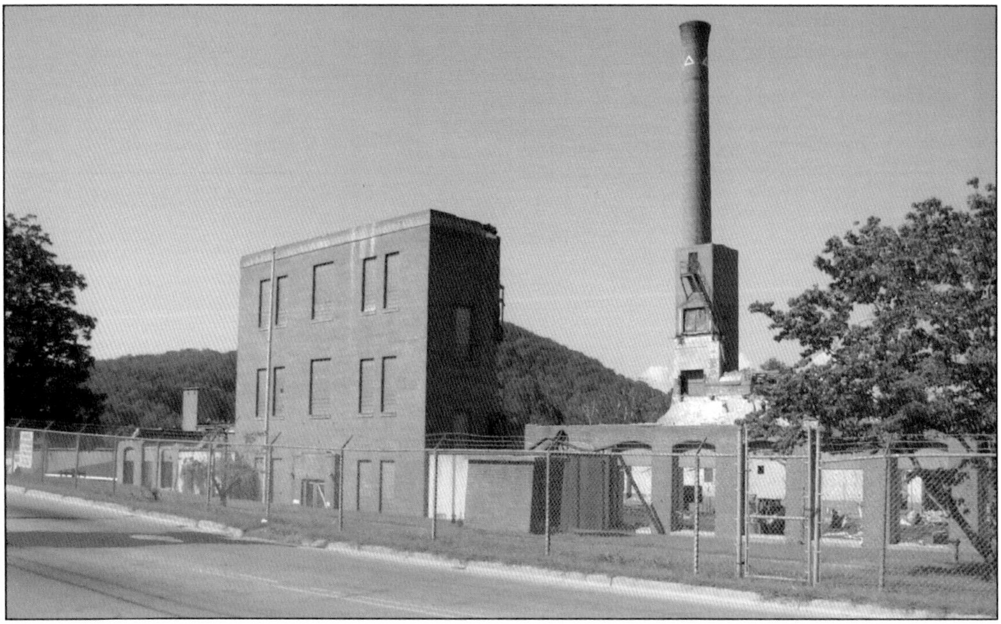

Mount Ida, which had been hidden from view on Baldwin Avenue in East Marion since Marion Manufacturing was built in 1909, reemerges as demolition of the mill nears completion in late 2011. The destruction of the mill building prompted an exhibit and reunion at the public library, newspaper remembrances, and spontaneous gatherings of former employees on the street out front. (Photograph by Kim Clark.)

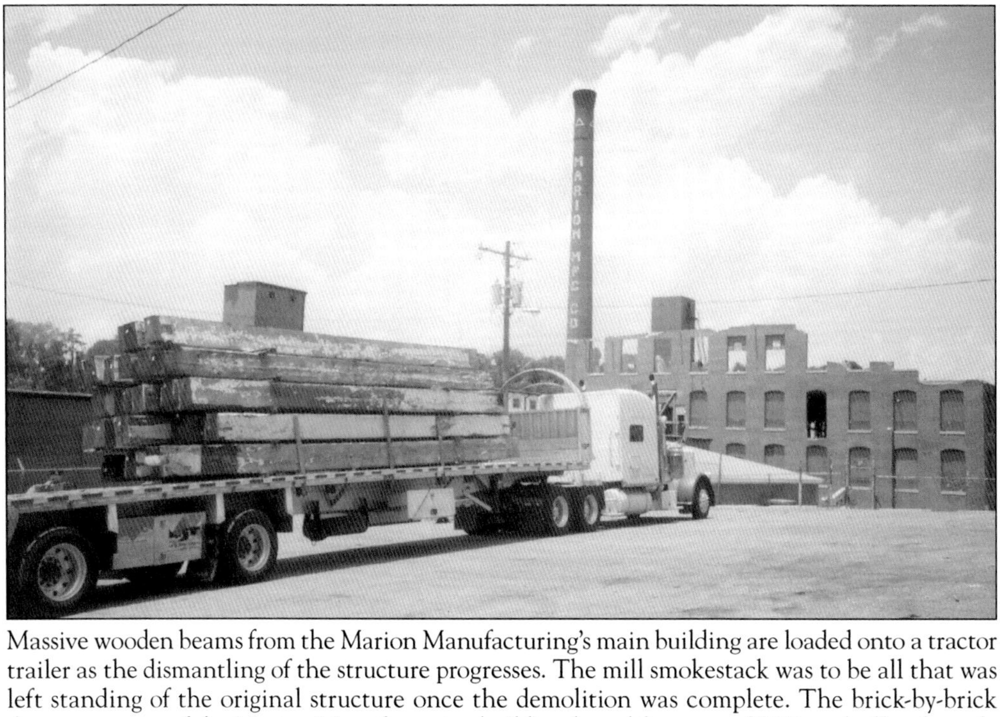

Massive wooden beams from the Marion Manufacturing's main building are loaded onto a tractor trailer as the dismantling of the structure progresses. The mill smokestack was to be all that was left standing of the original structure once the demolition was complete. The brick-by-brick deconstruction of the Marion Manufacturing building lasted for most of 2011 and offered ample opportunity for last looks and photographs. (Photograph by Jim Long.)

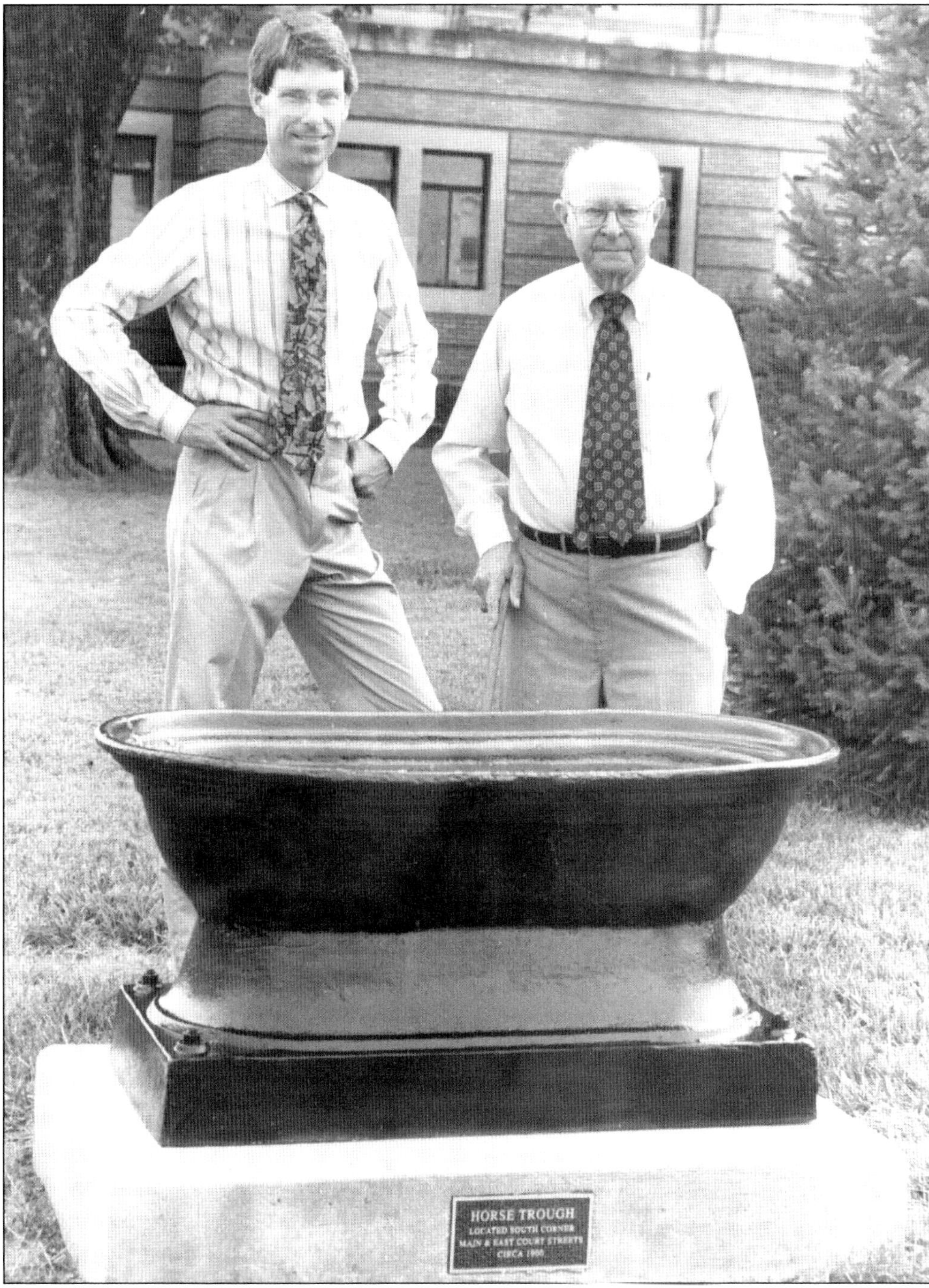

A circle of history was completed when a remnant of days gone by was welcomed back to the courthouse lawn by Warren Hobbs (left) and Frank Goldsmith. This horse trough had been in use on the site in the early 1900s, and its donation to the city was facilitated by Goldsmith. Hobbs devoted much of his energy and talents to historic preservation projects in McDowell County before his death at the age of 48 in 2002. Many of the photographs in this book are from his collection. (Courtesy of Carolyn Andrews.)